On this ⟨

in the era of

The Wars of the Roses

Dan Moorhouse

This book tells the story of the Wars of the Roses. It was a conflict spanning three decades, with many battles, plots, and controversies. The period includes some of the most famous names, events, and mysteries of English or British history: Richard III, the Princes in the Tower, 'Mad' King Henry VI, the end of the Hundred Years War, along with famous battles such as Bosworth, Barnet, Tewkesbury and Towton.

But it was much more than famous people, significant battles, and mysteries. It was a period in which several generations lived. When England and Europe were experiencing changes that would revolutionise the way that we communicate. A time in which the economic changes gathered pace, seeing feudalism in decline and the emergence of merchant classes as significant players on the national stage.

Within the book, you will learn about a wide range of things.

Alchemists and Astrologers feature alongside Necromancy and Witchcraft.

Featuring wool fleets, Mediterranean galleys, sea battles and piracy.

Love and lovers are found alongside marriage, bigamy, coronation ceremonies, annulments, and re-marriages.

Guns and cannons are found on the same battlefield as swords, pikes, bills, and longbows.

Executions and murder accompany treason, rebellion, revenge, and discontent.

A book of this nature cannot include everything that happened within a period. There is scope for a second volume should there be a demand. Daily entries were selected based on providing enough variety, availability of source material during lockdowns and existing coverage on some days.

You can find out about other events from the period on my Facebook page https://www.facebook.com/thewarsoftheroses or website https://schoolshistory.org.uk.

The book would not have been attempted were it not for conversations I had with Ian Dawson and Anna Coates. Many people have helped along the way, especially members of the Battlefields Trust, Richard III Society and Tudor Society.

On this day in the era of the Wars of the Roses is the first in a series of books in this format. The second book is currently being written, on The Hundred Years War.

A percentage of profits made from the sale of this book will be donated to Forgotten Veterans. This UK based charity assists former members of the British Armed forces. forgottenveteransuk.com

January

1st January 1461

The heads of Richard, Duke of York, The Earl of Rutland, and The Earl of Salisbury are on spikes overlooking the City of York. The Duke of York was mocked with a paper crown, and a sign placed proclaiming 'Let York overlook the City of York'. The symbolism of the crown, sign and prominent heads spiked high above the gates was clear to all. The Lancastrians were in no mood for further dissent and woe betide any who tried.

As the heads were being displayed, the Queen was cementing a relationship with the Scots. Her mission was clear, rid the country of the menace that was the Yorkist faction. In York, the Duke of Somerset was gathering his thoughts, thinking of the campaign ahead. With a sizeable army behind him and a Yorkist leadership now shattered, the prize of London and the release of King Henry VI seemed manageable.

In their way stood two significant figures. Richard Neville, the Earl of Warwick and Edward Earl of March and son of the deceased Duke of York. Neither were particularly experienced on the battlefield. Edward to this date had not commanded in any battle. Warwick had, but only twice.

What the Yorkists lacked in experience they gained in motivation. Both men had lost their father at the Battle of Wakefield. Neither had anything to lose. Crucially both had significant landholdings and retinues and the support of the City of London.

England was poised for a tumultuous battle for the crown. That conflict was to last a further 26 years.

2nd January 1471

Edward IV was in exile.

Edward's conflict with the Earl of Warwick had seen him initially under house arrest and, following a brief exile for Warwick, subject to a resurgent Lancastrian force. He and his younger brother Richard had been forced to flee in the face of an army led by Warwick but now fully supported by the fiery Queen Margaret of Anjou.

Edward fled to the safety of Burgundy, where, since 1468, his sister Margaret had lived as wife to Charles the Bold. Exile had not immediately resulted in aid being offered to Edward, despite the family ties. That began to change in late 1470. On 3rd December the French repudiated the Treaty of Peronne.

Peace between Burgundy and France was seemingly coming to an end. This changed the fortunes of the Yorkists in exile. By 31st December Charles, the Bold had set aside ships, troops, and a sum of £20,000 to support Edward in an attempt to regain his throne.

Plans were discussed on 2nd January 1471 at the first meeting of Edward and Charles during the formers time in exile. Burgundy agreed to support Edward. Edward in return would come to the aid of Burgundy against the French. The Yorkist plan to retake the throne was set in stone.

Were there any doubts on the Burgundian side, the French swept them aside on 6th January when they attacked St. Quentin. The agreements of 2nd January stood both Edward and Burgundy in good stead, they both needed allies.

3rd January 1458

Margaret Beaufort married Henry Stafford.

Margaret Beaufort is best remembered as being the mother of Henry Tudor. Her marriage to Edmund Tudor, Henry's father, was brought to an untimely and premature end in November 1456 when Edmund, imprisoned at Carmarthen Castle, died of the Bubonic Plague.

A young mother aged just 14, Margaret's position was one that was potentially quite precarious. Her lineage meant that her son was politically significant as a male descendant of John of Gaunt. Furthermore, her child's father was half-brother to King Henry VI. In a bloody war for the throne, this could spell disaster for the infant Henry.

Under the care of Jasper Tudor, the young mother, already married twice as she had been wed at an early age to John de la Pole, was hot property. Her inheritance from her father made her wealthy, and she and her son made her part of the extended royal family.

A decision was made by Jasper Tudor and Margaret to seize the initiative regarding a future marriage. Tudor set about befriending the powerful Duke of Buckingham. Soon an agreement was reached for the marriage of the Duke's second son, Henry, to Margaret.

This union would bind two powerful houses together, protect Margaret's interests, and offer security to the young Henry Tudor. Lady Margaret Beaufort married Henry Stafford on 3rd January 1458, possibly at Maxstoke Castle in Warwickshire.

4th January 1483

Francis Lovell is created Viscount.

Francis Lovell was one of the most ardent of supporters of Richard III. His elevation from Baron to Viscount was due to the service that he had given to the crown and to Richard, Duke of Gloucester.

Having spent much of his formative years in the wardship of the Neville family, he had also spent time under the care of the Kings sister, Elizabeth. Lovell had inherited the baronies of Deincourt and Bedale in 1474, making him one of the richest men in England not to hold an earldom or dukedom.

As he came of age Lovell enjoyed the patronage of Richard, Duke of Gloucester. When Richard was appointed to lead an expedition into Scotland, Lovell was among the nobles to rally to the cause, being knighted by the 'Lord of the North' whilst on campaign.

His support of Richard's Council of the North and standing as a magnate led to his elevation to Viscount. Lovell is however better remembered for his political roles which began in earnest once Richard had become King.

He played a significant role in crushing the Buckingham Rebellion of 1484 but had already been identified by the public as being a confidant of the King, as illustrated in the not so complimentary rhyme:

The Catte, the Ratte and Lovell our dogge
Rulyth all Englande under a Hogge.

5th January 1461

At Linculden Abbey Mary of Gueldres and Margaret of Anjou agree to Scottish aid for the Lancastrian campaign in exchange for the town of Berwick being granted to Scotland.

1460 had not been kind to Margaret of Anjou. From the ascendancy that her Court enjoyed following the Coventry 'Parliament of Devils' she had seen the fortunes of her family slump. Far from being assured of the longevity of a dynasty, she was faced with losing everything she yearned for her son to inherit. The exiled Yorkists had regrouped. They had marched on London. Salisbury besieged and took the Tower of London. Heading north the earls of March and Warwick had defeated a Royal army at Northampton. Worse still, they had captured the King.

There followed the return to England of Richard, Duke of York, who made a bid for the crown. Though thwarted, he forced the hand of Parliament who enacted the Act of Accord. The inheritance of the crown had been handed to the House of York, totally ignoring the rights of the young Prince Edward.

Incensed, Margaret headed into the Lancastrian stronghold of the north and gathered around her loyal nobles, headed by the Duke of Somerset. Knowing that all out war loomed, Margaret made diplomatic overtures to Scotland. This resulted in an alliance being agreed on this day in 1461.

The Scots would provide Margaret with an army,. In return, Margaret, acting on the Kings behalf, granted the Scots the much prized border town of Berwick. The result was an alliance that was beneficial to both parties, Margaret of Anjou gained military might that on the face of it seemed unassailable. Margaret of Gueldres, the Queen Consort of Scotland, gained the security of holding Berwick which had for years been a platform from which the English invaded Scotland.

6th January 1463

Alnwick Castle is taken by the Yorkists.

Following their disastrous defeat at the Battle of Towton the Lancastrian's were restricted to control of only a few areas of England and Wales. In Wales the Lancastrian Castles, Harlech excepted, fell, or submitted in quick succession.

In England, Lancastrian dominance only really existed in the North East. A cluster of Castles, Bamburgh, Dunstanburgh and Alnwick, held for King Henry VI. It was symbolically important; the anointed King of England remained a King in England.

Unsurprisingly, the Yorkists sought to overcome this resistance. As the rule of Edward IV was being established, it fell to the Neville's of Middleham to eradicate the Lancastrian resistance in the North East. It was a task the Neville's relished.

The Earl of Warwick held a large personal army that was battle hardened and controlled much of the shipping in the North Sea which was used to bring north ordnance for use in sieges: though it was used sparingly. Alnwick was besieged by the Earl of Warwick's men, and Queen Margaret and her French Captain Pierre de Breze were forced to flee to Scotland.

In Scotland, the pair organised a relief force for the Castle. The small Scottish army arrived at Alnwick on 5th January, forcing Warwick to abandon the siege. The relief force did not remain at Alnwick though, returning north soon afterwards,

Warwick now only had a token garrison to contend with. Short of manpower, the garrison of Alnwick surrendered to Warwick on 6th January 1463. It was the third time that the Castle had changed hands in two years.

7th January 1469

John de Vere, 13th Earl of Oxford, released from captivity in the Tower of London

John de Vere, 13th Earl of Oxford, had been imprisoned in the Tower of London in 1468. His crime had been treason, and he went as far as confessing that he had plotted against King Edward IV.

Oxford's motivation for plotting against the King is quite clear. His father and elder brother had both been tried, found guilty and executed by the Constable of England. Family power had been slowly eradicated through the grant of ancestral lands to other East Anglian landowners. The honour of being the Great Chamberlain of England, held by the de Vere family for generations had been taken away and handed to his brother-in-law the Earl of Warwick.

Yet Oxford had remained quiet about any grievance that he held against the crown. He had not become embroiled in the arguments at Court over preferred continental alliances, nor had he openly voiced an opinion on the promotion of the Queen's family.

However, he, along with other men, was named as a protagonist in a plot against the King. It resulted in his incarceration in the Tower. His release was most probably due to the influence of the Earl of Warwick.

Shortly after his release, when Warwick rebelled, he sided with the Lancastrians and became a thorn in the side of the Yorkists. Joining the rebellion and whilst in exile using a small fleet to harass shipping. He even went as far as to attempt a raid on Calais, before landing at Saint Michael's Mount and taking the Castle.

8th January 1471

A session of the County Court sat in Cheshire.

The legal system of the 15th Century saw most crimes tried on a local or regional level. Each county had 2 appointed officials, and the magnates too had a role in overseeing the administration of justice. Only more serious crimes were brought before the Constable of England or Parliament.

A sessional court might therefore seem routine, but in many areas of the country, the functionality of Government had collapsed during the Readeption of King Henry VI.

In Cheshire, there were no records entered into the exchequer from September 1470 to June 1471, illustrating that administration on a local level had been impacted upon by national events.

The court hearing itself tells us much about the atmosphere of the day. Lord Stanley chose to delegate oversight of the Court to his son, which was not particularly unusual as the Magnates often used their household to perform administrative duties. It would also be a method of training sons the mechanisms of the legal system.

Stanley may have been quite reticent about hearing cases himself. Under King Edward IV he had held the position of Chamberlain of the Court. When the Lancastrians regained power, he had lost this position. Though Edward had returned to the crown, this alone did not mean that his position was again secure.

During the turbulence of the Lancastrian seizure of power his property was ransacked, and he and others held to ransom by 15 known men and a mob estimated to be 500 strong.

Though released by the mob for the sum of 10 marks, he did not return to participating in the workings of the state.

9th January 1450

Adam Moleyns, former Treasurer, was murdered by sailors at Portsmouth.

An angry mob burst through the doors of the Dominus Dei church. They sought out Adam Moleyns. Then murdered him, inside.

A career cleric, Moleyns had risen through numerous posts before becoming the Bishop of Chichester. He had gained the favour of the King and Duke of Suffolk during his meteoric rise. So much so that Moleyns had been entrusted with diplomatic missions to the Vatican and to France.

It was his involvement in French diplomatic missions for which Moleyns gained notoriety. He became associated with the policies of the Duke of Suffolk and the regular complaints about late pay.

At this point in his career, he held not only his bishopric but was also Clerk of the Royal Council, a member of the Privy Council and keeper of the Privy Seal. These led him into a collision course with the Lieutenant-General of France, Richard, Duke of York. This clash led to accusations being made about Moleyns work, which led to him resigning government positions but remaining a Bishop. In January 1450 Moleyns was making his way to France.

The reason for his murder is debated. Some suggest that it was motivated by the money said to be on his person. Others thought that Richard had paid to have him assassinated. A third theory is that he was murdered because the soldiers in Portsmouth associated him with the heavy losses in Normandy. Whichever is true, he was brutally murdered in a church. The Vatican responded to this deed by excommunicating the whole of Portsmouth. This remained in place until a mass penance was carried out in 1508.

10th January 1463

Imported Pomegranates

It is worth reminding yourself that whilst there was a civil war underway, life went on as normal for most people. This is evident from the trading records for the period. The following is an extract from an entry from the Hull Customs Accounts for 10th January 1463. These poundage and tonnage records show luxury items such as pomegranates along with more routine items such as soap and bow staves being imported. The figures shown to the right are pounds, shillings and pence showing the value of goods. A pound is a pound in weight of silver or gold at the time. 13.4 is one mark.

Navis Garardi Derrykson vocata Jacok de Midelsburgh applicuit 10 die Januarii

Adreanus Johnson, a	8 C orenges 3 sauses 1 bar cum haberdash	1 C pomgarnettes 1 sheryngknff	£4
Antonius Nicholes, al Thomas Dalhouse	2 bar allecis albi 2 last allecis albi 2 ams vimi rensis 1 bar ohi	7 bar osmondes 3 C bowstaves 1 bar saponis	£13 4s £16
Robertus Fyssher	16 bar osmondes 1 bar olii	1 pipa nucum 60 bond allii	£4

11th January 1454

Petition of Walter Ingham

East Anglia had seen many low-level disputes in the late 1440s into the 1450s. This example shows how the rule of law was breaking down in the region and how people sought justice.

Walter Ingham's petition states that he had received a forged letter that was supposedly from the Earl of Oxford. And that this forged letter led to him travelling to Wivenhoe in Essex at the Earl's command. The letter was forged to enable an ambush, with Thomas Dennys having sent it with a view to ambushing and murdering Ingham.

The petition, part of which is shown below, was sent to Parliament. It asked for the arrest of Dennys. This did take place. He was sent to the Fleet Prison. Furthermore, Ingham asked for Dennys to be detained there until such time as the Chancellor had pronounced judgement upon Dennys, as Ingham did not feel as though he was safe should Dennys be released pending a hearing.

"Petition of Walter Ingham of Norfolk, gentleman, that Thomas Dennys sent him a forged letter at Dunston on 11 January 1454 making it look as though the letter came from the Earl of Oxford, who was totally ignorant of the letter, and that the Earl had commanded him to come to him at Wivenhoe, Essex on 13 January. The petition goes on to explain how Dennys prepared several men 'as if for war with jakkes, salettes, lange de boeufs, and boar spears in two ambushes in two places', plotting to kill Ingham. This action was because Ingham had worked with his father for a writ of sub poena against Dennys and Agnes, his wife. Ingham was seriously wounded, and now has to use crutches because of a wound to his right leg". Appendix to the Parliamentary Roll, Henry VI March 1453

12th January 1468

Three men outlawed by the County Sherriff at Macclesfield

Nicholas and John Clayton along with John Werneby, all yeomen, were outlawed by a manorial court in Macclesfield.

They had previously been charged with trespass. Having failed to appear at a hearing set for 3rd October 1467, the County Sherriff had been tasked with apprehending the men.

Having evaded the law and not responding to calls for them to hand themselves in, the punitive penalty of outlawing the men was used at the hearing held on 12th January 1468.

This is a good example of how localised courts worked. They regularly sat, in much the same way as a Magistrates Court would today.

Punishments were well known to the population, the pillory, imprisonment, hanging being commonly administered for differing levels of crime.

Here we also see how a case escalates through the system, from initial hearing to being placed on the equivalent of a wanted list.

Outlawing somebody was as harsh a punishment as could be given to somebody in their absence. They were quite literally beyond the law, and all their possessions forfeit, as too could be their lives without any punishment for anybody choosing to assail them.

13th January 1456

The resignation of Richard Duke of York from his role as Protector.

"Parliament met at Westminster, where the Duke of York and the house of Commons worked hard to obtain a resumption of royal grants, but most of the Lords resisted. [Indeed] they went to the King and brought him to Westminster: there, in the King's presence, the Duke of York resigned his office". Benet's Chronicle.

Following the First Battle of St. Albans Richard Duke of York was installed as Protector of the realm. This is widely believed to be due to a relapse of his previous unresponsive state, though some people question whether that was the reality of the situation.

Richard's Protectorship faced opposition from some nobles who were opposed to his reforms and to him personally. These nobles, aligned largely to the Queen, made his governance increasingly difficult.

When Richard attempted to have royal grants resumed, that Is continued, these nobles made moves to block the move. It was a political powerplay. The Queen and her followers saw an opportunity to regain control and bring an end to Yorkist dominance.

Their solution was to have the Duke of York removed from office. The only way that this could be achieved was through the return to the personal rule of the King. So, they brought King Henry to Parliament. Whether or not the King was aware is hard to tell. The message was loud and clear to Richard Duke of York though.

As a result, Richard Duke of York resigned from his position as Protector and retreated to his estates. This handed control of Government to Queen Margaret and her favourites.

14th January 1423

The opening of Parliament. This is the first session of the infant King Henry's reign.

The opening of any Parliament is a grand affair. There is a pomp and ceremonial aspect and often a sense of a new beginning. In 1423, that was most certainly the case.

When King Henry V died, his son and heir was just 9 months old. From a strong and much celebrated monarch one day to an infant as King the next. The contrast is not only huge but particularly important in terms of Medieval Governance. The Medieval system had Parliament and a council, but laws were done in the king's name and 'through the king', with his consent.

With an infant on the throne, this was impractical. A working solution needed to be established that recognised the rights of the King. At the same time, Government at all levels needed to be run efficiently. The matter was critical, England was occupying large parts of France, and there was a risk of indecisiveness threatening the agreements that Henry V had fought hard to win.

The first task of this Parliament was to determine how to rule in the King's name until he was old enough to rule in his own right. And it was no easy task. Establishing a Royal Council was of paramount importance, defining roles was a matter of contention that had to be addressed, agreeing the nature of the young Kings upbringing too was a matter for debate.

The outcome of the debates and subsequent decisions by Council was that the Duke of Bedford would hold seniority at Council and in Court. His younger brother, the Duke of Gloucester would also hold positions and act in Bedford's stead during periods when Bedford was in France.

15th January 1460

Raid on Sandwich

In 1459 the Yorkist leadership had fled into exile. The Earl of Warwick, as Captain of Calais, had chosen to go there with his father and the Earl of March.

Sitting back and allowing the Lancastrians to maintain the upper hand was not an option for Warwick. With the fleet and garrison of Calais loyal to his command, he had effective control of the Channel.

Just a small fleet, loyal to the crown, impeded total dominance. Warwick decided to be proactive. He knew which ports the fleet might be docked at and was convinced of the superiority of the Calais Fleet.

Warwick worked on putting together a raiding party. This flotilla then set sail across the English Channel with the intention of finding and engaging the crown fleet. The flotilla found the Lancastrian controlled fleet at Sandwich.

Warwick chose to send a detachment of ships under Sir John Dynham to attack. They did so at dawn on 15th January 1460, taking the Lancastrians by surprise, destroying the fleet and taking its guns.

"tooke the principall shippes of the Kynge's navie... well furnished with ordinaunce and artillarie."

During the raid, the Lancastrian commander, Richard Woodville Earl Rivers and his wife Jacquetta of Luxemburg were captured. Jacquetta was quickly released. Rivers was taken to Calais and ridiculed by the Yorkist leaders, though he was released reasonably quickly as he fought in the battles of Towton.

16th January 1456

Henry Holland, Duke of Exeter released

The Duke of Exeter had been imprisoned in the Tower of London due to a series of misdemeanours. These were sufficiently important for him to be required to answer charges against himself.

The Duke had been reprimanded by the Duke of York, the protector and most senior of the Royal Dukes. At one stage, the retainers of York's household had formed up in arms and marched on the Duke of Exeter to bring an end to a dispute. Something that York and his Government could ill afford to happen regularly

As a Lord, his case was heard in Parliament. Exeter had done nothing treasonable but was becoming something of a nuisance in the South-West, an area that had other serious feuds running through the period.

Parliaments function here is to keep him in line. In a manner like that used at other times with men such as the Earls of Northumberland, the options were to demote, strip lands and therefore wealth or to take a bond from him which was reliant upon his future behaviour.

Parliament opted for the latter; he was released on a bond of recognisances of 2000 marks to the King. His good conduct would then be reviewed later:

"Condition, that he [The Duke of Exeter] shall appear in person in chancery on the morrow of All Souls next, or at an earlier day upon warning received by writ of the great or privy seal, unless prevented by bodily infirmity, imprisonment or other reasonable cause". Official translation of the Parliamentary roll.

17th January 1461

Stamford, Lincolnshire is ordered by Council to put its defences in order

Queen Margaret's alliance with the Scots resulted in the formation of a large army. With a large army behind her, she intended to march south, free the King and finish off the Yorkists.

Such an eventuality was quite expected by the Yorkists. Buoyed by her victory at Wakefield, it stood to reason that she would hammer home her advantage. As early as 5th January funds were granted to the Earl of Warwick to prepare the defence of London.

Towns and Cities started to commit men to the Yorkist army, Norwich sending 120 on the 12th for example. As Margaret's army began its march south fears grew and so, as was the case at Stamford, defensive preparations were ordered at towns along the route of the Great North Road.

The fears held by Council and in towns on the route of Margaret's army were not unfounded. The march south was unruly. Towns and Abbeys were ransacked.

Fear grew along the route, to the extent that Margaret wrote to the citizens of London to try and reassure them. Her efforts were in vain, bad news travelled fast. Along the route, many people sought refuge.

This quote from the pro-Yorkist Croyland Chronicle shows this:

"This fact too, in especial gave us additional ground for apprehension, that numbers of persons who lived in the country, being desirous to provide for the safety of themselves and their sacred things, had fled with the utmost speed to this island, as their sole place of refuge".

18th January 1486

Marriage of King Henry VII to Elizabeth of York.

IN 1483 Henry Tudor declared his intention to marry Elizabeth of York, eldest daughter of King Edward IV and Elizabeth Woodville. It was a bold declaration. Tudor was in exile; Elizabeth was the niece of King Richard III and sister of the two missing Princes in the Tower.

The declaration was an astute one though. The mothers of both Henry and Elizabeth had colluded to form an alliance. For Margaret Beaufort the aim was to put her son on the throne, a marriage with a Princess from the House of York would help to legitimise such a move and would limit opposition. For Elizabeth Woodville, it offered an opportunity to protect the interests of her daughters.

The promise of a union of the houses of Tudor and York played a part in diminishing support for Richard III. It was not the only reason, but it contributed to the royal army at Bosworth being smaller than Richard may have anticipated.

Following Henry's victory, there were calls for the marriage to take place as soon as possible. It would go a long way toward pacifying those who had been on the losing side at Bosworth and enable the new regime to have a means of rapprochement with Yorkists.

Henry, however, had other ideas. He had himself crowned as soon as was practical. Then he opened his first Parliament, in which the Speaker implored him to proceed with the marriage. Henry's purpose in sequencing events in this order was clear: he was the King, there was no joint rule.

The marriage did then take place on 18th January 1486. 9 months later, Elizabeth gave birth to Prince Arthur.

19th January 1454

The Paston family of Norfolk rose in prominence in the years following the Black Death. By the time of the Wars of the Roses, they were landed, holding several manors and Caister Castle. They are a source of lots of detail about contemporary views as their extensive correspondence has survived.

This letter, from their collection, was written by John Stodeley to the Duke of Norfolk on 19th January 1454. It illustrates the state in which King Henry found himself upon the birth of Prince Edward.

"...at the prince's coming to Windsor, the Duke of Buckingham took him in his arms and presented him to the King in goodly fashion, beseeching the King to bless him; but the King gave no answer. Nevertheless, the Duke stayed with the prince by the King, and, when he could obtain no answer, the Queen came in, took the prince in her arms and presented him as the Duke had done, desiring the King to bless him: however, their labour was in vain, for they departed thence without any answer or expression from the King..."

The letter is quite telling. Firstly, it provides us with an insight into the condition of the King at the time. A lack of responsiveness to being presented with his son illustrates the depth of his disassociation. Second, it shows the way the Royal household operated. It was not the Queen who presented Prince Edward to the King but the Duke of Buckingham. Third, it shows that the King's condition and news of his lack of response had spread beyond the inner circle of Court.

20th January 1455

Papal Jubilee

A Papal Jubilee was traditionally reserved for those who had visited Rome or a major site of pilgrimage in the Holy Land. The English Government had pressed for one to be held so that the ordinary people of the country could see one and participate.

It was a propaganda piece in some ways, designed to put people in a good mood through a large communal celebration. England got one in 1455. The reason: a call to arms. A crusade against 'the Turks'.

The Archbishop of Ravenna arrived in England and was warmly welcomed. Records show he was granted gifts. A jubilee did indeed take place.

His purpose though was clear, to encourage the English to join a new Crusade. He had examples of how they could be beaten. He was confident of a victory for Christendom.

His timing was far from ideal though. His diplomatic visit coincided with Henry's recovery from his mental illness and the resultant changes within the Council. His initial talks had been with the Duke of York in his role as Protector. His final talks were with the reconstituted Council including Somerset.

Given the recent war in France, this being only 18 months after the battle of Castillon, and the hostile climate within England the Council had to politely decline to send a large army.

Some individuals did join Crusades whilst the Wars of the Roses were in progress, though never officially as representatives of England.

21st January 1479

Robert Stillington, Bishop of Bath and Welles was appointed along with Anthony Woodville, the Earl of Essex, and Bishop of Ely to treat with the French Ambassador.

The appointment of Robert Stillington is significant. It is he who was later cited as having married Edward IV to Eleanor Butler. He had recently been released from the Kings custody having been arrested on unknown charges, then released with a pardon, the previous year.

Evidence of Edward's earlier marriage can be found in a letter from the Burgundian Ambassador. In it, he says that Stillington married the King but also added that the King merely made promises to make sexual advances on Eleanor Butler.

Whatever the truth behind Edward being previously married, or not, it is highly improbable that he would entrust matters of such diplomatic importance to someone who had intimate secrets that could invalidate his son's inheritance.

The embassy to meet with France was at an important time. Burgundy was undergoing a period of adjustment as it tried to establish a Regent. France had already taken advantage of the political instability and nominally taken control of parts of the Duchy. This threatened agreements that the English had with Burgundy on trade.

Furthermore, a bullish France may renege on the terms of the Treaty of Picquardy. This would result in financial losses for those English nobles, and the King, who was in receipt of pensions from France.

22nd January 1478

Royal Joust concludes the festivities to mark the marriage of Richard, Duke of York to Anne Mowbray.

Though the groom was just 4 years old and his bride a year older, this did not stop a grand celebration of the marriage. The marriage was of the Kings second oldest son, Prince Richard to Anne Mowbray, sole heiress of the Duchy of Norfolk. It recognised Norfolk's close ties with the House of York and gave both bride and groom a sizeable and significant landholding.

The wedding ceremony itself had taken place a week before on 15th. The finale of the celebrations was a jousting contest. Jousting for the prize of elaborately embroidered letters which were to be presented by Princess Elizabeth of York.

Jousts and Tournaments were regularly used to mark special occasions or as part of diplomatic visits. They demonstrated strength, chivalry, friendship. Such events could be a place where negotiations were made. They also reinforced the image of a strong, powerful and just monarchy.

The best known of the contestants included the Marquis of Dorset, Earl Rivers, Edward Woodville and Richard Grey. These men entered in pomp and ceremony, with several horses each.

What is perhaps most remarkable is not who was present at this large family celebration but who was not. George, the Duke of Clarence, was imprisoned in the Tower of London as the festivities took place.

23rd January 1484

Parliament opens for its only session during the reign of King Richard III. Titulus Regius is passed.

Titulus Regis was the Act of Parliament that legitimised Richard III as King of England. It did so by confirming Parliament's decision of 1483 that the marriage of Edward IV to Elizabeth Woodville was invalid.

Edward's marriage was invalidated on the evidence of Robert Stillington, Bishop of Bath and Welles, who said that he had overseen an earlier marriage contract between Edward and Eleanor Butler. In medieval times an agreement to marry was binding, even if it never took place. To break an agreement required a process to be followed which, if such an agreement was ever made, was not done.

As a result, the children of Edward were declared illegitimate and could not inherit the throne. As George, Duke of Clarence had been attained his children were also unable to accede to the throne, leaving Richard as the rightful heir to the throne.

The Act also hints at the possibility of both Edward and George being illegitimate, further advancing the right of Richard to be the King. This is based partly on Edward having been born in Rouen whilst his father was Lieutenant of France.

Titulus Regius was the first item on the agenda of the only parliamentary session held in Richard's reign.

Following Richard's death at Bosworth and Henry Tudor becoming King, the Act was overturned thus legitimising Elizabeth of York to whom Henry Tudor was to wed, along with reinstating the rights of her sisters.

24th January 1483

William Catesby appointed as the speaker.

At the beginning of each session of a medieval Parliament, a speaker was elected by the commons. The tradition was that the speaker would then protest that they were not capable, then be confirmed to the role with an agreement that the actions of Parliament would not be held against them.

At the beginning of the only Parliament held during the reign of King Richard III, the commons elected Sir William Catesby to the role of speaker.

Catesby was the son of Sir William Catesby, a knight with landholdings in Northamptonshire. He trained in law at the inner bar before gaining employment in the service of William, Lord Hastings.

Following the death of his father, he inherited several estates in the Midlands. He also managed land for other lords, a common practice at the time as this allowed those lords to focus on other issues.

Through this work, he became acquainted with Richard, Duke of Gloucester and became close friends with the Duke. When Edward IV died, Catesby was one of the men entrusted with a position on the Regency Council. Closely allied to Richard, he secured the position of speaker when Parliament sat.

Catesby also held the role of Chancellor of the Exchequer under Richard and was a key advisor to him during his reign.

Catesby fought alongside Richard at the Battle of Bosworth. Captured following the battle, he was beheaded in Leicester on 25th August 1485.

25th January 1451

King Henry VI asserts his right to rule

The structure of Government in the 15th century placed the King as a figurehead and decision maker. Often, roles would be delegated but significant decisions were usually taken by the King and his Council.

In the late 1440s and 1450, King Henry VI had allowed his most trusted advisors to make decisions on his behalf. There are examples of only a few members of the Council presenting the King with policy documents for his approval.

That policy had backfired. With England in a state of turmoil and economic collapse, those trusted advisors had become the focal point of discontent. Anger at the state of the nation had been aimed at those men who had become viewed as being evil and wicked counsellors.

The Duke of Suffolk had been impeached for his handling of affairs, then murdered on his way into exile. The Bishop of Chichester, another key advisor, had been murdered by a mob in Portsmouth. The people of Kent had risen in rebellions led by Thomas Cheyne and later Jack Cade. England was in a dire situation on all fronts.

Following the expulsion then murder of Suffolk, the Duke of Somerset rose in prominence. King Henry, however, did not permit Somerset the same level of independent decision making that Suffolk had enjoyed. On 25th January 1451, the King informed Council that he would resume personal control over a number of areas that had previously been delegated. This is significant as it demonstrates that Henry was at times an assertive monarch.

26th January 1473

William, Lord Hastings leads an embassy to meet Charles the Bold of Burgundy

In 1472 the English, Bretons and Burgundians had agreed on an alliance against the French. Each agreed to wage war, at the same time, with set objectives and agreements over the spoils of war.

In early 1473 King Edward IV wanted to formalise the plans for this attack. Backed by Parliament to raise an army in England, he was confident that a three-pronged attack would be successful.

Hastings was sent to Burgundy with a simple but practical plan:

1) Burgundy would provide 10,000 men for a year, and the cost of this would be taken from English spoils of war.

2) Burgundy would attack on a different front to split the French army.

3) Burgundy was free to claim French territories except for Rheims as this was where Kings of France were crowned, and Edward wanted to claim the crown as his.

4) The English would land in Normandy in spring or early summer.

The plan seems quite logical but unfortunately for Hastings and later Edward, Charles the Bold had changed his priorities. Instead of focussing on France, he was now engaged in the conquest of the Duchy of Guelders.

It was an objective that had not changed by the time the English sailed and so a truce with the French, in England's favour, was agreed.

27th January 1458

Great Council meets

In 1458 King Henry VI attempted to heal the rift between the rival factions at Court. The Lancastrians and Yorkists had been at loggerheads for much of the 1450s, made worse by the First Battle of St. Albans in 1455.

There had been little opportunity for King Henry to deal with the divisions. Following the Battle of St. Albans, there had been a second protectorate. It was not until Henry assumed personal leadership once more that efforts to placate the factions could be undertaken.

Those efforts faced many problems. The sons of the nobles who had been killed at St. Alban's wanted revenge. The Yorkists too were unwilling to concede much, there was still much to be done.

Neither party trusted the other. This meant that large retinues began to be taken to meetings by the major nobles. Henry had struggled to get the nobility to attend Council in 1457 amid fears for their security.

Eventually, a date of 27th January 1458 was fixed for a Great Council to be held in London. The Lancastrian nobles and their retinues were accommodated outside of the walls, the Yorkists within the walls. This was to keep the parties apart and minimise the risk of clashes.

Henry also raised a force of men from the areas surrounding London and paraded them around the city as a show of strength: designed to warn the nobles against clashing. This did not stop the Lancastrians from attempting to ambush leading Yorkists.

The Council did not begin on time, some lords arriving late. The King then went to stay at Chertsey, resulting in little progress until his return to London in March, when he made his decisions about how to proceed.

28th January 1457

Henry Tudor born

Henry Tudor became the first of the Tudor monarchs following his victory over Richard III at Bosworth. At the time of his birth, such a position improbable. There were many men with better claims than his, he was born as an important baby but not a potential monarch.

Henry's mother, Margaret Beaufort, was a slightly built 12-year-old bride when she wed Edmund Tudor. She was also the heiress to the substantial Beaufort states. Edmund, on the other hand, was the son of Catherine of Valois, the widow of Henry V who broke with convention and remarried, to Owen Tudor.

Despite her young age and slight build, Margaret became pregnant. She gave birth to Henry aged 13 at Pembroke Castle in South Wales. Many marriages that were arranged would see the couple wait to consummate the relationship. In this case, if Margaret was to die at an early age, Edmund would gain more if there was a child: which is believed by some to be the reason for the childhood pregnancy.

Henry's father had died during Margaret's pregnancy. Edmund had been imprisoned by the Yorkists and died of Bubonic Plague when Margaret was 6 months pregnant.

The infant Henry and his mother were transferred into the care of Jasper Tudor. A year later Margaret married Henry Stafford, a son of the Duke of Buckingham.

This was largely to protect herself and Henry in a very volatile political environment. Aged 5 the Court decided to make Henry a ward of William Herbert, Earl of Pembroke.

Though Margaret still saw Henry on occasion, he was to all intents and purposes brought up without either parent present.

29th January 1449

William de la Pole, Duke of Suffolk imprisoned in the Tower of London

England was in a state of turmoil in 1448 and January of 1449. The economy was struggling, the war in France was going from bad to worse, and the Council was perceived to be mishandling both of the situations.

Attribution of the blame for the woes of the English army had already begun. Bishop Moleyns had resigned his government posts and then been murdered. Suffolk too was subject to accusations of being at fault, meddlesome and corrupt.

Suffolk chose to confront his accusers. On 22nd January he requested of Parliament that he be granted leave to challenge his accusers in the commons. In turn, the commons approached the speaker, asking for this wish to be granted. Furthermore, they asked that Suffolk be imprisoned to preserve the peace whilst a hearing was held.

The latter request was initially rejected, no charge had been made against the Duke, there were no grounds to restrict his movements. On the 28th such a charge was made and, on the 29th January, Suffolk was imprisoned in the Tower. A translation of the parliamentary roll shows that:

'the realm of England is about to be sold to the king's enemy of France... where he would be assisted by Suffolk, who had fortified the castle of Wallingford to act as a place where the French invaders might remain 'until the time they might achieve their evil purpose'.

The speaker consulted the Lords, and there was agreement that there was sufficient suspicion of treason to imprison the Duke. He entered the tower the following day.

30th January 1462

Edmund MacRichard Butler is appointed as governor of Ormond in Ireland.

Lordship in Ireland played a significant role in the Wars of the Roses. Support for both sides of the conflict came from Ireland: the Lancastrians supplying Harlech from Ireland, the Yorkists raising armies and invading from Ireland.

The Butler family had been Lords of Ormond for generations. Holding lands in England as well as Ireland, the family, often delegated local rule, as they did in this instance.

In 1462 the Butlers took advantage of the Wars of the Roses to settle some scores with their long-time foes the Desmonds. John Butler, 6th Earl of Osmond, travelled to Ireland with a retinue. Along with Edmund, his cousin, he marched on Waterford.

The Lancastrian supporting Butlers captured not only the town but the son of the Earl of Desmond. The Desmond's responded with regular encroachments into Butler lands.

Edmund decided to face them. He swept down the Suir Valley and found the Desmond armed band at Piltown.

The ensuing battle, the only battle of the wars of the roses fought in the Lordship of Ireland, was a disaster for the Butler's. 400 of their retinue died. Edmund was captured.

Desmond and Yorkist pre-eminence in Ireland was restored.

31st January 1464

John Tiptoft was appointed as the Chancellor of Ireland for life.

In 1464 much of Ireland was under the control of the English. The Dublin Pale and Ulster, in particular, were under English control. An English government of Ireland was in place in Dublin. Roughly replicating the English structure of Government, it had a range of administrative roles and offices.

John Tiptoft, Earl of Worcester or 'The butcher of England' as the Lancastrians called him, was given the position of Chancellor of Ireland in 1464. It was followed in 1467 with the role of Deputy Lord Deputy.

Tiptoft had earned his reputation. In England, he had been appointed Lord High Constable in 1462. It was a role in which he excelled and seemingly took delight in. He oversaw the trials of many Lancastrians. Many were executed. The executions were often gruesome with some being castrated prior to execution and others quartered and impaled alongside being beheaded.

Tiptoft was Edward's 'bad cop', and the same brutal administration of justice was to come to Ireland when he visited. The most famous example being the execution of Thomas Fitzgerald, 7th Earl of Desmond.

Tiptoft held other positions of state including that of Treasurer. His brilliant early career as a scholar had been very much forgotten when the Lancastrians regained control of England in 1470.

He was quickly attained and executed, his last words being a request to the executioner to make 3 strikes on his neck as a sign to the trinity.

February

1st February 1458

A letter written by William Botoner to Sir John Fastolfe on this date is within the Paston Letters collection.

The Paston Letters contain correspondence from several people linked to the family. This particular letter illustrates how the great magnates were operating in 1458. Armed retinues accompanying the Dukes and Earls shows how tense the situation was.

"The King came to Westminster last week; the Duke of York came to London with his own household, only to the number of 140 horse, as it is said: and the Earl of Salisbury with 400 horse in his company, four score knights and squires.

The Duke of Somerset came to London on the last day of January with 200 horse, and lodges outside the Temple Bar and the Duke of Exeter shall be here this week, with a great strong fellowship, as it was said.

The Earl of Warwick has not yet come, because the wind is not yet favourable for him: the Duke of Exeter is greatly displeased that my Lord of Warwick occupies his office, and takes upon him the keeping of the sea".

The letter shows how London was bursting to the seams with armed camps as tensions rose. The factionalism led to a spiralling effect of each side matching or beating, the other in terms of the size of the retinue that accompanied the Dukes and Earls. It was a powder keg.

2nd February 1461

Battle of Mortimer's Cross

The Battle of Mortimer's Cross is the first Battle in which Edward personally commanded. It is significant as it is the beginning of what became the Towton Campaign. The symbolism connected to this Battle remains in use to this day.

Edward IV was in Ludlow when he heard the news of the deaths of his father, brother, and the Earl of Salisbury. He needed to act fast and regroup with the Earl of Warwick.

His route to London was blocked though. On 2nd February he was faced with a Lancastrian Army at Mortimer's Cross in the Welsh Marches.

As the rivals squared up to one another, there was a fantastic sight in the sky. A perihelion appeared. A rare sight in which there seems to be 3 suns. It was taken as a sign from the gods.

The Yorkist army made good use of their local knowledge. The Lancastrian force had to advance across open land. Yorkist archers may have been located on higher ground. An account suggests that archers were deployed to force the Lancastrian infantry towards the River Lugg.

The Lancastrian army was routed at Mortimer's Cross. Contemporary accounts do not provide enough depth to state precisely what happened. Some suggest that Owen Tudor's detachment was overcome, followed by swift defeat.

Edward adopted the 3 suns as his personal symbol. It features heavily in the Edward IV roll, his personal genealogy and legitimisation of his rule.

3rd February 1399

The death of John of Gaunt. His son is denied inheritance by Richard II resulting in the crown's usurpation by Henry IV and the beginning of the Lancastrian rule.

Though John of Gaunt's death is 56 years before the Wars of the Roses outbreak, it is a pivotal moment in the conflict's long-term causes. Richard II's refusal to allow Gaunt's son to inherit led to the usurping of the throne by Henry IV. This led to questions about right and proper lineage with arguments over right being discussed in Parliament in 1460.

John of Gaunt had dominated the political scene in the reign of Edward III. By far the wealthiest of the barons he was patron to many.

His influence was not always viewed positively. In the Great Rebellion of 1381, Gaunt's head was called for.

Fearful of another powerful magnate who could challenge his rule, Richard II chose not to allow Gaunt's son, Henry, to enter into his inheritance.

It was to prove fatal for Richard. His cousin rose against him, captured him, imprisoned him, and took his crown, leaving Richard II to die in Pontefract Castle.

Later, this deed would lead to questions about the legitimacy of monarchs and genealogies of the Plantagenet family's various branches grew in visual significance as the country descended into the dynastic dispute that was the Wars of the Roses.

4th February 2013

Scientists from the University of Leicester announced that DNA testing has conclusively proven that the remains discovered underneath the car park at Greyfriars were those of King Richard III.

For centuries, the whereabouts of the remains of Richard III remained aa mystery. It was known that his body had been taken to Leicester. What became of it was unclear.

Contemporary sources did not help. Some suggested that Richard had been unceremoniously dumped into the River Soar, in which case his remains would be lost forever. Other sources hinted at a more dignified, yet simple, burial.

It was these sources that led to an investigation fronted by the author and historian Phillipa Langley. The evidence, and a feeling of 'here' from Langley led to identifying a possible site: A car park, adjacent to Greyfriars in Leicester City centre.

A multi-disciplinary team of experts set about the task of examining and painstakingly excavating the site. Unsurprisingly for a former churchyard, they found remains on the very first day. They matched physical descriptions of Richard III and bore the signs of injuries consistent with those that sources say Richard had died of.

DNA experts from the University of Leicester then traced living people directly descended from the same maternal line as the former King. They took samples from several people, including the current royal family. A comparison with the remains was carried out.

The DNA matched. Richard III had been found.

5th February 1451

The last day of hearings in Kent in which the King presided over the trials of key rebels.

In 1450 two uprisings had taken place in Kent and adjoining counties. The largest of these was the Cade Revolt. The rebels had marched on London, crossed London Bridge and summarily executed several nobles. The revolt was ended through a promise of a general pardon, except for the ring leaders.

It was a promise the Council had no intention of keeping. Once the rebels had returned to their homes, commissions were established to identify those involved in causing the revolt. Once those investigations were concluded many barons, judges and soldiers accompanied the King to Canterbury, where he and other nobles presided over hearings.

5th February 1451 was the final day of these hearings. Henry VI presided over the last of four days of judicial hearings in person. Resulting from these hearings were 9 beheadings at Rochester. A further 12 executions took place on a later date.

The heads were taken to London and placed on spikes along London Bridge. In Kent, the mass executions became colloquially known as the "Harvest of Heads". The executions sent out a strong message to the area: insurrections would not be tolerated.

The show of force by the crown attempted to prevent any further uprisings or sedition in the region. There been the revolts led by Cheyne and Cade. The South East was also the region in which the Duke of Suffolk had been murdered, and where the Peasants Revolt had begun 70 years earlier. A hardline was now taken. Control was being asserted—the hard way.

6th February 1455

A Papal Ambassador calls upon England to join a Crusade.

Pope Nicholas V was eager to tackle the problem of "the Turk" in Eastern Europe. The Ottomans had advanced and were fighting against Christian armies.

He dispatched the Archbishop of Ravenna to gather support in Western Europe for a Holy Crusade against this threat from the east. England was granted a jubilee, usually only offered to those who had visited the Vatican or Holy Land. It was one way of the Church reminding the ordinary people of England and their masters of their duties as Christians.

The ambassador met with the Royal Council twice. On both occasions saying how vital a Crusade was and assuring the Crown of a glorious victory.

He faced several obstacles, though. His embassy had arrived as Henry VI recovered his senses. The Council he met on the second occasion was quite different to that of his first meeting as the Yorkists had resigned by that point and Lancastrian nobles had returned to office.

Finances in England were also tight, this was the middle of a great economic slump and bullion crisis. England and France, who were also asked to join the Crusade, had only recently fought the Battle of Castillon. As far as both sides in that conflict were concerned, the war was not over.

Additionally, there was tension within England and growing lawlessness around the country. The Royal Council had little choice but to decline to participate.

7th February 1478

Henry Stafford appointed as High Steward.

Henry Stafford was the Duke of Buckingham. He was one of King Edward's liegemen and related to the King. The High Steward's position was administrative in nature but often a title to denote importance with officials doing most of the work. It did though include some essential duties.

The Duke of Buckingham's appointment was to fulfil a straightforward task. To pass the death sentence on George, Duke of Clarence. The Duke had been accused of treason. His accuser was none other than his brother, King Edward IV.

In a unique scenario, a senior noble's trial, heard in Parliament as was tradition, saw the monarch himself acting as the prosecutor. As you would expect in a trial, witnesses were called. All for the prosecution, George was offered no defence. George had little chance of being found not guilty.

Parliament passed its verdict. What was needed was a High Steward to pass sentence. That task went to the loyal Henry Stafford, who duly proclaimed the death sentence.

The Duke of Clarence was returned to the Tower of London. The sentence was not carried out immediately, and the House of Commons raised the matter of the execution with the King.

George was executed in private some ten days after sentencing. Legend has it that he was drowned in a vat of Malmsey wine.

8th February 1452

Thomas Mulso was raising men in the name of the Duke of York at Fotheringay.

In Medieval England, raising a force of men through array or muster was an act of war. It was the preserve of the King or an official acting on his behalf to undertake such a call to arms. For it to happen without official consent was unlawful. To do so meant that there was a severe conflict between the two parties.

The conflict between the Dukes of York and Somerset had reached a breaking point by early 1452. York was now resolved to tackle the matter through military might. Consequently, his men, such as Thomas Mulso, were dispatched to his lands to muster forces. York also called upon towns that he believed to be sympathetic to his cause to rally to his side, writing to the people of Shrewsbury:

"It is well known unto you... what laud, what worship... was ascribed of all nations unto the people of this realm, whilst the kingdom's sovereign lord stood possessed of his lordship in the realm of France and Duchy of Normandy; and what derogation, loss of merchandise, lesion of honour snd villainy, is reported unto the English nation, for the loss of the same, through the envy, malice and untruth of the Duke of Somerset... who ever prevails and rules about the kings person".

York is laying the blame for England's plight in Normandy and France, along with its economic consequences, firmly at the door of Somerset. His intention is to force Somerset's hand and for himself to be in the ascendency. This letter had an adverse effect, it was forwarded to the King, and the Council began a muster to confront the Duke of York. That confrontation took place later in the year at Dartford.

9th February 1450

Thomas Cheyne is hanged, drawn and quartered.

Cheyne, or Bluebeard as he called himself, was from Kent. In 1449 and 1450, the region's people were becoming increasingly dissatisfied with the Government of the area.

Taxes were an issue; The Wars with France had ravaged the local economy and spent the lives of many local men, and there was a sense of injustice around how local administration was managed.

Cheyne, whose brother was an influential Lollard, chose to act. On 31st January he made a rallying call for the men of Kent to revolt against the 'evil counsel' of the Duke of Suffolk, Bishop of Salisbury, and Lord Saye.

Men gathered and were riotous. The uprising was short-lived though as Cheyne was soon apprehended.

He was found guilty of treason and on 9th February executed in brutal fashion. He was drawn, hanged, then had his entrails cut out and burnt before being beheaded and quartered.

If this was intended to scare the population into quiet compliance, it did not work. Soon after the same area rose again under the leadership of Jack Cade.

10th February 1463

Commission to William Stanley to arrest deserters from the Yorkist Army

The Yorkist victory at Towton was staggering in its size and significance. In one day, the political landscape of England was transformed. The Lancastrian army was devastated. Most leading Lancastrians were dead on the battlefield or executed shortly after that.

Morale amongst the victorious Yorkists was, you would imagine, unbelievably high. But a threat remained. Henry, Margaret, and the Prince of Wales had escaped to the north. The Yorkists had a mopping up operation to do.

This element of the Wars of the Roses was not one that was popular with everybody. Despite the almost certain eventual victory, long sieges were a drain on manpower and had a detrimental effect on local affairs.

When Edward IV called for his followers to pursue the Lancastrians into the North East and Scotland, the response was not as he had hoped. This led to commissions such as the one given on this day in 1463 to arrest those men who had failed to march with the King.

Edward's concern seems justified, several men, including the Earl of Northumberland, were soon to switch allegiances and a strong Yorkist army would be best equipped to tackle these issues.

11th February 1466

Birth of Elizabeth of York

11th February 1503

Death of Elizabeth of York

The eldest child of King Edward IV and Elizabeth Woodville, Elizabeth was destined to have a life of significance. As a Royal Princess, Elizabeth would be courted by the Kings and Dukes of Europe's most prestigious states. However, she was born amid a civil war. Her early years saw the crown taken from her father before it was retaken.

Her significance came to bear upon the death of her father. Rumour was rife that her uncle, Richard, intended to marry her and unify the Yorkist cause. Whether that rumour was true or not, we do not know. Her mother had other ideas. With her brothers taken to the Tower and disappearing from public view, presumed dead, the Princess was key to the Woodville family's continued power.

Elizabeth of York was also key to bringing an end to the conflict, which was realised not only by her mother but also by Margaret Beaufort. As Richard faced rebellions, Elizabeth Woodville and Margaret Beaufort negotiated Elizabeth's marriage to Henry Tudor should he claim the throne.

Henry Tudor used this to nullify some potential opposition to his invasion. Elizabeth married Henry Tudor in January 1486, unifying the houses of Lancaster, Tudor, and York.

12th February 1462

The arrest of John de Vere, Earl of Oxford and his son, Aubrey

Whilst the Yorkists had won a decisive victory at Towton, it did not mean that they had total control of the country. There was armed resistance in pockets and strong Lancastrian sentiment in large parts of England and Wales.

In early February 1462, the King received reports of growing unrest around the country. The North-West was unruly, virtually lawless in places. The same was spreading into other remote parts of the country. Sedition was on the rise. Outbursts of violence were happening.

The administration of local justice and estate management was, in places, severely hampered. Action was needed, and on 12th February, two significant decisions were taken by the crown.

First, a commission of 23 barons and 10 judges was appointed to investigate and deal with the insurrections.

Secondly, news of a plot reached the court, and the response was fast and decisive.

The plot implicated the Earl of Oxford. Action was swift. Oxford and his eldest son were arrested on 12th February 1462.

They were tried by the Constable of England, John Tiptoft, becoming the first senior noble to be beheaded due to the court of the man who was to become known as 'the butcher of England'.

13th February 1471

Commission established by the Earl of Warwick to enable an alliance with Louis XI of France

Upon taking control of the Government following the Readeption of Henry VI, the Earl of Warwick sought to change England's foreign policy. Warwick was in a strong but potentially precarious position. If Queen Margaret was to assert her authority, then Warwick could find himself ostracised and powerless.

Also, the Duke of Burgundy was hostile towards Warwick. Warwick, who had always favoured the French, sought change. But doing this was to prove difficult. London's wool merchants would prove to be formidable opponents of such a shift in allegiance: Burgundy was a highly profitable destination for English wool exports.

To encourage merchants to support a change, the French held free fairs for English merchants in the port of Caen, and pro-French sentiment was encouraged by an embassy. Warwick also used his influence in Calais to persuade the Staplers of Calais to support his policy.

On 13th February 1471, he established a formal commission to work with the French on a binding agreement. He had already told the French that he would commit to war against Burgundy in this agreement. Within this agreement was an assurance that Warwick would receive Zeeland and Holland.

The agreement with the French had dire consequences for Warwick. It led to Charles of Burgundy quickly deciding to back Edward IV's invasion of England, a matter that until Warwick's alliance with France, he had been quite content to put to one side.

14th February 1452

The Duke of Buckingham and Lord Bonville appointed to deal with the Yorkist uprising

Throughout 1451 and early 1452, Yorkist propaganda had grown in volume. Its tone also became increasingly belligerent. The Duke of York had numerous complaints.

France and Normandy were being mismanaged, something he resented having previously been the Lieutenant of France.

The economy was in a dire state, partly due to the great economic slump affecting all of Europe but also due to administrative mistakes and poor governance.

On governance, he was scathing of the counsel being given to the King.

Perhaps frustrated at being on the periphery of Government he ramped up his 'loyal opposition' and had begun asking his followers for support. Not just vocal support but a call to arms.

The King responded quickly and in strength to this threat. As well as appointing Buckingham and Bonville, who were to deal with Yorkist agitation in the South West, Henry called upon many barons to attend him with their retinues.

The ensuing politicking and shows of strength between the King and his most powerful subject led ultimately to the confrontation at Dartford. York appeared to gain the upper hand on the day but was politically outwitted and eventually quite humiliated. The uprising did not result in a clash but was a sign of things to come.

15th February 1474

The Earl of Oxford surrenders at St. Michael's Mount.

Oxford and Lord Beaumont had captured St. Michael's Mount on 30th September 1473 with a force of around 400 men. Though relatively insignificant in terms of overall control of the region or country, Oxford's seizing of the Castle was the only military threat posed by Lancastrians to Edward at this time.

Edward soon tired of having the Earl of Oxford holding a castle. He ordered that it be retaken and commissioned John Fortesque to lead a siege. The castle was subjected to a naval blockade and Fortesque brought in the Royal artillery under the command of John Wode. Free pardons were offered to all, including Oxford and Lord Beaumont, who surrendered. The Warkworth Chronicle summarises the end of the siege:

"And so this proverbe was fayne to yelde up the seyde mount, and put hyme in the KyngEs grace; if he had not done so, his owne menne wulde have brought hym oute. And so Fortescu entrd into the said mount, the xv day of Februarij the yere afore sayde, in whichewas vytayle enogh tylle mkdsomere aftere. And so was the Erle aforseyd, the Lord Bemonde, two brotheres of the seide Erles,and Thomas Clyfforde, brought as a presonere to the Kynge; and alle was donne by ther oune foly".

In short, the Chronicle says that the King decided to bring an end to the long siege and that pardons and promises remained in place. If the siege continued, Oxford's own men would bring him out: they were being starved out. On the 15th Fortesque entered the Mount and Castle and took the Earl, Lord Beaumont, Thomas Clifford, and other men into custody. Oxford did not receive a pardon.

16th February 1495

Beheading of Sir William Stanley.

Sir William Stanley was the younger brother of Thomas, Lord Stanley. William had been heavily involved in the Wars of the Roses. He fought at Blore Heath for the Yorkists which led to an attainder being issued by the Lancastrian Parliament.

He then went into exile along with other attained Yorkists but returned with the Calais contingent. As part of that group he marched with Edward north in 1461 and fought bravely at the Battle of Towton.

He was rewarded for this service with the grant of Clifford lands including Skipton Castle in 1465. When the Lancastrians tried to oust Edward in 1471, it was William who captured Margaret of Anjou following the Battle of Tewkesbury.

This earned him great favour, particularly with the Duke of Gloucester. Despite Richard's patronage as both Duke and King, William chose to change sides at the Battle of Bosworth. This decision arguably proved decisive in winning the day for Henry Tudor.

The new King was very grateful for William's intervention, resulting in him being appointed Lord Chamberlain and Chamberlain of the Exchequer. Despite his status and royal favour, Sir William became implicated in the Perkin Warbeck plot to overthrow King Henry VII. The evidence against him was quite flimsy by modern standards, but leniency on a crime of this nature could lead to many more problems. Sir William Stanley was sentenced to death, the execution, beheading, taking place this day in 1495.

17th February 1461

Lancastrian victory at the Second Battle of St. Albans

Following victory in the Battle of Wakefield, the Lancastrians were full of confidence. Their force bolstered by the arrival of Scottish troops. Margaret of Anjou had agreed to a treaty with the Scots to this effect.

The Lancastrians headed south, their goals being the release of King Henry VI, control of London and an end to the Yorkist threat. The advance was quite unruly with several towns being ransacked. This boosted the resolve of the Citizens of London to support the Yorkist cause.

The Earl of Warwick was in London. Edward, now the Duke of York by right, had not arrived with his force. Margaret had to be slowed down or stopped altogether. Warwick chose to confront the advancing Lancastrians at St. Albans.

It was a location he was familiar with, the Yorkists had been victorious there in 1455. Defences were constructed around the town. Warwick was satisfied that his position was secure, and the advance would be halted. His planning was thwarted, though. Lancastrian cavalry managed to outflank the defenders and take advantage of a weak spot in the town's defence.

Faced with the prospect of his army being annihilated, Warwick ordered a hasty retreat to London. The retreat needed to be quick. So quick that he chose to leave behind the prized possession: the King. The day was a resounding success for the Lancastrians. Warwick had been driven back with few losses for the Lancastrian army. More importantly, the King had been found guarded by two Yorkist knights on the battlefield.

18th February 1478

The trial and execution of the Duke of Clarence.

George, Duke of Clarence, was King Edward IV's younger brother and older brother of Richard, then Duke of Gloucester. Clarence was a flamboyant figure but easily led.

As political divisions re-emerged once more in the late 1460s, he chose to ally himself with the Earl of Warwick. Following Edward's landing at Ravenspur in 1471, he changed his allegiance and reverted to his brothers cause.

The elimination of a credible Lancastrian threat did not stop Clarence from being a political nuisance, though. Both himself and Richard married women of the Neville family. They bickered over the distribution of lands and their wives inheritance.

In 1477 one of his retainers was found guilty of necromancy and wishing the King dead, the latter being a treasonable offence. Clarence himself was not implicated in either case, but as Thomas Burdet was led onto the scaffold, Clarence shouted his support for the man. Edward was incensed. He derided George for the:

"most serious [misconduct] … in contempt of the law of the land and a great threat to judges and jurors of the kingdom' and prompted his imprisonment" (The Crowland Chronicle Continuations)

Clarence was summoned to the King. Parliament was hastily convened. George was accused by King Edward himself and put on trial. Witnesses spoke against Clarence. He was found guilty the same day.

He was executed at a later date. Legend has it that he was drowned in a vat of his favourite Malmsey wine. Clarence was also attained by Parliament, ruling out his heirs from the inheritance of his titles, including the crown.

19th February 1461

A letter from the Milanese ambassador on the situation in London

The events in England of 1459-61 were tumultuous. In London, ambassadors and merchants from other countries and Duchy's observed events with interest as they could have consequences for their trade or relations with England. One of the most complete collections of reports and letters by an ambassador is that of the Milanese Ambassador, whose words about February 1461 are noted below.

As Margaret's army drew closer to London, the city took steps to defend itself. News of other towns being ransacked had reached the Capital. So too had the word of the Lancastrian victory at St. Albans. The letter sums up the mood:

"In the meantime they keep a good guard at the gates, which they keep practically closed, and so through all the district they maintain a good guard, and those who are here, thank God, feel no harm or lack of governance. Yet the shops keep closed, and nothing is done either by the tradespeople or by the merchants, and men do not stand in the streets or go far away from home. We are all hoping that, as the Queen and prince have not descended in fury with their troops, the gates may be opened to them upon a good composition, and they may be allowed to enter peacefully. God grant this may happen! otherwise ... favour, and thus we are not without great fear, as ... the least lack of control would ruin everything. God be our protector, and may He not consider our sins!"
Milan State Papers, Parliamentary Archives 1461.

The citizens of London had chosen their side in the conflict. It was a decision that was to stand the Yorkist cause in good stead for much of the Wars of the Roses.

20th February 1478

Petition to Parliament of Roger Twynyho.

Roger Twynyho's wife was blamed by George, Duke of Clarence for the death by poisoning his wife. Isabel, Duchess of Clarence, had, in fact, most probably died because of complications following childbirth.

It is believed that King Edward IV did not know of Clarence's actions concerning Ankarette Twynyho until after the execution of his brother. The following is an extract from Roger Twynyho's petition, dated this day in 1478:

"[They] took from her all her jewels... and also, on the Duke of Clarence's behalf as though he had used the King's power... they then caused her to be brought to the guildhall at Warwick before justices of peace in the county then sitting in session and caused her to be indicted by the same name... of having... given to the said Isabel a venomous drink of ale mixed with poison, of which she sickened until... she died. The justices arraigned Ankarette and a jury appeared and found her guilty, and it was determined that she be taken from the bar there to the gaol at Warwick and from thence should be drawn through the town to the gallows and hanged until she was dead. The sheriff was commanded to do the execution and so he did."

The petition shows that ordinary people had the right to go to Parliament with a concern. Such petitions usually concerned economic or land rights but could include many other issues.

Twynyho received a sympathetic hearing from Parliament. It arrived two weeks after the Duke of Clarence had been found guilty of treason and just days after his execution.

21st February 1456

Bale's Chronicle notes this as the date upon which Henry VI resumed personal rule.

"[on 21st February 1456] the king resumed his rule and discharged the Duke of York of the protectorship".

Henry is recorded as having attended Parliament in this week, and the Protectorship did come to an end at around this time. As is quite common, dates in sources do not match precisely. However, there was parliamentary activity on this date, detailed below, so it is quite conceivable that the decision to resume personal rule had been taken and the transfer of power back to the King was being managed at this point. The parliamentary roll suggests 25th for Henry officially resuming control.

The same date saw Parliament deal with a petition regarding Italian merchants. The commons asked for protectionist measures to ensure that prices and profits were at an adequate level. From the Parliamentary Roll:

"Italian merchants travel round the county to buy woollen cloth, wool, wool fells and tin they are able to see the poverty of the people and, by offering to pay for the goods with ready cash, keep prices low. From 21st February 1456 they should be allowed to buy those goods only in the ports of London, Southampton and Sandwich, upon pain of forfeiting the goods bought. And the said merchants should sell all their imported goods to the King's lieges within four months, and if they fail to sell them may export them without paying custom. But if they do not sell to the King's lieges and do not depart as soon as weather permits after four months they should forfeit all their goods. If they are storm driven to another port they may buy woollen cloth there."

22nd February 1461

The Earl of Warwick and March rendezvous in the Cotswolds

Following the Yorkist defeat at Wakefield, the Lancastrians had marched south. The Earl of Warwick intercepted them at St. Albans, where his army was defeated. It was now imperative for their cause that the two main bodies of men joined together to face the threat posed by Queen Margaret's army. This happened on 22nd February 1461.

Warwick was in retreat from his defeat at St. Albans. Edward was fresh from his victory at Mortimer's Cross. Ahead of them lay London, apprehensive about the future as the spectre of Margaret of Anjou's rampaging army loomed large behind the troops of the two Yorkist Earls.

London was busy preparing its defences. So tight was the security that a group of Aldermen were forbidden from leaving the city. Warwick and Edward had to think quick, strategically, and pragmatically.

Warwick did so, almost immediately. He informed Edward that he was now the rightful King. With his father dead, he inherited the claim. The Lancastrians had broken the Act of Accord. By right of genealogy and legally he could claim the crown.

And that claim is precisely what was declared later, in London. The popular young Earl of March was welcomed and heralded as King Edward IV. Now, he needed to win the right to keep the title. He did not have long to wait for that to happen.

23rd February 1447

Duke Humphrey arrested on charges of treason.

Duke Humphrey, the King's uncle, was a hugely popular figure with the general population, and he was a constant thorn in the side of two of the most powerful men in the Council: Cardinal Beaufort and the Duke of Suffolk.

They clashed over the direction of the campaigns in France. Another source of conflict was Beaufort being a senior representative of both the King and the Church.

In 1441 Humphrey was forced to take a back seat in national politics. His wife, Eleanor Cobham, was found guilty of necromancy. The scandal was too damaging to his reputation, and so he avoided court.

In 1447 the Duke of Suffolk had a policy in France that was incredibly unpopular. Civil unrest was on the rise, and the people were whispering of a return of 'Good Duke Humphrey' to lead a challenge on Suffolk.

A Parliament was called for February 1447. As Humphrey approached Bury St. Edmunds, where Parliament was being held, he was met with a message commanding him to go straight to his lodgings and stay there.

Shortly after, Viscount Beaumont, the Duke of Buckingham, Marquis of Somerset, Earl of Salisbury, and Lord Sudeley arrived at his lodgings. They arrested Humphrey on a charge of treason and imprisoned him. He died in custody days later so the full nature of the charge can only be assumed. It was most possibly a conspiracy charge of planning uprisings against Suffolk, perhaps with additional charges of wishing to overthrow the King in his own favour.

24th February 1462

King Edward IV heads north to address the Scottish threat

There was a threat to the fledgeling Yorkist regime with several castles holding out for the Lancastrians and Queen Margaret's alliance holding firm.

Edward was keen to crush this. He planned a campaign that would flush the Lancastrians out of the north and make the Scots think twice about interfering in English affairs.

The date set for his march north was 24th February 1462.

11 days before this, a plot was uncovered. The Earl of Oxford intended to follow Edward north with an army of some 1000 horse. It would appear to be following in support of the King, then act as a potent threat to his rear as Battle commenced.

As this happened in the north, the Duke of Somerset would sail from France and land on the south coast, taking a relatively undefended London.

King Henry would march south at the same time, leaving King Edward isolated and surrounded.

With the plot uncovered, Edward was able to make plans to prevent the Lancastrian's scheming from succeeding.

In the meantime, the Lancastrians struggled to raise large armies, though Edward's own Commissions of Array had not been as successful as he would have hoped.

25th February 1425

The title of Duke of York is restored. The title had been stripped because of Richard of Cambridge's treason in 1415. This had been followed, at Agincourt, of his brothers, the 2nd Duke of York's, death. Cambridge's son, Richard, becomes the 3rd Duke of York.

In 1415 Richard, Earl of Cambridge was executed on the eve of the English invasion of France.

He had been implicated in the Southampton Plot, tried by the peers of the land and upon being found guilty of treason, sentenced to death by beheading.

The Earl of Cambridge was the second eldest son of Edmund of Langley, 1st Duke of York. His brother, Edward the 2nd Duke of York was childless in 1415, and so had he not been executed, Cambridge would have been heir to the Duchy of York.

Edward was killed fighting at the Battle of Agincourt, leaving Richard Plantagenet, son of the Earl of Cambridge as his heir.

But Richard could not inherit his father's lands or titles as an attainder had accompanied the death sentence. The attainder was lifted as the young Richard grew up.

On this day in 1425, he was granted the right to his inherited title, becoming Richard, 3rd Duke of York.

The title itself did not mean that Richard had all of the rights and lands. They were all restored but at later dates as the Duke reached adulthood.

26th February 1462

John de Vere, 12th Earl of Oxford, beheaded. There is a conflict of dates as the Short English Chronicle suggests the 23rd.

The 12th Earl of Oxford played little role in the military aspects of the Wars of the Roses. He was however quite significant politically as he was appointed to oversee investigations into Yorkist behaviour.

The 12th Earl of Oxford had managed to stay out of the bickering that had blighted English politics throughout the 1450s. It was not until 1459 when he, like other barons, was faced with a decision over who to back as war became seemingly inevitable.

He chose to back the King and he and his eldest son Aubrey were noted in chronicles as being close to the Queen. Indeed, Oxford must have been close to Queen Margaret as, in the aftermath of the Parliament of Devils, he was appointed to lead an Anti-Yorkist Commission of Array.

His execution of that array was not forgotten. Following the Yorkist rise to the ascendancy in mid to late 1460 he failed to attend Parliament, claiming ill health. Following Towton, his continued support for Margaret and his previous actions sealed his fate.

He and Aubrey were arrested on charges of treason. Both were found guilty, and on this day in 1462 John de Vere, 12th Earl of Oxford was executed by beheading on Tower Hill. His son had been executed 6 days previously.

27th February 1461

Edward and the Earl of Warwick arrived in London

The Earl of Warwick had rendezvoused with the Earl of March in the Cotswolds as they made their way to London from St. Albans and Mortimer's Cross, respectively. On route, Warwick had persuaded Edward that he had the right to be King and that now was the time to assert that claim.

Upon their arrival in London, the Yorkists set about strengthening their position with their armies behind them. They needed to persuade the people to support them and protect the City against Queen Margaret's army.

Persuading the City was not as straightforward as it may seem. Though London was Yorkist in its leanings, Henry was a crowned and anointed monarch. Furthermore, the Lancastrians had defeated the Earl of Warwick at St. Albans and plans had been mooted for welcoming the royal party back into the capital.

Days of military preparation and political negotiation were to follow. Key to the success of both was a simple fact: Edward was everything that Henry was not: young, affable, athletic, and not tainted with any of the scandals, mistakes, or losses of the previous 15 years.

Soon the Yorkists had persuaded the City that they were rightful rulers and that they could fulfil the task. In March, Edward was proclaimed King.

It did not stop Queen Margaret's army advancing to the gates of London. They did so before retreating to the north. The chase given to them by the Yorkist army was to secure the throne.

28th February 1458

Great Council Meeting

The divisions between rival families and factions throughout England had reached boiling point by February of 1458. It was clear that to preserve peace, agreements and compromises would have to be made and accepted. In the build up to a Great Council Meeting, held on 28th February 1458, several meaningful discussions took place.

Rivalries between noble families were having a detrimental impact on the functioning of court and Government. The political factionalism had already resulted in the First Battle of St. Albans. The Protectorship of Richard Duke of York had seen some of the court party removed from office. In general, a consensus government focussed on improved fiscal management had been the objective.

Old wounds had reopened in the time after the return of King Henry VI to the throne. In the North, the Earl of Northumberland's men continued to clash with those of the Neville family. In November 1457, the Percy family, holders of the Earldom of Northumberland, were persuaded to agree to arbitration with the Neville's, who also agreed to participate.

Talks such as these went a long way to ensuring that the Great Council could take place. The two families made agreements regarding future conduct. This was expected to apply to their retainers as well.

The Great Council meeting itself paved the way for the Loveday Parade later in the year. It established the need for conciliatory tones and actions. The nobility agreed that this was in everybody's best interests. So Queen Margaret proceeded with plans for an elaborate Loveday at which the rivals would agree to peace and at which terms of compensation would be settled.

29th February 1452

Richard Duke of York crosses the Thames to Dartford. He had been refused entry to London. Now, the Duke was pursued by a Royal Army commanded by Lord Bonville and the Duke of Buckingham.

The political situation in 1452 was quite complicated and very precarious. Following the loss of France, the rivalry between the Dukes of Somerset and York had become more intense. The two became more entrenched in their views, and on most matters, there was no middle ground.

Coupled to this was the Duke of York's stance on how Government was being managed. For him, it was unwieldy, inefficient, and corrupt. Since the impeachment then the murder of the Duke of Suffolk, it appeared that little had been done to halt poor practice.

Hailed by the commoners, particularly in the South East, the Duke of York had become the leader of the 'loyal opposition'. He had support within the nobility for his views, though not a majority.

Furthermore, Richard Duke of York had been frustrated by a lack of role at the heart of Government. He, at this time, was heir to the throne. He was the most senior prince of royal blood. Yet he had no particular role at the time.

These frustrations had boiled over by February 1452, and he had issued calls to arms amongst his supporters and towns he believed to be sympathetic to his views.

Aware of these actions, a royal army was mustered to face the Duke. It was supported by many prominent nobles. Now they were in pursuit of Richard. His crossing of the Thames took him to Dartford, where the two sides would face on another.

March

1st March 1484

Elizabeth Woodville left the sanctuary of Westminster Abbey. She paid homage to Richard III in exchange for his public promise to find suitable marriage partners for her daughters.

The decision to leave Westminster Abbey's sanctuary cannot have been an easy one for Elizabeth Woodville to make.

Her family had been targeted by Richard as he wrestled control of the machinery of Government. Her sons had gone to the Tower to prepare for a coronation then, under Richard's care, vanished from public view.

Her marriage had been declared invalid by Richard's parliament and her own lands forfeit. Yet there were signs of a rapprochement toward her family by Richard.

There were also rumours circulating about the future husband of the former Queens eldest daughter, Elizabeth of York.

As her thoughts are not recorded, it is conjecture to work on regarding Elizabeth Woodville's reasoning behind leaving the sanctuary. That it was predetermined is known as messengers and heralds frequently visited her.

Perhaps she felt that there was no further threat to herself or her family. Perhaps the failure of Buckingham's Rebellion resigned her to a new and different role?

Or was she already confident in the success of plots being hatched with Margaret Beaufort for her daughter's future marriage to the Tudor claimant?

2nd March 1484

Foundation of the College of Arms.

The College of Arms was established in 1484. It acted as the overseer of all matters concerning heraldry in England and Wales. It remains in existence to this day.

The heralds were granted a common seal and the authority to act in the name of the King. Furthermore, they were given a building, Coldharbour House, where they could administer all matters relating to heraldry. The Duke of Norfolk, the Earl Marshall of England, was assigned as patron of the body. The charter for the Royal College of Arms summarises its function as:

"...)the Garter King of Arms of England, the King of Arms of the Southern parts, the King of Arms of the Northern parts, the King of Arms of Wales, and all other heralds and pursuivants of arms... for the time being, shall be in perpetuity a body corporate in fact and name, and shall preserve a succession unbroken."

The College had responsibility for the heralds who organised tournaments. Through this, the College of Arms became known as the source of expertise in armour and, as coats of arms are hereditary, noble genealogy as well.

The College of Arms has retained a role in the modern world. Though the need for heralds at Tournaments diminished over time, heraldry's use grew in other areas. For example, the use of Coats of Arms on town and corporate liveries became part of the College of Arms' function.

The most visible work of the heralds of the College of Arms remains state functions. They are prominent at Royal weddings, funerals, the opening of Parliament and at State Banquets.

3rd March 1452

The Duke of York and the Royal Party had confronted each other at Blackheath. The Duke had made demands of the Government. Both parties had been backed by sizeable retinues in a very tense standoff.

The Duke of York's demands at Blackheath had been agreed to by Henry VI.

They were:

- To be named heir, which by blood he was.
- The arrest and trial of Somerset.

King Henry VI had agreed to both of these demands. The former was a case of a hereditary right that the Duke of York had wanted to be made clear to all. The latter was a continuation of the clash between the two Dukes, and Henry probably felt as though he had little choice but to agree. After all, it would be the Lords who determined such a case, not himself personally.

Somerset was duly taken into custody and was being taken toward a ship as a prisoner when Queen Margaret realised what was afoot. She intervened and forced his immediate release.

By the time the Duke of York arrived at King Henry's tent, Margaret and Somerset were already there.

This resulted in York outlining his complaints followed by a heated exchange between the King and Queen. The outcome was not in York's favour. Somerset was free, and no trial was called for.

Once in London, York was made to swear an oath of allegiance in St. Pauls Cathedral on 10th March before being allowed to return, rather humiliated, to Ludlow.

4th March 1464

Lancastrian rebels are defeated at Dryslwyn by John Dwnn and Roger Vaughan.

In 1464 a series of pro-Lancastrian uprisings took place. In the North West of England, there was a rise in lawlessness. The unrest spread into Wales as a series of rivalries re-emerged.

Around Dryslwyn Castle in South Wales, this took the form of a bitter uprising. Lands in the area had been farmed by men who politically were opposed and between whom there was no love lost. Thomas ap Gruffyd was one landholder. He was a staunch Lancastrian.

His neighbour and foe was Henry ap Gwilym, both had men they could call upon: and they did so as part of a planned revolt. As unrest spread around the country, tensions in the Dryslwyn area grew. A plot had been hatched that would see Dryslwyn become embroiled in national scheming.

The Duke of Somerset, even though he was effectively under surveillance, planned a coordinated uprising. He would oversee rebellion in the North of England. In the North of Wales Roger Puleston and John Hanmer were entrusted with leadership. In the South of Wales, leadership fell to Jasper Tudor, with much assistance from Philip Castle of Pembroke, Philip Mantel of Gower, Hopkyn ap Rhys and Lewis ap Rhydderch.

Such a widespread and coordinated uprising could pose severe problems for Edward IV. But, in South Wales, it was suppressed quite quickly. As trouble flared John Dwnn, the Captain of Carmarthen and Aberystwyth and Roger Vaughan organised a defence. At Dryslwyn, they overwhelmed the rebels and crushed the uprising. Dwnn was rewarded handsomely for his quick thinking and actions.

5th March 1486

Elizabeth Woodville is restored to her Dower lands.

Dower lands are the estates granted to a noble lady. For a Queen Consort such as Elizabeth, these lands would be expected to raise revenue to sustain her personal servants, court and living expenses.

Elizabeth's Dower lands were forfeited during the reign of Richard III. This deprived her of income and was most probably motivated by a desire to limit her ability to interfere in the establishment of Richard's government.

The removal of Elizabeth's Dower lands was also part of the move to block Elizabeth's family's influence. Richard III had had Earl Rivers, the Queen's brother, executed on the same day that he was invited to take the throne.

Henry Tudor took a rather different view. It was Elizabeth who had brokered the deal with his own mother for his marriage to Elizabeth of York. As the mother of his bride, Elizabeth Woodville was of high status and was deserving of a lifestyle that required substantial funds.

His restoration of her Dower lands illustrates her importance and that he was willing to reverse decisions made earlier that had adversely affected Yorkists, so it was conciliatory as well as deserving of his mother-in-law.

Elizabeth herself had little use of substantial Dower lands following her daughter's marriage to King Henry VII. She retired from public life and lived out the rest of her life in the relative solitude of a nunnery.

6th March 1450

A group of plotters in Bury St Edmunds plan to kill King Henry VI and replace him with Richard Duke of York.

From the Kings Bench Ancient Indictments

"[William Oldhall amongst others], proposing to depose the King and put the Duke of York on the throne and realising they could not do this while he remained powerful with his lords about him, plotted his death and destruction at Bury St. Edmunds on 6th March... [Bills were posted] on men's doors and windows that the King following counsel of the late Duke of Suffolk, the Bishops of Salisbury and Chichester, Lord Saye and others , had sold the kingdoms of England and France...

England was a tinderbox of discontent in 1450.

The economic problems coupled with high taxes and the losses in Normandy and France were incredibly damaging to morale. Anger had been directed mostly at the Duke of Suffolk. To a lesser extent at the Bishops of Salisbury and Chichester, the latter had been murdered earlier in the year.

Now the ire was aimed at the King's person. The solution proposed by rebels was the deposition of Henry VI and the crowning of the Duke of York. This had political implications for the Duke of York. He was now being touted as a potential King, which was when large parts of the country were in revolt, caused by things that the Duke himself was complaining about.

Oldhall was executed for his role in the plot. The Duke of York was in no way implicated, but the calls from the commons for him to lead was one that would reappear at several points over the coming ten years.

7th March 1470

King Edward IV hears of a rebel Commission of Array

Edward was at Waltham Abbey on 7th March 1470. He had been joined by many barons, including Henry Percy, Earl of Northumberland, the Earl of Arundel and Lord Hastings.

His reign had faced a significant test. The Earl of Warwick had, for a period, kept the King under virtual house arrest. Government had been in the King's name but by Warwick's hand. Edward's 'release' had diminished Warwick's influence at court but did little to address the Earl and his supporters' complaints about Edward's rule.

Rebels were known to be preparing and some, Lord Welles and Dymmock, were held captive by the King. The news that the King received on 7th March was potentially devastating. The rebels had issued a Commission of Array, gathering a large army to use against the King.

Edward intended to march north to tackle the northern rebels. He was told that Sir Robert Welles was raising an army of 100,000 men (chroniclers are prone to exaggeration). This would mean facing two rebel armies, and he was unsure of the intent of the Earl of Warwick.

The solution was simple. As Sir Robert Welles was the son of his captive, Lord Welles, he wrote to him and stated that he would execute Lord Welles if his force did not disperse.

Robert dispersed part of his army. Edward went ahead and executed Lord Welles despite the dispersal of his son's army.

8th March 1464

Here we have an example of Medieval debt recovery. In much the same way as in the modern world, a debtor would be taken to court. Here, the defendant initially states that they have no case to answer. Therefore, a hearing date is set where both sides can make their case. This involves attorneys. The defendants, failing to attend the second hearing, are ordered to pay the plaintiff, and recovery measures are set down.

Court of Common Pleas, CP 40/812, rot. 251

Term: Easter 1464. County: London. Writ type: Debt (sale of goods)

Damages claimed: £10. Damages awarded: 30s

Case type: Sale of goods

Pleading: Edward Pygott states that on 10th May 1458, in London, Elizabeth, wife of Peter Hous, when she was a single woman, bought from him 160 hides of grey, and 30 hides called 'rygges' of grey for 48s 1½d. Also, on 16th September 1460, she bought 42 hides of budge and 10 black lamb hides for a further 30s 8d, and on 8th March 1461 she bought 300 miniver skins, 57 ermine skins, 7 marten skins and 3 skins of white leather for £3 16s 8d, all payable on request. However, Elizabeth has not paid for any of these items, either before or after her marriage to PH, to his damage of £10.

Cases such as these could take several hearings to be resolved. Both parties had the right to legal representation. They could make arguments at each hearing. Attorneys could attempt to agree out of court settlements, though this did not happen in this case. Should the debts not be repaid on time, there was the provision to place the debtor into gaol until such as time as the court's orders had been fulfilled. The cost of imprisonment was often borne by the prisoner.

9th March 1484

Robert Brackenbury receives grants from Richard III.

Robert Brackenbury was one of Richard IIIs most loyal servants. He lived in County Durham, where his family's lands bordered those held by Richard in lieu of his wife, Anne Neville.

Brackenbury had entered Richard's service during his overlordship of the North of England, becoming one of his retainers and feoffees. By 1479, he was the treasurer of the Duke's household.

When Richard became King, Brackenbury was soon rewarded for his previous service with important roles. He was one of the few Northern knights to receive a royal appointment early in Richard's reign, being appointed as Constable of the Tower of London.

In this role he would have been one of the few who had access to the Princes in the Tower, leading some to believe that he was responsible for their presumed murder.

Brackenbury's continued loyalty and service bore fruit following the failure of the Buckingham rebellion. As Richard attained those who had risen against his rule, he used forfeited lands to implant loyal supporters from the north. Brackenbury was one of the chief recipients.

The grants made on 9th March 1484, with more to follow on 23rd, allocated him lands forfeited by Earl Rivers and the Cheney family. The lands were chiefly in Kent, with additional manors being granted to him in Suffolk and Sussex. The income from these estates, some £500 per annum, and his appointments were higher than most barons.

Brackenbury remained loyal to the end, he died on the battlefield at Bosworth.

10th March 1463

Henry Beaufort, Duke of Somerset, is pardoned by Edward IV. This followed his surrender on terms of Bamburgh Castle to Sir Ralph Percy on 24th December 1462.

When the Duke of Somerset surrendered Bamburgh Castle in December of 1461, he did so on terms. One of these was an agreement that he would swear allegiance to King Edward IV and receive a general pardon for his role as a Lancastrian commander.

It seems astonishing that a man at the heart of the Lancastrian strategy to this point could be pardoned in this manner whilst many with much lesser ties to the Lancastrian regime had been summarily executed. Somerset, however, was a wholly different case. As a Duke, he was as senior a subject as one could get. He personally commanded the respect of many lords, knights, and commoners.

Edward wanted to utilise this. Somerset at Edward's court would reduce Lancastrian agitation. For a while, Somerset proved loyal, participating in sieges in the North East and advising the King on strategy.

By 1463 though, he was plotting with Lancastrians once more, encouraging uprisings around the country. He switched sides openly to fight for Henry VI in March 1463 when he surrendered two castles he held for Edward to Margaret of Anjou's cause.

Somerset then fought in the Battle of Hexham the following year. Captured after his defeat, he was summarily executed.

11th March 1461 and 11th March 1471

Edward moves to secure his crown

The pursuit of Margaret of Anjou to the north in 1461 began with the first Yorkist troops leaving London under the command of Fauconberg.

William Neville, Lord Fauconberg was commander of the vanguard of the Yorkist army. With such a large force making the journey north, with forces from Yorkist estates in the midlands and Wales joining en route, the march up the Great North Road was staggered to not result in men and baggage becoming backed up. There followed armies commanded by the Earl of Warwick and the King. The army departing from London comprised many from the Yorkist lords' personal retinues and recruits from the South East and London. Men recruited by the likes of the Earl of Warwick in the midlands joined the army as it headed north. Forces under the Duke of Norfolk's command were raised in East Anglia, they took a different route north.

Exactly ten years later, Edward once again embarked on a campaign to secure his crown.

On 11th March 1471, Edward IV, his exiled army and allies set sail from Burgundy.

Having been forced into exile by the Earl of Warwick's armies, Edward had endured a period of exile. He had travelled to Burgundy, where his sister Margaret was married to Charles the Bold. Initially, the Burgundians showed very little interest in Edward. If anything, his presence was rather embarrassing. Suddenly, in early 1471, this changed. France changed its policy toward Burgundy and allied with the Lancastrian establishment in England. When the French attacked St. Quentin, Charles the Bold saw the need for a Yorkist England as an ally. A Burgundian fleet and army was assembled. It sailed on this day in 1471, eventually landing at Ravenspur, Yorkshire, several days later.

12th March 1470

Battle of Losecote Field

Edward IV was faced with rebellion. He was determined to overcome the threat posed by the rebels. He had already told Sir Robert Welles, leader of the revolt, that his father, a prisoner of Edward, would be executed if his army did not disperse.

As Edward marched north, much of Welles' army returned home. Some, however, remained. Edward found them near Empingham.

With scouts reporting that Robert Welles had only retreated as far as Stamford, Edward chose to be very direct. His army drew up to face the rebels. Lord Welles was dragged before them. And, in sight of the rebel army, beheaded.

The Royal artillery then opened up on the rebel force, and a rapid advance was led by Edward himself.

The rebels panicked, turned, and fled. Many discarded their armour and padded jackets to enable a faster escape: hence the name Lose Cote (coat) field.

In reality, this was more a rout than a battle. The rebel army had fled as soon as Edward's artillery opened fire.

Inspection of items found amongst the rebel baggage, it was discovered that the Duke of Clarence and Earl of Warwick were both implicated in the rebellion.

13th March 1461

King Henry VI correspondence of this date within the Plumpton Letters.

A letter was written by Henry VI to Sir William Plumpton. It makes Henry's thoughts on the situation clear.

Edward is viewed as a traitor. You can infer that his title is considered forfeited by Henry by reference to the 'late Earl'.

He is also clearly concerned, asking for support to come in all due haste.

The Plumpton's to whom he wrote were a family of merchants. Many letters from their archive have survived.

By the King R.H. Trusy and well beloved, we greete you well, and for as much as we have very knowledg that our great traitor, the late Earl of March, hath made great assemblies of riotous and mischeously disposed of people, and to stirr and provoke them to draw unto him, he hath cried in his proclamations havoc upon all our trew liege people and subjects, theire wives, children, and goods, and is now coming towards us, we therefore pray you and also straitely charhe you that anon upon the sighy hereof, ye, with all such people as ye may make defenaible arrained, come unto us in all hast possible, wheresoever we shall bee within this our Realme, for to resist the malitious entent and purpose of our said trator, and fails not hereof as ye love the scurty of our person, the weale of yourselfe, and of all our trew and faithfull subjects, Geven under our signet at our Cyty of York, the thirteenth day of March.

14th March 1471

Edward IV lands at Ravenspur.

Having set sail from Burgundy on the 11th, Edward IVs fleet disembarks at Ravenspur on this day in 1471. His fleet of 36 ships carried a small army of 1200 men, including those provided to him by Charles the Bold.

Edward's voyage had not gone according to plan. It had been intended for the invasion force to land on the coast of East Anglia where he would see his force bolstered by the retinues of John Mowbray, Duke of Norfolk and John de la Pole, Duke of Suffolk.

However, when his fleet arrived at the shore of East Anglia, his agents who went ashore discovered that both Dukes were in captivity and the coast was guarded.

Edward chose for his fleet to head north, to the isolated stretch of land that is now known as Spurn Head. From here his army marched to York, harassed by men in the Livery of Lord Montagu.

The Earl of Northumberland, the main potential threat in the north, chose to take no action against Edward's band.

Once at York he had to persuade the City to allow him entry. Which they did on the basis of him being the Duke of York.

Edward began to muster men to his cause. His restoration campaign was now well and truly underway.

15th March 1450

Suffolk is 'stole away' from Westminster.

London was becoming increasingly unsafe for the King and his chief counsellors. With unrest and sedition on the increase, the Duke of Suffolk quickly and quietly left the city and his accusers.

He had gone to a house near Bury St. Edmunds, and when this was discovered, he made to leave England. That voyage to France, on 1st May, proved to be his last deed. He was murdered at sea.

"[On 15th March]` the Duke secretly stole away from Westminster and rode no one knew where. The commons of the land were angered at this and several of the Duke's men were seized by watchmen of the city during the night, only to be freed again soon after. [On 29th March] one John Ramsey, servant to a vintner in London, was drawn, hanged and quartered because he had said London should put the King from his crown, and, on the Monday following, Parliament was moved to Leicester". Bale's Chronicle

Ramsey's views were considered traitorous at the time. It was an act of treason to wish the King dead or wish harm to the Kings person. Views such as these were all too common in the first half of 1450 with several plots revealed and two uprisings in the South East being put down.

Suffolk was not the only official to steal himself away from London. Adam Moleyns too, was murdered whilst on his way overseas. The atmosphere was highly charged, and emotions ran high as England suffered reverse after reverse in France and Normandy.

16th March 1485

Queen Anne Neville died.

Anne Neville died as Queen Consort of England, her husband being Richard III. That she would marry somebody of high status was never in doubt, and she played an important diplomatic role during her life.

Anne was the daughter of Richard Neville, 16th Earl of Warwick and Anne Beauchamp. The Earl of Warwick was one of England's leading magnates. Her great aunt, Cecily, had married Richard, Duke of York, meaning that she was related to the royal house of York by marriage.

The fact that Anne was of Yorkist blood made her marriage one of significance diplomatically. Her father realised this, and the potential benefits for the family, and arranged for Anne to marry the Lancastrian Prince of Wales, Edward of Westminster, in 1470.

It was a short marriage due to Edward's death the following year in the Battle of Tewkesbury. However, had the Lancastrians prevailed her place in the court may have had a similar effect to the one that Elizabeth of York had after Bosworth.

Her husband and father both killed in the battles of 1471, Anne was courted by Richard, then Duke of Gloucester. The couple married in spring of 1472, a union resulting in the birth of one child, Edward of Middleham.

Anne was crowned alongside her husband in 1483. In April 1484 Edward of Middleham suddenly died. The grief-stricken Anne fell ill herself and died, possibly of tuberculosis, on this day in 1485.

17th March 1477

The York House Books contain a note about a John Collins. Collins was accused of being an envoy of the Scots. It resulted in messages being sent to his place of birth to obtain a testimony of his origins.

Collins was from Darlington, but the requirement to prove that he was English is indicative of relations between England and Scotland at the time.

"[When John Collins] was defamed by certain children of iniquity to be a Scot [an envoy was] sent to the place where he was born, namely Darlington, County Durham, to bring in a letter containing clear testimony that John was born an Englishman in the village of Cockerton in the parish of Darlington..."

Anglo-Scottish relations had remained fraught throughout the era of the Hundred Years War and Wars of the Roses. Scotland regularly worked in alliance with France to thwart English ambitions and act as a thorn in their side.

In 1477 England was negotiating with the French and as such was wary of Scottish incursions into the North. Such forays were regular as Border Reivers raided deep into English territory. At a time of diplomatic activity on the continent, the risk of a larger, invasion force, was heightened.

It was with this in mind that efforts to identify Scottish spies were increased. In this instance, John Collins appears to have been accused merely for having a northern accent. His identity was confirmed via his local priest who could testify that he was indeed from Darlington.

18th March 1471

Edward gains admission to the City of York

The army of Edward was by no means assured of victory when it made its way through northern England in the spring of 1471.

Lord Montagu had offered limited resistance. The Earl of Northumberland had avoided any intervention. Yet Edward's army at 1200 men was incredibly small and vulnerable.

He sought support from the City of York. But initially, the gates remained closed to him. Edward drew upon several devices to gain entry, albeit with just 17 guards to accompany him inside the walls.

He used the same ploy that had been successful for Henry Bolingbroke as Richard II was overthrown, in that he stated that his business was to claim his rightful Ducal title.

Perhaps more persuasive were letters from the Earl of Northumberland, he held sway over most of the region.

From York, Edward recruited loyalists from the North of England and set about creating the army that was to go on to regain the crown following successes at Barnet and Tewkesbury. Edward gambled on the loyalties of men in the North, and it paid off.

His policy towards Henry Percy, Earl of Northumberland, paid dividends in that he could enter the heart of Yorkshire relatively unchallenged. From that point onwards, he was able to recruit and plan his assault on the Lancastrian regime. Once again, he was to achieve his goal incredibly quickly.

19th March 1487

The date given in John de la Pole's attainder, as the start of his treasonable behaviour.

John de la Pole, Earl of Lincoln, was the nephew of Richard III. Following the Tudor victory at Bosworth, he had been reconciled with the new regime. It was not to last, though. He became disenchanted. Whilst disgruntled with the Tudor regime, a clergyman called Symonds introduced Lincoln to a young man named Lambert Simnel. Simnel bore a striking resemblance to Richard, Duke of York, one of the Princes in the Tower.

Lincoln decided that this presented an opportunity to raise support once more for the Yorkist cause. His aunt, Margaret of York, now Duchess of Burgundy, was willing to back a venture. This led to a mercenary army being recruited under the command of Captain Martin Schwartz. Lincoln, Schwartz and the pretender, Simnel went to Ireland to muster a pro-Yorkist army.

The army sailed to England in June 1487, landing at Piel Island. As they marched through northern England, some Yorkist sympathisers and lords swelled their ranks. They marched quickly, some 200 miles in 5 days. Now an army of some 8000 men, it was a formidable challenge to the crown.

Henry Tudor had, however, been preparing. Sir Edward Woodville commanded cavalry that skirmished with the advancing army, slowing its progress. Rhys ap Thomas marched from Wales. The cannon of the royal artillery was brought north. Lord Scales arrived with substantial reinforcements. Battle was met at Stoke Field on 16th June. The Earl of Lincoln was killed in a decisive victory for Henry Tudor's army. He was posthumously attained, the date of the start of his treasonable actions being stated as this day of 1487.

20th March 1470

The Duke of Clarence and Earl of Warwick seek assistance

The Battle of Losecote Field had made the Duke of Clarence and Earl of Warwick's involvement in the Lincolnshire rebellion quite clear. Items in the baggage train had implicated them.

Furthermore, the confessions of captured men, such as Sir Robert Welles, also frequently reference the pair. For Clarence and Warwick, this meant find support quickly, or flee.

On 20th March 1470, the pair headed to Manchester to seek the Earl of Warwick's brother in law, Lord Stanley's support. As the Paston's recorded a week later, it was to no avail for Clarence and Warwick:

"And when the Duke of Clarence and Earl of Warwick heard that the king was coming toward them, incontinent they departed and went to Manchester, hoping to have had help and succour of Lord Stanley; but in conclusion there they had little favour, as it was informed the king, and so men say they went westward..." Newsletter to John Paston 27th March 1470.

Warwick and Clarence did secure additional support for the rebellion. Soon they had Edward IV in flight to Burgundy where he spent a short amount of time in exile and, initially, quite isolated. It enabled Warwick to reinstall King Henry VI as monarch and establish a Lancastrian Government, with Warwick himself in virtual control of the country.

The Readeption of Henry VI saw many local governance systems collapse, with some counties recording no accounts for the duration of the re-established Lancastrian regime.

21st March 1522

Death of Christopher Urswick. Urswick had been a diplomat, agent and confessor to Margaret Beaufort and Henry Tudor.

Christopher Urswick is a lesser-known figure but one who has left a lasting legacy.

The visible legacy is to be found in Hackney, London, where the church he ordered to be rebuilt remains part of the small but significant remains of early Tudor London.

Less well known but perhaps more significant is his role as confessor to Margaret Beaufort. In this role, he is believed to have offered counsel and worked as a go-between as Margaret plotted her son's rise.

The link with Margaret Beaufort resulted from Urswick having been educated at the expense of the Stanley family. Having grown up in Furness, deep in the heart of Stanley territory, he had been sent to Cambridge to train in law at the Earls expense. He was also ordained as a sub-deacon. When Margaret and Earl Stanley married, Urswick became her confessor.

It is known that Urswick was sent by Margaret to the continent in 1483 to warn Henry Tudor of the plans that Richard III had in place. He also fled following the failure of the Buckingham revolt. In 1486 Urswick noted that he had been acquainted with Henry Tudor for some 15 years, and to Elizabeth of York for 4 years.

Urswick was undoubtedly respected by Henry Tudor, holding a similar role for him early in his reign. Though overlooked in modern histories of the period, he was not ignored at the time. He features, briefly, in Shakespeare's play Richard III.

22nd March 1455

The death of Chancellor John Kemp.

John Kemp had risen through the ecclesiastical and administrative ranks during the reign of Henry V. A highly capable man, he was involved in the execution of the war in France and heard the confessions of English soldiers on campaign.

Henry V had so much faith in Kemp's abilities that he promoted him to senior positions and he returned to London to play a significant role in the country's governance whilst the King was in France. This role soon became combined with diplomatic tasks, Kemp being one of the key dignitaries in the negotiations with France that secured the Treaty of Troyes.

When Henry V died, Kemp was one of the men sitting on the Council in London. As such he played a role in formulating how the country would be governed during the Minority of King Henry VI.

Promoted within the Church to Archbishop of York, he was also given high office within Government. Firstly, as Keeper of the Privy Seal and then as Chancellor. He resigned the bishopric to concentrate on his work in Government, before, in old age, being created Cardinal-Archbishop of Canterbury.

When Henry VI became unwell, it was John Kemp who many in Government turned to. He was viewed as an impartial figure and held Government together. Indeed, before Kemp's death, there had been no suggestion of appointing a Protector, there had been no need under his strong leadership.

R.G Davies wrote of Kemp: Had he survived until the King recovered his health, the civil wars might not have happened; with his death, they were certain.

23rd March 1430

The birth of Margaret of Anjou.

Margaret was born in Pont-a-Mousson in France. Her parents were Rene, the King of Naples, and Isabella the Duchess of Lorraine. By birth, she was a member of the Royal House of Valois-Anjou.

Margaret was contracted to marry King Henry VI of England and became Queen Consort in 1445. Her life as Queen Consort was complex and is subject of many studies.

As the King suffered from prolonged breakdowns, Margaret sought to manage his interests, their sons' interest and matters of state. The latter contributed to the growth of factions, with herself becoming the head of the Lancastrian faction.

She was a fiery woman, described by Shakespeare as being the she-wolf of France. She managed to wrestle control of the Council and Parliament on several occasions. This brought her into conflict with the Duke of York, particularly after Parliament passed the Act of Accord in 1460.

Margaret forged an alliance with Scotland and drew upon support from many nobles, most notably the Duke of Suffolk and following his murder, the Duke of Somerset.

In the face of defeats during the wars of the roses, she tended to bounce back, regrouping, and finding support for her cause.

Margaret ceased to play any significant role in politics after the death of her son, Prince Edward, in battle and that of her husband, both in 1471. She died in Anjou in 1482.

24th March 1458

Loveday Parade at St. Pauls Cathedral.

A Loveday was a traditional method of arranging for disagreements to be dealt with in the middle ages. However, it was unusual for all the senior nobles to be called into attendance at one, making this a rather unique event.

The Loveday Parade of 1458 took place at St. Pauls Cathedral, making it a large public show of conciliation. It had been preceded by many talks. These concerned the clashes that many nobles were having and the grievances that had arisen from the First Battle of St. Albans.

Alongside the Loveday were agreements of compensation and bonds of good future behaviour. These included:

The Duke of York was to pay the Duke of Somerset 5000 marks.

The Earl of Warwick was to pay Baron Clifford 1000 marks.

The Earl of Salisbury was to cancel fines imposed on the Earl of Northumberland and Lord Egremont.

Lord Egremont was to pay a bond of 4000 marks and keep the peace (with the Neville's) for 10 years.

Lords of the Lancastrian faction were to promise not to seek vengeance for losses at St. Albans.

Yorkist Lords were to endow the Abbey of St. Albans to pay for prayers for those lost in battle in perpetuity.

25th March 1470

Henry Percy reinstated as Earl of Northumberland.

Henry Percy had been removed from his position as Earl of Northumberland because of his defection to the Lancastrians.

That change of sides had resulted in several castles returning to Lancastrian control and had prolonged the process of securing control of the north by Edward IV. Much of the Percy land, and the title Earl of Northumberland, had subsequently been granted to Lord Montagu.

As was often the case with the Percy family, Henry managed to rehabilitate himself in the eyes of the crown. Therefore, Edward chose to reinstate Percy, with Lord Montagu being granted lands elsewhere by way of compensation.

For the crown, it was prudent to re-establish Percy control over Northumberland. The family had a long history of governance in the region, were well respected by their tenants and had the confidence of the major cities of York and Newcastle.

Additionally, the Percy family were well-versed in Anglo-Scottish politics and had acted as Wardens of the Eastern Marches for many years. Politically it was prudent to return the Percy family to their position. It would limit the risk of insurrection in the region, enhance control of the border, and ease future negotiations with the Scots.

The move paid dividends for Edward. When he landed in staunch Percy country in 1471, the Earl did nothing to stop his progress.

26th March 2015

The reinternment ceremony for the remains of King Richard III held at Leicester Cathedral.

In June 2012 it was announced in Ricardian Bulletin, the journal of the Richard III Society, that archaeological digs would begin searching for the remains of Richard III.

The Looking for Richard Project, led by the society, had identified several potential sites for his remains, acquired funding and established partnerships with Leicester City Council and the University of Leicester to undertake the dig.

Human remains with features consistent with those of Richard's descriptions were discovered on the very first day of the excavation. Following the exhumation of the remains, DNA tests were conducted. These based on mitochondrial DNA of the living descendants of Richard's sister, Anne of York, proved that the remains were those of the King.

A legal battle then ensued as various groups sought control over where the King ought to be laid to rest. The University of Leicester agreement as they entered a partnership for the dig was for reinternment at Leicester Cathedral.

After legal hearings, it was determined that this agreement was legally binding. Richard was given a funeral service not dissimilar to a state funeral.

The funeral was attended by representatives of the current royal family, the Duke of Gloucester attending along with distant relatives of Richard III which included the actor Benedict Cumberbatch.

27th March 1454

Richard Duke of York named as Protector of the Realm.

The death of the Chancellor, John Kemp, on 22nd March meant that the Council could not function in the King's name during his illness. With the King unable to respond to questions of importance, it became clear that the lords would have to accept that Henry was incapacitated and act in the country's interests by formulating an alternative means of governing.

Consequently, a solution had to be found and fast. Given the tension between senior nobles and the faction emerging around the Queen, this was not going to be an easy task.

The solution was to appoint a Protector and Defender of the Realm. Who should be was a matter of great debate. The Queen is believed to have argued that she should act as Regent. This approach would be acceptable in her native France, but royal ladies' elevation to such positions was frowned upon in England.

The Duke of Somerset had political backers but also was held responsible by some lords for the loss of Normandy. This left Richard, 3rd Duke of York. He was highly experienced as an administrator and soldier and of royal blood. Ideal, except he had also raised an army against the King just two years earlier.

With all the options having serious flaws, the seniority and popular backing of the Duke of York won the day. He acted as Protector and Defender until Henry recovered.

28th March 1461

Battle of Ferrybridge

The Yorkist army had marched north up the Great North Road. As it drew closer to the enemy, it was to face a large and daunting obstacle, the River Aire.

The geography of the north the region funnelled any advancing army into a relatively small area. They could cross at Ferrybridge or ford at Castleford, but nowhere further east as the river grew too wide and deep.

This meant that an entire army would need to cross at a very narrow point. It provided a perfect defensive position, one which the Lancastrian army sought to exploit fully.

A first assault on the bridge was repelled. It was too difficult for the Yorkists to engage in numbers. A second assault was launched. Lord Fauconberg also chose to send a force 3 miles up the river to use the ford at Castleford.

The Earl of Warwick was injured during the fighting for control of the bridge. This limited his involvement in the ensuing battle at Towton. The Earl recovered in time to pursue the Lancastrians to the north in the weeks that followed.

Faced with this flanking manoeuvre, The Lancastrian defenders tried to destroy the bridge before beating a hasty retreat. They then resisted Yorkist advances in a skirmish at Dintingdale, at which Baron Clifford and many of 'The Flower of Craven' were killed.

The exact timings of the battle of Ferrybridge are a matter of debate. Some historians suggest it took place over two days, ending on the 27th, others that it was a series of assaults that flowed into the later battle at Towton.

29th March 1461

Battle of Towton

Fought in blizzard conditions on Palm Sunday, the Battle of Towton was a decisive, regime changing, victory for the Yorkists. The Lancastrian army, commanded by the Duke of Somerset, had chosen the site of the battle. They held the high ground. Any advance by the Yorkists would be over undulating land, ideal for defending.

Edward's smaller army would have to advance uphill, into artillery fire and a hail of arrows. Then it would face a larger, less tired Lancastrian army. Logic says this was going to be a great day for the House of Lancaster. It did not work out that way.

The blizzard hampered the vision of the Lancastrians. Lord Fauconberg, realising this, ordered the Yorkist archers to advance before loosing arrows and then to fall back. With the wind behind them, the result was that Yorkist arrows found targets whilst the Lancastrian ones fell short.

Fierce fighting then ensued as the main battles of the two sides engaged. For hours, the battle could have gone in either direction. The Yorkists though were quite lucky. The Duke of Norfolk had been delayed in his march north. They arrived as the battle raged.

Their arrival resulted in a large part of the Lancastrian force being forced back, and many turned and fled. This led to a rout. Fleeing down a hill towards Cock Beck, thousands of men were cut down by arrows or run through.

Contemporary sources vary greatly on the numbers who died. Most suggest a figure of around 28,000 dead. Some historians, probably more realistically, put the figure at about 9000.

30th March 1486

Death of Cardinal Bourchier.

Thomas Bourchier played a significant role in English politics throughout the Wars of the Roses. He was appointed Archbishop of Canterbury in 1454, leading to a role as an arbitrator between the various parties as tensions grew.

In 1458 Bourchier was one of the people involved in setting up the Loveday parade and negotiating agreements between various parties. During the period of Richard Duke of York being protector, he had been Chancellor and was not viewed as being particularly partisan.

When war flared up in 1459, Bourchier sided with the Yorkists. He presided over the coronations of Edward IV, Elizabeth Woodville, Richard III and Henry VII.

Edward IV sought to have the Archbishop elevated to the rank of Cardinal as early as 1465. This was in recognition of his work and because England had no clergy of that rank at the time. The creation of Bourchier as Cardinal was eventually agreed upon by the Vatican in 1473.

Clergy played an important role in diplomacy and execution of the law. When Edward IV invaded France in 1475, Bourchier was appointed to negotiate the Treaty of Picquigny. This treaty saw the French make large payments to Edward IV and some English nobles, in return for halting the Campaign of that summer.

Bourchier persuaded Elizabeth Woodville to send Richard of Shrewsbury to join his brother, Edward V, in the tower. Bourchier had sworn allegiance to Edward V, though went on to preside over Richard III's coronation.

31st March 1448

Edmund Beaufort created Duke of Somerset.

Edmund Beaufort's brother had been the Duke of Somerset. Upon his death, the title had been unused and, when Edmund was given the title, it was created for a second time making Edmund the 1st Duke of Somerset in its second creation.

He gained the Dukedom due not only to his lineage but also his roles to that date. In 1436, he had lifted the Siege of Calais then, during a period of peace, acted as Lieutenant of France shortly after his elevation to Duke.

The Beaufort line held claim to a Dukedom due to its descent from King Edward III. Edmund Beaufort was the third eldest child of John of Gaunt, his mother was Katherine Swynford. John of Gaunt was the third eldest of Edward IIIs sons to survive childhood. Therefore, he was a prince of royal blood: though King Henry IV had barred the descendants from John of Gaunt's union with Katherine Synford from inheriting the throne.

It was this role that led to him clashing with the Duke of York. From August 1449, the French began attacking Normandy. Somerset's policy and tactics failed. It set the tone for the future relationship between the Dukes of Somerset and York, though Somerset grew ever more important as a senior advisor to the King and Queen Margaret.

Despite his seniority, Edmund only inherited a sum of around £300. In contrast, the net worth of Richard 3rd Duke of York was some £5800. The King's attempts to provide additional income for Beaufort led to clashes with other nobles, which became more bitter because of events and failings that he was associated with. Edmund Beaufort, Duke of Somerset, died at the First Battle of St. Albans in 1455.

April

1st April 1450

Ordnance confirms that Members of Parliament would be paid expenses to attend Parliament if it were called to sit outside London.

Not every member of Parliament was an incredibly wealthy baron or knight. Some had relatively limited means when the expenses associated with their households, and ties to their overlords were taken into consideration. This meant that for some members of Parliament, leaving their estates was quite prohibitive financially.

To counter the problems associated with attendance at Parliament, and the regular changes of location, it was determined to pay expenses in certain circumstances.

Those circumstances were:

- Where Parliament was to be held outside of London.
- The Members income was less than 40s per annum.
- The Member held a rank lower than that of Lord.
- Such expenses were capped to £3 per annum.
- Expenses were to be forfeit where the member was a commissioner, or should they fail to appear before a commissioner.

This is one of the earliest occasions where Parliament was reformed to make attendance open to more people. Though it remained the case that members were men of some standing, it ensured that those with limited means could represent the counties that had elected them.

2nd April 1478

Thomas Thwaites became Chancellor of the Duchy of Lancaster.

The Duchy of Lancaster was and remains an asset held by the crown. It provided an income for the royal household from its large landholdings.

Despite the name, these estates were held in many parts of the country, replicating in many ways the spread of lands allocated to the nobility. As a large estate, it needed effective and efficient governance. To that end, Chancellors were appointed to the Duchy to have oversight of its management.

Thomas Thwaites was appointed to the role whilst also holding the position of Chancellor of the Exchequer. He combined these roles in the particularly challenging scenario of a general European economic slump and bullion crises.

The Chancellor of the Duchy of Lancaster's role gave Thwaites oversight of land management aspects within the crown's estates. He was charged with overseeing rents, appointments, administration, management of disputes and the justice system within the Duchy and organising Arrays. These were linked to magnates' roles in areas neighbouring the Duchy's lands, but Thwaites answered to the King.

The prime concern was to ensure that the estates continued to be profitable for the monarch. Revenue from these lands paid towards the upkeep of the Royal Household and contributed toward the cost of waging war and maintaining royal castles.

3rd April 1454

Chancery Patent Rolls confirm the nature of Richard Duke of York's appointment as Protector.

"Appointment, during pleasure, by the advice and assent of the lords spiritual and temporal and the commonality of England in the present Parliament, in consideration of the king's infirmity whereby his attendance [would be] prejudicial to his swift recovery, of Richard Duke of York, as protector and defender of the realm and church and principal councillor of the king, [the] authority of the duke ceasing when Edward, the king's first born, arrives at years of discretion, if he should then wish to take upon himself the charge of protector and defender".

This Chancery Roll confirms the decision made on 27 March.

Prior to Richard's formal appointment as the Protector, there had been earlier temporary decisions that enabled the continuance of Government in the King's absence.

For example, the Chancery Rolls also have an entry dated 13 February 1454 regarding Richard's role in the monarch's absence.

"Power to Richard Duke of York, by assent of the council, to hold in the king's name Parliament on 14 February at the palace of Westminster, as the king can not be present in person, and to do all the things for the good governance of the realm, [and] to dissolve that Parliament by assent of the council".

Here we see that appointing a protector can take some time and that the role may change.

4th April 1461

Letter from William Paston and Thomas Playters to John Paston

"Please you to know and weet of such tidings as my Lady of York hath by letter of credence under the sign manual of our sovereign lord King Edward, which letter came unto our said lady this same day, Eastern Even, at 11 clock, and was seen and read by me, William Paston.

First, our sovereign lord [King Edward IV] has won the field and, on the Monday next after Palm Sunday, he was received into York with great solemnity and processions. And the mayor and the commons of said City made their means to have grace by Lord Montagu and Lord Berners, which before coming into the said City desired him of grace for the said City, which granted them grace...

... King Harry, the Queen, the Prince, the Dukes of Somerset and Exeter, Lord Roos, been fled into Scotland, and thy be chased and followed.

We sent no ere unto you because we had none till now, for unto this day London was as sorry City as might..."

The Paston Letters, though bias in their allegiance, often illustrate the political situation very well. The solemnity of Edward's entry into York is hardly surprising, just days earlier the City had been the significant base of the Lancastrian leadership. The letter also shows that no time was being wasted in the pursuit of the remaining Lancastrians. Additionally, the letter shows how fast news could spread. In London, news of the events at Towton (29 March) arrived six days later.

5th April 1485

City of York records shows Royal Proclamations were made forbidding seditious talk suggesting that the King had poisoned his Queen, Anne Neville, to facilitate a marriage to his niece.

"And where it is soo that diverse sedicious and evil disposed personnes both in our citie of London and elleswher within this our realme, enforce themself daily to sowe sede of noise and disclaundre agaynest our persone... to abuse the multitude of our subgiettes and averte ther myndes from us, if they coude by any meane atteyne to that ther mischevous entent and purpose, some by setting up of billes, some by messages and sending furth of false and abhominable langage and lyes, some by bold and presumptuos opne spech and communicacion oon with othre, wherthurgh the innocent people whiche wold live in rest and peas and truly undre our obbeissance, as they oght to doo, bene gretely abused and oft tymes put in daungier of ther lives, landes and goodes... fromhensfurth as oft as they [all officers and loyal subjects] find any persone speking of us... othrewise than is according to honour, trouth and the peas and ristfulness of this our realme... they take and arrest the same person... [or] answere unto us at your extreme perill." York House Book vol 1. p359-60

Rumour around the country was rife that Queen Anne had been poisoned. It was, so went the rumour, to allow the King to marry his niece, Elizabeth of York. The origin of such tales is unknown, but they had a severe effect. So much so that Royal Proclamations were issued concerning such seditious talk. On 30 March, Richard had felt obliged to vehemently deny the rumours at a meeting of London Councillors. The sheriff had then been ordered to arrest those found to be spreading the rumour. It did not stop the gossip though, and a subsequent order had to be made in the City of York, a place where Richard was held in high regard.

6th April 1471

King Edward IV sees a sign from God.

Edward IV is well known for having used hard to explain sights as motivation tools. The Sun in Splendour was adopted as his personal badge resulted from his men seeing a parhelion before the Battle of Mortimer's Cross. Now, ten years later and once more on his way to fight for the crown, he sees and uses another vision.

On this occasion, Edward and his companions see a vision in a church at Daventry. It is recorded in Edward's history of his restoration, the Arivall, which he commissioned says:

"So it happened that, the same Palm Sunday, the King went into procession, and all the people after, in good devotion as the service of that day asks, and when the procession was come into the church, the King knelt and devoutly honoured the rood. ...in a pillar of the church a little image of St. Anne, made of alabaster, standing fixed to a pillar, closed and clasped together with four boards [as iy] had been from Ash Wednesday to that time. And suddenly boards, compassing the image about, gave a grest crack and a little opened, which the King well perceived and all the people around him. And then, after the boards closed together again, without any man's hand or touching and as though it had been a thing done with violence, with a greater might it opened all abroad, and so the image stoodd open and discovered, in the sight of all the people there. The King, seeing this, thanked snd honoured God snd St. Anne, taking it for a good sign, and token of good and prosperous adventure, that God would send him aid in what he had to do, and remebering his promise... gsve his offerings."

7th April 1446

King Henry VI gives a special order to Sir Thomas de Ashton to perform Alchemy.

Sir Thomas de Ashton does not fit the stereotype of a medieval knight. Despite his memorial stained glass window depicting him in full plate armour, adorned with the House of Lancaster's symbol, he is not recorded as having ever undertaken any military service. That itself is not unusual, many knights were busier with administrative roles, serving as members of Parliament, or working within the royal family's household's or for magnates.

Sir Thomas was none of these. Though his father was an accomplished soldier, he chose a different path. It was one that saw him gain royal approval and protection. His preferred method of serving the monarch was through the field of alchemy.

Sir Thomas de Ashton and Sir Edmund de Trafford were granted a special licence to undertake work as alchemists on this day in 1446. The order forbade any subject of the King from molesting either of the men. The two knights, both from Lancashire, were to pursue their experiments in the field of base metals.

Upon the licence being issued, there were clashes between another party interested in alchemy, the Booth family, and the local clergy. Granting the licence may have been due to close ties that Ashton had with the court.

Local legend has it that the alchemists sent King Henry VI gold that they had made from base metal. In 1456/7 Henry's Government undertook an inquiry into the potential revenue that could be earned from alchemy. This made men such as Sir Thomas prized assets.

8th April 1460

John Clifford is appointed Warden of the West Marches.

John Clifford, 9th Baron Clifford was a young man in 1460. He had inherited his father's title and estates following his father's death in the First Battle of St. Albans.

Spurred on by anger at his father's bloody end and a longstanding rivalry with the Neville family, Clifford had become increasingly involved in local and national politics.

The bickering between the Neville family and the Earl of Northumberland, to whom Clifford allied himself, had boiled over not only at St. Albans but in skirmishes and attempted ambushes. When the Loveday of 1458 took place, it required compensation to be paid to Clifford by the Neville's.

Those Loveday agreements did not last for long. Local clashes continued, and the factionalism on the national stage erupted into war, at Blore Heath, in 1459. Soon the leading Yorkists had fled into exile, followed by their being attained at the Parliament of Devil's.

In the period of Yorkist exile, Clifford was granted many Neville lands in the north and the role of Warden of the Western Marches. The role of warden of the western marches placed Clifford in command of defences against Scottish invasion. In doing so, it also provided him with control over the North West's military capabilities, command of castles and management of the well-oiled system of array.

9th April 1483

Death of King Edward IV.

Edward died an early death, aged 40. His son, Edward V, was young. The governance of the country in the eventuality of his early death had not been established. In historian Charles Ross's view, he was the first king in true control of his crown not to ensure the safe passage of the crown to his son since the Norman Conquest.

"[Edward IV] remains the only King in English history since 1066 in active possession of his throne who failed to secure the safe succession of his son. His lack of political foresight is largely to blame for the unhappy aftermath of his early death".

In hindsight, his premature death is not so surprising. The Croyland Chronicle, usually sympathetic to the Yorkist regime, wrote of him in the late 1470s that he was:

"a man of such corpulence, and so fond of convivial company, vanity, debauchery, extravagance and sensual enjoyment.."

He had, however, performed exceptionally well as a military commander. From his victory at Mortimer's Cross to securing the crown at the Battle of Towton took just a matter of weeks. Upon returning from exile, he was similarly fast in securing London, then won decisive battles at Barnet and Tewkesbury that ended the Lancastrian line.

Edward had not left his throne secure in his son's hands though, nor were all potential claimants dealt with at the time of his death.

His legacy, therefore, is mixed. He is charged with putting pleasure ahead of affairs of state. Yet in 1461 and 1471 he launched two of the most effective, decisive, and fast military campaigns seen in England's history.

10th April 1471

There is an account in the Warkworth Chronicle of King Henry VI riding around London on this date.

There is a remarkable account of both anointed Kings of England being in London simultaneously, in the same place, just before the Battle of Barnet.

King Edward IV was ruling, King Henry VI was about to become his prisoner. Yet Henry opted to ride through the City days before the large Yorkist army was due to face the one fighting in Henry's name.

Though the following account comes across as being somewhat convivial, the arrival of Edward signals Henry's placing in more secure lodgings. From the Warkworth Chronicle:

"King Harry and, with him, the Archbishop of York rode about London and desired the people to be true to him; and every man said they would. Nevertheless, Urswick, recorder of London, and divers Aldermen who had the rule of the City, commanded all the people who were in arms, protecting the City and King Harry, to go home to dinner; and during dinner time King Edward was let in, and so went to the Bishop of London's palace, and there took King Harry and the Archbishop of York and put them in ward..."

It is hard to establish whether Henry and men loyal to him were fully aware of the military situation. It is quite hard to believe that they would have remained in London if they knew that Edward and his army were closing in on the capital. Yet, Henry had already survived years as a prisoner, so perhaps nothing untoward was suspected?

11th April 1447

Death of Cardinal Beaufort.

Henry Beaufort was a grandson of King Edward III, being a legitimised son to John of Gaunt to his then mistress Katherine Swynford.

Beaufort was the 3rd son and was raised with positions in the church in mind. This bore fruit as he was consecrated as Bishop of Lincoln aged just 23.

He was also an able administrator and was appointed Lord Chancellor soon after the crown's usurpation by Henry Bolingbroke, Henry IV.

Beaufort was a strong willed and sometimes obstinate character. He led an English army on Crusade upon his appointment by Pope Martin V as Cardinal.

Upon returning to England, he became a dominant figure in the Regency council of the infant King Henry VI. His political acumen, political position and financial clout led to a faction forming around Beaufort.

Through the revenues of his diocese, Cardinal Beaufort financed many of the campaigns in France. His finances making such large contributions to the costs of the ongoing wars in France meant that his thoughts on the conflict carried much weight. As a result of this, he clashed with other senior members of the Council, most notably Duke Humphrey, over the policy on France and the economy.

His death left a vacuum in Government. His opposition to some policies had usually been reasoned and considered; it was a gap soon to be filled with a different type of factionalism.

12th April 1477

Arrest of Ankarette Twynho

On 12 April 1477, a band of men in the service of George Duke of Clarence made their way to Keyford near Frome in Somerset. The 26-man strong party led by Richard Hyde of Warwick and Roger Strugge of Beckington was there to make an arrest.

At 26 strong, the party would easily overcome any resistance in this sleepy manor.

The arrest was that of Ankarette Twynho, the midwife who had presided over the birth of the Duke of Clarence's last-born child. The Duchess of Clarence was believed by George to have been poisoned. Perhaps consumed in grief, he sought no other explanation and had decided who was to blame.

Hyde and Strugge found Twynho at her husband's house. They arrested her and took her, via Bath and Cirencester to Warwick where she arrived on the 14th.

On the 15th, she was accused of having poisoned Isabel, Duchess of Clarence. Further, the poison had brought Isabel's life to an end, on 22 December of 1476.

The jury who had been assembled had been appointed in haste and by Clarence's household. They found Ankarette guilty, and she was executed immediately.

The common suggestion is that George believed that Isabel died because of problems during labour. However, Isabel had died over two months after giving birth, and the child outlived Isabel by ten days, suggesting that the death of Isabel was not linked to complications at birth: such deaths were typically soon after labour.

13ᵗʰ April 1459

Clifford's Inn in London is damaged in a "battle" between the men of the court and the men of Fleet Street.

The Annals of London record this clash.

"On one occasion, in a broil between the students of the Inns of Court and the inhabitants of Fleet Street, the Queen's attorney was killed; and, in consequence, the principals of Furnival's, Clifford's, and Burnard's Inns were committed prisoners to Hertford Castle, and Alderman Taylor and others were committed to the Castle of Windsor". Annals of London

It took place at a time of great unrest within the Capital. There had been clashes between people within the City who aligned themselves with different court factions for some time. Clashes had taken place in the 1440s and earlier in the 1450s.

The Loveday of 1458 had attempted to defuse the political situation. It simply reaffirmed the reasons for animosity as it led to further violence that was caused by the settlement. Some became cocksure, others were offended at having to pay compensation

For some, particularly in the north, those agreements were an indirect approval to take revenge by way of property, theft, or destruction. The armed bands that had threatened London in 1458 had not gone away. The divisions between those loyal to Queen Margaret and her opponents, centred around the Duke of York, had worsened.

This led to the affray on Fleet Street of 12 April 1459. It was a short, violent, clash between people associated with the rival factions. At least 8 people died in the clash of 13 April 1459: more than died at the rout at Ludford, which is counted as a battle in many histories of the Wars of the Roses.

14th April 1471

Battle of Barnet.

In Barnet, the morning of the 14 April 1471 was misty. It was in this visibility that two large armies drew up to face one another. King Edward IV had marched from London the previous day and billeted in the town. The Earl of Warwick, Earl of Oxford, the Marquis of Montagu and Duke of Exeter had marched south and camped outside of Barnet. Scouts had skirmished, cannon been fired through the night. Now, it was time for the real fighting to begin.

The exact location of the battlefield is not certain. Accounts of the battle do make its course as clear as is expected of any medieval clash though. Mist obscuring the sight of both armies played an early role. Edward, seeing the mist forming, began moving his men closer to the Lancastrian lines. It would limit his foe's ability to bring to bear the artillery that they would have brought with them for the battle.

The plan worked, and much of the Lancastrian shot simply flew over the heads of the Yorkist lines. A Yorkist advance soon followed. A critical moment in the battle happened at this point. The Yorkist advance failed and was pushed back by the battle commanded by the Earl of Oxford. Oxford, not wanting to become too isolated from the remainder of the Lancastrian army, stopped short of pursuing the Yorkists and retreated toward the main Lancastrian line. He and his battle were mistaken for a Yorkist assault, the mist working against the Lancastrians.

It proved a decisive error. The Yorkists pounced on it and soon had the Lancastrian army in flight. Furthermore, they had the Earl of Warwick, dead on the battlefield.

15th April 1464

Prince-Bishop Booth of Durham is released from House Arrest

In 1464 Lawrence Booth was held under House Arrest. It had led to his removal, temporarily, as the holder of the temporalities of the palatinate of Durham.

His initial arrest and release were the result of the politics of the North East of England at the time. Booth was a longstanding supporter of the Lancastrian cause. He had served as Chancellor in the Government dominated by Margaret of Anjou and as the Keeper of the Privy Seal and Lord of the Privy Seal.

He was held in such high regard that he was appointed by Queen Margaret as guardian of the young Prince Edward of Westminster. His loyalties to the Lancastrian cause and his fierce defence of the palatinate's rights brought him into conflict with the Neville family.

They clashed over the rights to the lordship of Barnard Castle. The matter was raised several times, with King Edward IV himself having to make a final judgment on the matter. Edward judged that the crown owned the rights and gave control of the Castle and other lands to the Neville family. This brought Prince-Bishop Booth into conflict with Durham Prior.

The conflict became bitter enough for Booth to be placed under house arrest and his powers, temporalities, removed. He was released on 15 August 1464. This was a politically important time in the region, 10 days before this peace negotiations with the Scots had begun, the Battle of Hedgely Moor was fought soon after, Booth's release was, perhaps, an attempt to maintain law and order and 'normality' as far as was possible.

16th April 1471

Attempted Civic Coup in Salisbury

The turmoil that beset the Lords of the land had localised consequences. In many parts of the country, the trades that exported were closely aligned with one, or other, faction. In this respect, the Earl of Warwick had an advantage over other nobles through his Wardenship of the Cinque Ports and Captaincy of Calais.

For local economies to function most profitably, they needed the export market to be operating well: and this made the increasingly important merchants very aware of the implications of deals with France or Burgundy. In Salisbury, those economic interests had seen two of the most influential merchants, William Swayn and John Halle, become aligned to the Houses of York and Lancaster, respectively.

Salisbury had agreed to raise 40 men for Warwick's army, in the name of King Henry VI. Swayn had already decided to send men of his retinue to the Yorkist army. The Battle of Barnet changed all of this. It happened before the civil authorities in Salisbury had mustered. This led, on 16 April, to the Civic Authorities discussing the repercussions.

Do they send men to the army of the victorious Edward IV? They eventually opted to raise the 40 men but deploy them in defence of the town.

Whilst the authorities discussed these options, Swayn attempted to wrestle the position of mayors of Salisbury for himself. This would give him local pre-eminence and reflect the national success of the House of York. The initial choice to deploy the 40 men to defend Salisbury may have been made to stop the local power struggle from getting out of hand.

17th April 1471

King Edward IV lead his army toward the south west to face the threat posed by the newly landed Lancastrian army.

A second Lancastrian army had landed in the South-West on the same day that the Battle of Barnet took place. Upon hearing of this second threat, Edward IV had little choice but to face it.

Having disposed of the threat that Warwick had presented, he now faced the once dominant and still fiery Margaret of Anjou. This invasion force was potent in its threat. If not because of its size, which was relatively small before meeting up with supporters, but for who was present.

Not only did Margaret of Anjou return to English shores but with her was Prince Edward of Westminster. In the eyes of many, Edward was the Prince of Wales and the heir to Henry VIs throne. His very presence may result in people joining the Lancastrian cause. Edward IV set out at once to face them.

From the Warkworth Chronicle:

"When the King heard that they were landed, and had gathered many people, he took all his host and went out of London the Wednesday of Easter Week [17 April], and manfully took his way towards them. [When] Prince Edward heard thereof he hastened himself and all his host towards the town of Chichester; however, he did not enter the town but made his way to Tewkesbury, and there he made a field not far from the River Severn."

The aim of Edward IV was to prevent the Queen and Prince Edward's force from meeting forces being arrayed in Wales by Jasper Tudor. For the Lancastrian force, the aim was to achieve that before engaging the Yorkist force.

18th April 1468

King Edward IV writes to Sir John Paston

The Paston Family of East Anglia were significant landowners. The family had grown in power and significance following the Black Death. They invested sensibly, and marriages were arranged that served them well. The family knew the importance of having well respected professionals within the family, so invested in education. In just a few generations, they rose from the lower echelons of the gentry to a position of holding castles, several manors and being respected enough to receive personal letters from the King himself.

Edward IV to Sir John Paston, 18 April 1468

"…it is accorded between us and our cousin the Duke of Burgundy that he shall wed our dearest sister Margaret and in a short while we intend to send her into Flanders for the accomplishment and solemnisation of the marriage; at which time it [is fitting for] her to be accompanied by great nobility of this realm… We therefore, well understanding and remembering the good affection you bear towards us, our pleasure is [that] you will dispose yourself to the said intent and purpose…"

John Paston III had travelled to Burgundy for the marriage of Margaret of York to Charles of Burgundy. His goal was to take advantage of any mercantile opportunities that may arise at the time of the marriage. John too wrote of the wedding and ceremonies that accompanied it. On 8 July 1468 he wrote to Margaret Paston:

"And she was brought the same day to Bruges to her dinner, and there she was received as worshipfully as all the world could devise, as with procession with ladies and lords best beseen of any people that ever I saw or heard of…"

19th April 1471

King Edward IV establishes a command post at Windsor

Edward IV had heard the news of the Lancastrian landing in the South-West on 17 April. The situation dictated rapid action. The South-West had several significant Lancastrian Lords, Jasper Tudor would be recruiting in the South of Wales and forces from the Midlands may be drawn towards Margaret's army.

Every passing hour would see her strength increase. To counter this threat, Edward established a command post at Windsor on 19 April. From here, scouting parties could track the movements of any Lancastrian forces approaching London. It was a good place for his army to regroup as some had disbanded following the Battle of Barnet.

Coupled with the establishment of a Command post at Windsor was the organisational aspect of the forthcoming campaign. A campaign against a formidable Lancastrian army may be short; however, it may turn into a protracted campaign with pockets of resistance to deal with.

The experience of the Towton Campaign had shown that a great victory did not necessarily result in a war being won. So, victuals were ordered to ensure that the army was well provisioned. Ordnance was brought forward so that it could move with the army. Sheaves of arrows were readied for transport. Weapons and armour were cleaned. And all the possible routes that Margaret could take would have been considered and plans formulated.

20th April 1456

Richard Neville, 16th Earl of Warwick was appointed as Captain of Calais.

The Earl of Warwick's main reward for his part in the First Battle of St. Albans was being given the role of Captain of Calais. He retained the Captaincy, in practice if not in appointment, until his death. The Captaincy of Calais was a significant role. It, along with the Cinque Ports wardenship, another role given to Warwick, included control of the Calais Fleet, Garrison, Wool Exchange and Treasury. It was England's route into Europe, a prized and most valuable possession.

This appointment's significance became apparent when England's political situation turned against Warwick and the leading Yorkist lords. Whilst Richard, 3rd Duke of York, went to Ireland, the remaining Lords chose to flee to Calais. From here the Calais Fleet was used to distribute pro-Yorkist propaganda along the South Coast. It also pressured merchants from London who were exporting to the continent to make decisions about where to trade: which put pressure on the Lancastrian authorities.

The main benefit in the military aspects of the Wars of the Roses was the opportunity this appointment gave Warwick to go on the offensive. For example, a raid was made on the Port of Sandwich, resulting in many Government controlled ships being damaged.

It was from Calais that the Earl sailed to discuss plans with the Duke of York in Ireland. There followed the invasion fleet of 1460. It was again used to launch Warwick's return to impose the Readeption of King Henry VI. In short, Warwick's appointment as Captain of Calais gave him control of the English Channel and its shipping.

21st April 1471

Edward IV Issue Roll

The Issue Roll is the administrative account of how many people were in the Tower of London. This issue roll covers the period from 21 April to 14 May 1471. It shows that there was a garrison of 100 men staying in the Tower with the Constable, John, Lord Dudley. Documents also show that Queen Elizabeth was in residence along with the Princes and Princesses. The royal family's presence at the Tower during this period was for their protection: the starting point of this period being after the Battle of Barnet but before the Battle of Tewkesbury. Furthermore, it is known that King Henry VI was held at the Tower of London at this time.

The significance of the document is that it relates to a period during which King Henry VI died. There has been discussion about where he died and who did it—a popular theory being that he was killed by Richard Duke of Gloucester in the Wakefield Tower. However, records also show that upon returning to London of Richard Duke of Gloucester, he and a great number of his men also took up residency within the Tower. It had been besieged by the Bastard of Fauconberg, and so troop numbers were kept high until terms were made with him.

With this being the case, it is very uncertain where Henry VI would have been held. Senior Yorkists would probably have been assigned the better accommodation within the Castle and Henry would have been downgraded. There is little evidence to support theories about where, or how Henry VI died. The earliest theories date to after the end of the Wars of the Roses. The Issue Roll is one of the very few documents that offer anything concrete on the period during which he died. It does not tell historians anything conclusive on Henry's demise.

22nd April 1472

Papal dispensation is given for Richard Duke of Gloucester to marry Anne Neville.

In the Medieval Era, religious laws set out by the church stated that people could not marry if they were related within 4 degrees. Richard Duke of Gloucester and Anne Neville faced this impediment to their union. It was not insurmountable; they could apply to the church to receive a dispensation to marry.

"Richard Duke of Gloucester, layman of the diocese of Lincoln, and Anne Neville, woman of the diocese of York, wish to contract marriage between them, but as they are related in the third and fourth degrees of affinity, they request a dispensation from the same. Item, with a [littera] declaratoria on third and fourth".

Richard and Anne were related in several ways. They shared descent from Ralph, Earl of Westmorland, and Joan Beaufort. They were also both descended from Edmund of Langley. Therefore, they applied for the dispensation from the Pope.

It was not as simple as just asking for permission, though. Anne was a widow and with her came a large inheritance. Her sister had recently married the Duke of Clarence, Richard's brother, George. George claimed guardianship rights over Anne, and she was moved into sanctuary for her 'safety'. It was part of a struggle between the two brothers of the King over lands. Anne was found and that land dispute settled by Act of Parliament.

The petition to the Vatican was duly agreed to on this day in 1472. Richard and Anne married and had one child together, Edward of Middleham, who died quite suddenly during his father's reign as King.

23rd April 1445

Marriage of King Henry VI and Margaret of Anjou.

"[Henry VI] took to wife Margaret, daughter of Rene Duke of Anjou and King of Sicily, a young lady exceeding others of her time, as well in beauty as wisdom, imbued with a high courage above the nature of her sex, as her noble acts have manifestly declared..." Polydor Virgil

The marriage of King Henry VI to Margaret of Anjou was a diplomatic one. Marriage to Margaret brought with it no dowry, unusually for the period, but bought a two year long truce with France which, given the state of affairs in the Hundred Years War, was of much value to the English Government.

The marriage had been negotiated by William de la Pole Duke of Suffolk. He stood in for King Henry at the betrothal ceremony, held in France in May 1444. The Royal wedding, set for 23 April of 1445, was to be a lavish affair. Margaret's journey from her father's castle at Angers was to be full of pomp and ceremony. She travelled first to Pointoise where she was greeted by the Lieutenant of France, Richard Duke of York, and escorted to Rouen despite her being ill. Margaret was escorted then to Harfleur from where she sailed to Porchester, landing on 7 April. A short voyage to Southampton followed on which she was heralded by trumpeters.

The marriage ceremony took place at Titchfield Abbey. It was presided over by the King's Confessor, William Aiscough, bishop of Salisbury. Little of known of the ceremony itself, though we do know that Margaret's wedding ring was a gold ring with a large ruby set into it.

24th April 1457

John Neville, 1st Marquess of Montagu, marries Isabel Ingoldsthorpe.

John Neville was the younger brother of Richard Neville, Earl of Warwick. As his brother became more important on a national scale, John assumed more significance in the North East. Having been involved in the ongoing feuds with the Percy family from an early age, John was a seasoned veteran of skirmishes when the Wars of the Roses broke out. He had fought in early battles and, despite being on the victorious side, been imprisoned for a period following the battle of Blore Heath. He was then captured at the Second Battle of St. Albans and was imprisoned until the day following the Battle of Towton. He then assumed responsibility for eradicating the Lancastrian resistance in the North East, for which he was elevated to the peerage as Lord Montagu.

Isabel Ingoldsthorpe was the heiress of her father, Sir Edmund Ingoldsthorpe and of her uncle, John Tiptoft, Earl of Worcester. As such, she stood to inherit lands and titles of considerable worth.

A union between an heiress of this calibre and a second son is quite unusual, typically such a lady would marry a firstborn son and enhance the joint inheritances. John, however, was from the most powerful non royal family in the land. It seems too, from a Paston letter, that the Earl of Worcester may have encouraged this marriage:

"the Erle [of Warwick's] yonger broþere maryed to Ser Edmund Ynglthorp's doughter upon Seynt Markes Day; the Erle of Worcestre broght aboute the maryage".

Queen Margaret insisted that Isabel was a ward of the crown and so John had to pay a fee of £1000 for the marriage. The marriage took place at Canterbury Cathedral and was officiated over by Archbishop Bourchier.

25th April 1464

Battle of Hedgeley Moor.

By 1464 Edward IV was in a position where the resistance to his rule was in an isolated pocket of the North East of England. The Lancastrians in the area were surviving due to support from Scotland and France. For Edward, it made sense to isolate Scottish support and thus deprive the remaining Lancastrian outposts of supplies and the military assistance they needed to survive.

To enable this, he wanted a treaty with the Scots. A meeting was to be held in York to negotiate terms. Lord Montagu would march to the border and escort the Scottish delegation to York in safety.

The Lancastrians had one chance to stop the treaty from being agreed. Led by the Duke of Somerset, they opted to confront Montagu's force. They did so at Hedgeley Moor in Northumberland.

Scant evidence exists about this battle, though it appears that Montagu had a force of around 6000 men to that of 5000 led by the Duke of Somerset and Sir Ralph Percy. Following the usual exchanges between the archers of each army, the Yorkists advanced. As they did so, part of the Lancastrian army broke and fled the battlefield.

The Duke of Somerset tried to regroup his force, but in the chaos of the battlefield men became isolated and cut down, including Ralph Percy

The Duke of Somerset was able to flee the battlefield. Montagu and his army were victorious and able to meet the Scots, who they then escorted to York, where a treaty was agreed upon.

26th April 1469

John Neville is paid for the deployment of archers for 9 days from this date to suppress the Robin of Redesdale Rebellion.

The Robin of Redesdale Rebellion was an uprising in the North of England that was orchestrated by the Earl of Warwick as part of his revolt against King Edward IV. The rebels protested high taxes and unjust rule. In particular, the rebels were angry with the role of members of the Woodville family in running state affairs.

Robin of Redesdale is a legendary figure. Several people have been cited as potentially being the true man behind the name. These are Sir John Conyers, his sons John and William, Sir Robert Welles, or Lord Ogle. Each was connected to Richard Neville, Earl of Warwick, and had a connection to his stronghold at Middleham, close to where the uprisings began.

The northern uprising was quashed by Lord Montagu. He received his payment on this date of 1469 for the deployment of archers on the campaign. However, the name Robin of Redesdale reappeared later in the year in a larger uprising that culminated in the Battle of Edgcote.

The Warkworth Chronicle describes the uprising:

"After that, by their assignment, there was a great insurrection in Yorkshire, of divers knights, squires and commoners, to the number of 20,000; and Sir William Conyers was their captain, who called himself Robin of Redesdale..."

27th (or 28th) April 1442

Birth of Edward, future King Edward IV to Richard Duke of York and Cecily Neville at Rouen, Normandy

Somewhat surprisingly for someone of noble birth, the precise date of Edward IVs birth is not known. Most modern histories state that it is the 28 April, based on the Annals of William of Worcester. This is translated as saying:

"1442 Edward, King of England and France, the second son and heir of Richard Duke of York, was born, on Monday 28 April after midnight in the second hour of the morning, at Rouen."

However, the same writer notes elsewhere that:

"The Lord Edward was born… in the city of Roeun, on 27 day of the month, after midday, at 14.45, in the ongoing year of Our Lord 1442."

To add to the confusion, 28 April 1442 was a Saturday, not a Monday.

Edward's birth is not only confused in terms of which day he was born. Questions have also been asked about where and when he was conceived. One, mostly posthumous, method of discrediting Edward was to call into question his own legitimacy. This was hinted at in Titulus Regius. The argument here is that Richard Duke of York was campaigning 9 months before Edward's birth and as such could not have been the father of the child. It is an argument that has some merit, but given the movements of field commanders to and from the front, there is nothing concrete to prove that Edward was illegitimate.

28th April 1489

Henry Percy is lynched at Cook Lodge House, Topcliff

Henry Percy, 4th Earl of Northumberland, was a rarity in the Percy family: he had formed up for battle on the Yorkists' side. Having had his inheritance denied and then seen it handed to Lord Montagu as a result of his fathers' attainder, Henry Percy finally had livery of his lands in 1473. He was given the traditional Percy roles of being Warden of the East and Middle Marches, securing the border against Scottish raids. At the Battle of Bosworth, Percy fought for Richard III, commanding one of the battles that formed up against Henry Tudor.

That action led to Percy, along with several other Lords, being imprisoned for a period as Tudor secured his throne. Accounts of the Battle also led to criticism of Henry Percy from loyalists to Richard III who believed that the Earl of Northumberland had not committed his men to Richard's cause. In 1489 Percy took residence at Cook Lodge House on his Yorkshire Estates near Thirsk. He was charged by Henry VII with gathering taxes for the Breton Wars.

Tension was high in the area, and Percy wrote to a retainer asking for armed men to be secretly brought to him from Scarborough. They arrived too late. Percy was confronted by an angry mob, led by John Chamber, and killed.

It is widely believed that Percy had let down Richard III at Bosworth and that this was a motivation for his assassination. The uprising itself was in protest at the tax of a tenth.

29th April 1483

Richard Duke of Gloucester met with the party led by Earl Rivers that is escorting the young King Edward V south for his coronation.

When Edward IV died on 9 April 1483, Council agreed that an escort of some 2000 men would be sent to Ludlow to accompany the new King, Edward V, to London. The young Edward was under the care of his uncle, Earl Rivers, at Ludlow. Not convinced that the Woodville family were to be trusted, William Hastings sent a message to the Dukes of Gloucester and Buckingham informing them of events.

The new King and Earl Rivers received word of Edward IVs passing on 14 April. Buckingham a day later. Richard Duke of Gloucester, possibly a few days after that. Upon receiving word of his brother's death, Gloucester wrote a series of letters. To Earl Rivers he made it clear that he would meet the entourage and that there would be severe repercussions should the King not be freed to a guardianship set out by Council: To the Dowager Queen Richard wrote that he would:

"come and offer submission, fealty, and all that was due from him to his lord and King, Edward V".

The Duke of Gloucester headed south, stopping in York to lead prayers in his brothers' honour. He also had the local nobility swear allegiance to the new King, himself being the first to do so.

The two Dukes met with Earl Rivers at Northampton, on 29 April 1483. According to Polydor Virgil it was on this evening that Richard Duke of Gloucester informed the Duke of Buckingham of his intention to seize the throne. Virgil's account is widely disputed due to bias.

30th April 1483

Earl Rivers, Sir Richard Grey and Sir Thomas Vaughan are arrested by Richard Duke of Gloucester. They were imprisoned at Pontefract Castle.

Having spent a seemingly pleasant evening with the Dukes of Gloucester and Buckingham just the night before, Earl Rivers finds himself arrested by the pair on the morning of 30 April 1483. Richard Duke of Gloucester wrote to the Council to inform them of his actions and explain why. Earl Rivers was arrested along with his leading officers, including Sir Richard Grey and Sir Thomas Vaughan.

News of the arrests sent shockwaves through London. Elizabeth Woodville immediately took herself and her other children into the Sanctuary of Westminster Abbey when she heard the news. Council was shocked. But Richard's letter was reassuring. It affirmed that he had the best interests of the young King at heart. The letter and the words of William Hastings to support it placated the Council. That the Earl has been placed in custody was of no concern, Richard discredited him in writing, and a fair hearing would be given in due course. Preparations for the Coronation of Edward V were to continue being made. Richard had acted to protect the young King and to ensure that ill counsel was eradicated.

Whether or not this is part of a premeditated plan to seize power is a matter of opinion. Some believe it was. Tudor historians such as Polydor Virgil certainly make the most of these events in portraying Richard in a poor light. But there was no coup at this stage, weeks were to pass before any events took place that altered the line of inheritance.

May

1ˢᵗ May 1464

Secret marriage of Edward IV and Elizabeth Woodville.

The marriage of Edward IV and Elizabeth Woodville took place in secret with just a handful of witnesses.

Edward, as King, was expected to marry somebody of royal blood. Marriage was a diplomatic tool, cementing alliances. Indeed, the Earl of Warwick was negotiating such a marriage.

Elizabeth Woodville was far an ideal choice as a royal bride. She was the widow of a Lancastrian noble killed in battle fighting against Edward, though her mother was Jacquetta of Luxemburg.

It is widely believed that Elizabeth had refused Edward's suggestions that she should become his mistress. The theory goes that he was so besotted that he chose to marry her. Though Elizabeth herself came from noble stock, the marriage when revealed sent shockwaves through court.

Nonetheless, the marriage lasted to Edward's death and produced many children, the most notable of whom were the uncrowned Edward V and his brother Richard, The Princes in the Tower, along with Elizabeth of York who was destined to marry Henry Tudor and, like her mother, become Queen Consort.

Following Edward's death at an early age, the legality of the marriage with Elizabeth Woodville was questioned. It was stated that Edward was precontracted to marry Eleanor Butler, an assertion accepted by the Three Estates which declared the marriage null and void. This was stated in Titulus Regis, though overturned upon Henry Tudor's accession to the throne.

2nd May 1450

Murder of William de la Pole Duke of Suffolk.

The Duke of Suffolk was a controversial figure. A favourite of the King he had significant influence over policy at home and abroad. His management of crown affairs brought him into conflict with both the commons and his peers among the nobility.

This discontent was to the extent that at the Leicester parliament of 1449-50 there were calls for his execution on the grounds of treason. The murder of a close ally, Adam Moleyns, and increased political pressure led to Suffolk asking for the right to be heard. He was subsequently arrested and impeached by Parliament.

The impeachment hearing found the Duke guilty, and he was then sentenced to a period of exile. This sentence would remove the Duke from the heart of English politics, diminish his wealth and authority upon his return and severely limit his chances of gaining senior positions again.

The Duke was spared execution due to his affinity with the King. Suffolk made for a life on the continent. He left his wife and son behind and began his journey into exile. It was at this point that his unpopularity among the commons was to prove his undoing. Bale's Chronicle summarises it:

"...the Duke of Suffolk... rode to the sea, when he was at sea between Dover and Calais he was taken and beheaded, his body cast upon the sands at Dover and his head put upon a stake".

3rd May 1415

Birth of Cecily Neville.

Cecily Neville was the wife of Richard Duke of York. She lived throughout the whole course of the Wars of the Roses, into the Tudor regime.

Her lineage was significant. She was a great-granddaughter of King Edward III, being John of Gaunt's granddaughter through both maternal and paternal lines.

Cecily was the mother of Kings Edward IV and Richard III, grandmother to Edward V and Elizabeth of York and great grandmother of King Henry VIII.

Cecily spent much of her married life overseas, moving to occupied France during Richard's posting there as Lieutenant and later to Dublin when Richard was the Lieutenant of Ireland.

Her life and how she was treated by the various monarchs as the wars ebbed and flowed provide an insight into how women of noble birth were viewed at court.

When her husband was killed at Wakefield and posthumously attained, she was awarded an income of 1000 marks a year.

As would be expected, her sons provided amply for her upkeep once they were in power, with Edward granting her lands and income worth 5000 marks as early as June of 1461.

Henry Tudor too provided for the Yorkist matriarch quite handsomely, ensuring that arrears of monies due to her were paid and extending licences for her to export wool.

4th May 1471

The Battle of Tewkesbury.

A Lancastrian force including Prince Edward and accompanied by Margaret of Anjou had landed on the south coast on the same day that the Battle of Barnet was fought.

The army headed north, intending to join forces with men raised in South Wales by Jasper Tudor. King Edward heard of the landing quite quickly. Though some of the army from the Battle of Barnet had disbanded, he quickly established a command post at Windsor and sent messengers out to gather a large fighting force once again.

The speed of both armies was important. If the Lancastrians were to merge forces before Edward had gathered a large force, the odds could be overwhelming. Similarly, if Edward could head off the Lancastrians before they combined, the odds would be in his favour.

Edward acted quickly. His army aimed to cut off the march. They did so at Tewkesbury. The battle was decisive.

The Yorkists not only secured victory but Prince Edward was summarily executed when captured soon after the fighting, thus removing any future claim to the throne from this branch of the House of Lancaster.

Margaret of Anjou was soon in Yorkist hands and placed under close guard.

Those Lancastrian leaders who had not fallen in battle were captured and following a brief trial presided over by Richard Duke of Gloucester, executed. In a day, the Yorkists removed the most severe threats to the throne at that time.

5th May 1487

John de la Pole and Lord Lovell land in Ireland with 2000 Swabian and Swiss Troops.

The remaining senior Yorkists remained resolute in their bid to regain the crown. The Earl of Lincoln, John de la Pole and Lord Lovell gathered support on the continent.

This support, from Margaret Duchess of Burgundy, enabled them to hire 2000 mercenaries. These mercenaries were highly skilled, coming from forces well versed in the most modern military techniques.

With Lambert Simnel at their head, having been proclaimed to be Prince Edward and therefore the rightful Yorkist King of England, they sailed to Ireland.

In Ireland, they were sure of a warm welcome. The Irish had, by and large, been incredibly supportive of the Yorkist cause throughout the wars.

The sight of 2000 well-armed mercenary troops would encourage many Irish to offer support and join the Yorkist army. Sympathetic lords joined the Yorkist force. The pretender was even crowned King in Dublin.

The army grew in size, though the raw recruits' quality of training and arms was questionable. It was a significant force though, and additional, battle-hardened men were expected to join the cause upon taking the fight over the sea to England.

This would then allow them to follow Richard Duke of York's footsteps and make a landing in Northern England or Wales from where they could make their bid for the crown.

6th May 1471

Richard Duke of Gloucester, sat in judgement over Lancastrians captured after the Battle of Tewkesbury.

As Constable of England Richard Duke of Gloucester was able to preside over the trial of perceived traitors. After the Battle of Tewkesbury, several leading Lancastrians had been captured.

Others had sought sanctuary in Tewkesbury Abbey. The Yorkists were in no mood to leave these men safely in the Abbey. So, 2 days after the battle, they were dragged out to face an immediate trial.

The Dukes of Gloucester and Norfolk took charge of proceedings. The Duke of Somerset was the most senior Lancastrian within the Abbey. He had also previously been given opportunities by the Yorkists to work within the court, one that he had quickly deserted to re-join the Lancastrian cause. He had sealed his own fate; he was quickly found guilty and summarily executed. So too was Hugh Courtenay and the influential Sir John Langstother and other lesser nobles also being condemned.

Such actions have been questioned: was it, or was it not a breach of sanctuary rules? Was it right to execute the nobles? The answer to the latter was clearly yes from the perspective of the Yorkist regime. The Lancastrians had rebelled against the Act of Accord. In power, they had attained leading Yorkists several times, and had some executed. They broke promises and plotted with people, resulting in changes of allegiance. For Edward and his advisors, this needed to be put to an end and executions would do just that.

7th May 1471

Milanese State Paper. A curious assessment of the unity within the Lancastrian camp at the time of the two-pronged assault on Edward IVs reinstated regime,

The outcome of the Battle of Barnet was well known by this date. That was not the case of Tewkesbury, though.

This led to a discussion about the consequence of the death of the Earl of Warwick. Having been powerful but quite unpopular amongst the nobility, it was believed by some that his death may improve the standing of Queen Margaret's army.

It was in this context that a letter was sent from the Milanese ambassador in Bruges to Milan on this date in 1471:

"the Earl of Warwick and his brother have been slain by King Edward. A Spaniard, who left London on 24th April, relates that King Edward has set out with his power to look for the Queen and the Prince... We have heard nothing since... There are many who consider the queens prospects favourable... because it is reckoned, she ought to have many lords in her favour, who intended to resist her because they were enemies of Warwick..."

The letter is curious. The Milanese seemed to be reliant on hearsay from merchants at this time. This does bring into question the reliability of their sources of information.

Nonetheless, it is quite telling. It shows that the planning surrounding the Angers Agreement may well have been flawed from the start: would the nobility have rallied around a Government out of deference to King Henry and Queen Margaret if they knew Warwick would be in real control?

8th May 1483

Richard Duke of Gloucester was named Lord Protector.

On this date, the Council formally announced that Richard Duke of Gloucester would act as Lord High Protector of the realm.

Council also sent out writs summoning members to attend Parliament in June. These are important administrative decisions. As was seen in the infancy and incapacity of Henry VI, the system of government needed either an alert, adult king or a Protector to act on his behalf.

Parliament was called to confirm decisions made for the minority rule and would also usually make grants of taxation to the new monarch. These two decisions enable governance to continue as smoothly as possible with the Protector making decisions with input from Council and Parliament continuing to have its rights.

The system could work, similar arrangements had for some of Henry VIs minority and in many ways during his incapacity. In this case, things changed quite quickly, the reign of Edward V being over upon the acceptance by the Three Estates of the invalidity of Edward IVs marriage to Elizabeth Woodville on 25th June 1483.

In the period in which Richard was Lord High Protector the roles that needed to be undertaken included governance of the country and preparations for the coronation of Edward V. Planning the coronation was made more difficult because the royal treasury was severely lacking in funds. Richard paid for his own coronation from his personal wealth, rather than from the crown's funds.

9th May 1467

Milanese State Paper

An intriguing entry in the Milanese State Papers shows us that the Earl of Warwick's dislike of the situation, as early as May 1467, may lead to unrest. From Chartres, a paper written on this day in 1467 noted:

"There has been talk of treating with the Earl of Warwick to restore King Henry in England, and the ambassador of the old Queen of England is already here."

This is over 3 years before the Angers Agreement and 18 months before the Earl of Warwick, or the Duke of Clarence made any kind of public move against King Edward.

Whether the rumour as accurate or not is hard to determine for that time. King Edward summoned the Earl to respond to the suggestion: The Earl declined but responded in writing. That was accepted by the King, and it was not unusual for a leading magnate to be busy with other matters.

However, the following summer, Warwick's deputy in Calais, Lord Wenlock, was conspiring with the Lancastrians. Later, in early 1469, the Earl of Oxford was known to be plotting on behalf of the exiled Queen Margaret and her son, with the Lancastrian line's restoration in mind.

Clearly, Warwick was plotting at some point before it became clear to the Yorkists. When that began is a matter of debate. Warwick's discontent was fuelled by the rise of the Woodville family and his own reduction in influence. This was the case by mid-1467, but whether it had been the case long enough to turn him against his long-time ally by this point is not known.

10-14th May 1471

Thomas Neville, known as the Bastard of Fauconberg, raided up the Thames.

One element of the Lancastrian plan in 1471 was to seize London. In particular, the Tower, as this would hopefully result in the return of King Henry to his own supporters.

Thomas Neville held a command in Calais. His role in the Lancastrian invasion was to use the Calais Fleet and a supporting army against London. Early sources give varying sizes for the fleet, the Arrivall suggesting 43 ships, others noting that Fauconberg had command of all of the fleet previously held by Warwick and another saying 46 ships.

At first, the fleet sailed up and down the Thames, attempting to harass Yorkist forces and encourage the City of London to support their cause. Artillery was fired at the Tower of London and at other places along the river.

The harassing lasted several days until the land-based Lancastrian force was in place to lay siege to London with supporting artillery fire from the Calais Fleet.

The Yorkist force returning from the Battle of Tewkesbury was able to overcome the threat posed by Fauconberg. Earl Rivers and the Duke of Gloucester's men secured the Tower, the walls and drove off the Lancastrian force, which retreated down the Thames and eventually to Sandwich.

Fauconberg negotiated with the Yorkists and for a period was retained in their company before eventually being executed. Early accounts, however, suggest he was taken and executed at Southampton before the end of the mayoral year, in October.

11th May 1486

The Stafford brothers seek refuge in Culham Abbey.

Humphrey Stafford, his younger brother Thomas, and Francis Lovell had all been close to King Richard III. Having fought at Bosworth, attainders had been issued that stripped the families of their titles, rights, and lands.

To avoid harm, the three had taken up sanctuary in Colchester, during which time they formed a plot and Lovell headed north, to Yorkshire, to drum up support for a rebellion.

Meanwhile, Humphrey Stafford drew up fake documents that said that he had been pardoned. The ruse worked, and the Stafford brothers made their way to Worcester.

The early Tudor regime was alert to the possibility of rebellion and acted quickly. The Stafford brothers attempted to gather a force to head north, which never materialised.

In the north, King Henry VII arrived at Pontefract and found no large rebel force to contend with: he turned and marched south, on the Stafford's.

News of the kings advance reached the brothers, who escaped. They travelled to Culham Abbey where they took up sanctuary on 11th May 1486. However, the chasing pack, led by John Savage, broke sanctuary and arrested the men.

The brothers' trial made an important legal precedent, it determined that sanctuary would no longer apply to those accused of treason. The brothers were tried, and Humphrey executed for his treasonable rebellion attempt on 5th July. Thomas received a pardon.

12th May 1480

Richard Duke of Gloucester was created Lieutenant-General of the North.

Richard Duke of Gloucester had held several key positions in the north prior to this newly created position. It gave him extensive powers, largely military in nature.

Following the reinstatement of Edward IV as King, there had been attempts to improve relations with the Scots. Initially, the English had to relieve Berwick, but after that, ambassadors had met to try and improve relations and reduce unrest along the border.

By the late 1470s and into 1480 the number of border raids had increased again. As Warden of the West March, Richard was charged with the defence of the border in that region. Now though, the raids were large in number and increasingly frequent.

The solution that King Edward, no doubt with input from his brother, came up with was the position of Lieutenant-General of the North.

As Lieutenant General, Richard could call commissions of array across most of the north of England: Westmoreland, Cumberland, Northumberland, and the ridings of Yorkshire.

This meant that he could raise a substantial army if required, without needing to wait for messages to get to and from London and meant a coordinated approach to dealing with the raids, and Scotland, across the entire border.

This position strengthened Richard's control over the region, reinforcing the notion that he was 'Lord of the North'.

13th May 1461

The Earl of Warwick was commissioned to suppress disturbances in the North Riding

Following the Yorkist victory at the Battle of Towton many Lancastrians had fled to the north. A campaign had been launched very quickly by Edward to secure as much of the region as possible.

Lord Fauconberg and Lord Greystoke were sent into the East Riding to secure Hull and Beverly. The King himself travelled as far north as Newcastle, overseeing the execution of some captured Lancastrian nobles, including the Earl of Wiltshire.

A force led by Sir John Conyers and Sir Robert Ogle almost captured King Henry at Carham. Lancastrian resistance remained though.

In Northumberland, several castles held out. In the North Riding, many people remained loyal to Henry, fuelled by years of animosity between the Percy and Neville families.

With a crown to secure and the threat of Scottish assistance to the Lancastrian enclave, Edward commissioned Richard Neville, Earl of Warwick, and his retainers to suppress all opposition in the North Riding.

The Neville's utilised their own retainers along with ordnance from the Royal Armouries to besiege the castles that held out in the region. They faced a stubborn defence by the Lancastrians, who were supplied and assisted militarily by their Scottish and French allies.

With attempts by the crown to raise a larger force to crush the resistance proving difficult, it took some time to flush out the Lancastrians. The North East saw some resistance until the Yorkist victory at Hexham.

14th May 1471

Siege of London

Thomas Neville, the Bastard of Fauconberg, had been harassing London from the River Thames for several days. On 12th May the land forces that had been mustered for the Lancastrian cause demanded entry to the City of London. This was flatly rejected.

An attempt to storm across London Bridge was repelled by the retinues of the Lords who had stayed to guard the city. On 13th May a combined naval and land attack was made, mainly to the West of the city. On the 14th simultaneous assaults on London Bridge and the East Gate, backed by artillery from the Thames, stretched the defences. But they held. Earl Rivers then sallied from a postern gate, forcing Fauconberg to retreat.

"so aftar continuynge of muche shote of gonnes and arrows a greate while, upon bothe parties, th'Erle Ryvers, that was with the Qwene, in the Tower of London, gatheryd unto hym a felaship right well chosen, and habiled, of iiij or v{c} men, and ysswyd owt at a posterne upon them, and, even upon a poynt, cam upon the Kentyshe men beinge abowte the assawltynge of Algate, and mightely laied upon them with arrows, and upon them with hands, and so killyd and toke many of them, dryvynge them from the same gate to the watar syde. Yet netheles, three placis wer fiers brennynge all at ones. The Maior, Aldarmen, and many of the sayde citie, were anone in theyr harnes, and parted theyr felashippe into divers partes, as them thwoght moste behofefull, but a great parte of the citizens were at Algate, and with them many gentlemen and yemen, which all made the defence that they best myght; and shott many gouns, and arrows, amonge them; but for thy Kentishemen spared nat to assayle at bothe the gates, so that the sayde lord and citizens determined in themselve to arredy them in good array, and to ysswe owt upon them, in hands, and put them to flyght and discomfiture". Arryvaile of Kynge Edward IV.

15th May 1464

Battle of Hexham.

The Duke of Somerset moved the Lancastrian army through Northumbria in April of 1464. It gathered troops from the garrisons in the area.

Learning of this, Richard Neville, the Earl of Warwick, was sent as a forward vanguard of Edward's army to the North East. Neville's force arrived quickly. Neville's brother, Lord Montagu who had already been victorious at Hedgeley Moor, marched his army along the Tyne. They found Somerset camped near Hexham.

The Battle itself appears to have been brief. Accounts suggest that the Lancastrians were ill prepared for the sudden arrival of a Yorkist force.

They hastily threw up a defensive line by their camp. Behind them was the River Tyne. As the size of Montagu's army became visible to the defenders, many deserted. Those that did not probably numbered around 500. They were quickly overwhelmed and forced into the river.

As the battle ended the Earl of Warwick arrived. At this point, any faint hope of turning the table was over.

Though the battle was small in terms of the numbers involved, it was of significance. The Duke of Somerset was captured and immediately executed.

The Lancastrian baggage train included some £2000, a considerable amount at the time.

16th May 1464

Lords Roos and Hungerford were found after the Battle of Hexham.

The Battle of Hexham had been a Lancastrian attempt to prevent Yorkist forces marching north to escort Scottish negotiators to York. At the battle, Lords Hungerford and Roos had jointly commanded the left flank of the Lancastrian army. Their line was broken and fell into disarray with men scattering. As the vanguard was defeated, the Lancastrians were forced to flee the field, bar Sir Ralph Percy who made a last stand.

Yorkist forces found Lords Hungerford and Roos hiding in woods the day after the battle, 16th May 1464. The pair were taken to Newcastle, where they were tried for treason and beheaded the following day.

Roos had been a committed and loyal subject to Henry VI having fought at Wakefield, the Second Battle of St. Albans and being one of those who accompanied the King north following the defeat at Towton. Lord Hungerford had fought in the French campaigns.

Captured by the French at the siege of Chastillon he was released in 1459. He was one of the Lords who went into the Tower of London for refuge when the Yorkists landed and took London in 1460. He fought at Towton and like Lord Roos went into exile with Henry VI following the defeat.

Hungerford spent time on the continent trying to raise funds and armies for the Lancastrian cause, an act that saw him once again imprisoned in France. He was soon released though, and upon his return to England, he soon saw conflict. It was the battle that was ultimately to cost him his life.

17th May 1468

Treaties announced to Parliament

Edward IV was eager to renew the English claim to the throne of France. He was also keen to improve English trading relations on the continent, as the treasury under his rule had been under financial pressures.

When Parliament resumed on 17th May 1468, the Chancellor made a series of announcements on trade and diplomacy. Diplomatically two key items were announced. Firstly, a 50-year truce with the Scots. Secondly, the diplomatic marriage of Margaret of York to Charles of Burgundy.

These were both designed to strengthen the English position against France. So too were some of the trade related treaties that were announced. Though these would be unpopular with some elements of the London Mercantile class, one was a new treaty with the Hanseatic League. Another was with Aragon.

Treaties were also concluded with the King of Naples and with both the Dukes of Brittany and Burgundy. Edward's diplomats had tied almost all of Frances neighbours into formal agreements with England and removed the threat of a counter strike from Scotland should a French War begin.

It was a complex web of treaties designed to isolate and weaken France whilst bolstering the English economy and continental support for campaigns against the French.

18th May 1471

Richard Duke of Gloucester was created Lord High Admiral and Great Chamberlain.

The reward for Richard Duke of Gloucester for his role in the campaign to retake the throne and secure it was further promotion.

Already the Constable of England and a senior royal, he was given the two significant roles of Lord High Admiral and Great Chamberlain.

This made him de facto head of the navy and in charge of the workings of the Palace of Westminster.

This was a period where the threat to Edward's crown was still real: the very same day as this appointment saw the Lancastrian Calais fleet depart from the vicinity of London, it was of paramount importance that the most trusted and capable men held key positions.

It followed therefore that it was Richard who subsequently negotiated with Thomas Neville, securing the Calais fleet. In doing so, Richard persuaded the Bastard of Fauconberg to surrender himself and the Calais Fleet to the crown: and Fauconberg must have believed the sincerity of Richard's words.

Command of the Calais Fleet was soon to be needed. The Earl of Oxford made an abortive attempt at a seaborne raid on Calais, which may have fallen had the fleet remained in the hands of Lancastrians. Oxford then raided the south coast and engaged in piracy, which was limited by Richard's ability to put the fleet to sea.

19th May 1483

Edward V enters the Tower of London to prepare for his coronation.

One of the most famous mysteries in English history begins to take shape on 19th May 1483. Edward at the time was seen as King Edward V. He is more popularly remembered as being the elder of the Princes in the Tower, was taken to the Tower.

There is nothing unusual in a king going to the Tower to prepare for his coronation. It had happened many times before as the Tower is the safest place for the soon to be crowned monarch and, by this date, tradition dictated that this should occur.

Delays in the coronation and the imprisonment of Woodville, Grey and Vaughan at Pontefract Castle made the young King's stay longer than anticipated. There was an air of suspicion around the court with different people playing for power.

Richard and his chief aides wanted the young King to be accompanied by his younger brother, Richard of Shrewsbury Duke of York. This was problematic as the young prince had been taken into Sanctuary at Westminster Abbey.

Shortly afterwards his mother, Elizabeth Woodville, was persuaded to allow the younger Prince, Richard, to accompany Edward in the Tower. The decision was likely taken partly through persuasion and partly through coercion: armed men had surrounded the place of sanctuary.

The coronation never happened. It was delayed for several reasons, not least of which was the treasury had no reserve of funds at the time. Little over a month later the boys were declared illegitimate and Richard invited to become King. They later vanished from public view and their fate remains an unproven mystery to this day.

20th May 1476

Death of Isobel Ingoldisthorpe (Neville).

Isobel is an interesting example of how noblewomen conducted themselves and the role that society dictated for them.

Upon her father's death, she became an heiress of some value. She had been a ward of Queen Margaret, showing how noteworthy she was. This made her an attractive proposition for bachelors of similar rank who could increase their worth through marriage.

This led to her marriage to John Neville, Lord Montagu. They lived mainly in the north of England, in the Neville estates. However, when war broke out, her husband was captured and imprisoned. In cases such as this, or where the Lord was absent for other reasons, the Lady often assumed many estate management duties.

Later in the Wars of the Roses, John was killed in the battle of Barnet. He had switched sides and opted to fight alongside his brother against the King. At the time it was common for widows to remarry. It was something of a necessity in many ways, heiress of not.

Isabel married William Norreys a year to the day after John Nevill had died. She had also been allowed to keep wardship of her children from her first marriage. Given that they were the children of someone who had died fighting against the crown, this may be unusual. Or it may be a reflection of the way that Isabel was viewed by King Edward. She died four years after her marriage to William and was buried alongside her first husband at Bisham.

21st May 1471

King Henry VI dies

"King Edward came to London, King Harry, being inward in prison in the Tower of London, was put to death, the 21st day of May, a Tuesday night, between 11 and 12 o'clock, being then at the Tower the Duke of Gloucester, brother to King Edward, and many others..." Warkworth Chronicle

Accounts of how King Henry died vary. Melancholy was the official line. It is most probable that his execution, in private, was ordered. As a result, there are no definitive accounts of who killed him, or how. His fate had been sealed with the loss of his son in battle and the surrender of Margaret of Anjou. To truly secure the crown, Edward needed the Lancastrian line ended.

Other sources, all from the Tudor era, say:

"Henry the sixt … was put to death in the tour of London. The contynuall report is, that Richard Duke of Gloucester killyd him with a sword". Polydor Virgil

"…slew with his own hands King Henry the Sixth, being prisoner in the Tower…as men constantly say". Sir Thomas More

Soon after his death, a Cult emerged around the King's memory. His tomb became a pilgrimage site, soon becoming the second most visited pilgrim site in England, after the tomb of Thomas Becket. For a monarch who is much derided, this may seem quite strange, but his pious nature and devotion to god were well known and admired within his lifetime.

22nd May 1455

First Battle of St. Albans.

Widely considered to be the first battle of the Wars of the Roses. Following King Henry VI's recovery, a Great Council was called to be held at Leicester. The council being held in a Royalist stronghold raised suspicions amongst the Yorkist leaders: were they about to be attained as traitors?

The decision was made to prevent the King from reaching Leicester. So, the Yorkists blocked the Royal party, accompanied by its army, at St. Albans. There was a long attempt to negotiate a peaceful solution through parley. It failed.

Richard Duke of York ordered his men to storm the barricades erected by the much smaller Lancastrian force. These attacks had little success. Yet the battle was not to last for long. Whilst the barricades were being assaulted, the Earl of Warwick led a second Yorkist force through the alleyways and backstreets of St. Albans.

This force entered the marketplace where the Lancastrian reserve was resting, and unready to fight. They were quickly surrounded and beaten. In the chaotic scenes, the Duke of Somerset was killed as he tried to flee from the Castle Inn, where he had been taking refuge. The Lancastrians on the barricades were now attacked from both sides. Baron Clifford, commanding the defence, was hacked to pieces. The battle was won in little over half an hour.

More importantly for the Yorkists, the King was now in their possession, having forced his entourage to surrender. The victory put the Yorkist faction firmly in the ascendancy at court, an advantage that it could be argued they did not press home.

23rd May 1463

John Neville is summoned to Parliament at Lord Montague.

John Neville was the third son of the Earl of Salisbury and younger brother of Richard Neville, Earl of Warwick. He rose in prominence in the 1450s.

John and his brother Thomas were knighted at the Tower of London alongside Edmund and Jasper Tudor. That he was dubbed alongside the King's own half-brothers shows the importance of the Neville family.

Based in the Neville's estates in the North, John soon began to make a name for himself. In the family feud with the Percy family, the Earls of Northumberland, he played a pivotal role. In 1453 he was one of the Neville commanders who ambushed Thomas Percy, Lord Egremont on Heworth Moor near York and fought what is sometimes called the Battle of Stamford Bridge.

The rivalry in the north soon became part of a broader national conflict. When the two sides fought at St. Alban's in 1455, John Neville was in the centre of the fighting. His reward for fighting on the victorious Yorkist side was a half share of lands forfeited by Sir William Skipwith.

In 1457 he married Isabel Ingaldesthorpe, after which his military career continued. He fought alongside his father at Blore Heath. Though on the winning side, he was captured during the rout and imprisoned. He was attained whilst in gaol but released and reinstated to his estates following the Battle of Northampton.

John's elevation to Marquess of Montagu resulted from his ongoing command in the north, coming after he took Neworth and Bamburgh Castles, but before his victory at Hedgely Moor.

24th May 1487

Lambert Simnel is crowned King at Christchurch Cathedral, Dublin.

Following Richard III's death at the Battle of Bosworth, there were several rumours about the whereabouts and fates of important Yorkist children.

In 1486 a rumour spread that the Princes in the Tower were alive. This prompted an Oxford priest, Richard Symonds, to note a supposed resemblance between a local boy called Lambert Simnel and a youthful Edward IV.

He decided to pass Simnel off as one of the missing Princes. Soon after, another rumour spread, that Edward, 17th Earl of Warwick had died.

Symonds changed his mind and decided that Simnel could pass for the less well-known Edward of Warwick, son of the Duke of Clarence and, attainder excepted, a claimant to the throne.

He promptly set about taking Simnel to Ireland where there were many Yorkist sympathisers. With senior Yorkists such as the Earl of Lincoln and Margaret of Burgundy willing to use the boy as a figurehead, the Irish accepted that he was Edward Plantagenet, Earl of Warwick.

And so, they crowned him King in defiance of the Tudors who had yet to make any headway into controlling Ireland.

The coronation of the pretender was important to the Yorkist cause. It attracted more men to the army that they were recruiting for the invasion of England.

25th May 1455

Richard Duke of York took the role of Constable of England for himself.

The role of Constable of England is one of the great offices of state. It was the most senior prosecutor in medieval England. As such, the position was given to nobles who were senior and commanded the crown's respect or had sufficient authority to enforce their will.

The position was used at several points during the Wars of the Roses to initiate trials and executions at very short notice, perhaps most famously after the battle of Tewkesbury.

25th May is the anniversary of two appointments to this position. The first, in 1450 of Henry Percy, Earl of Northumberland. This was a reward for his work as a warden of the marches, keeping Scottish raiders at bay. The position also potentially influences events in the North East where relations between his family and the neighbouring Neville family were frayed.

The second was not so much an appointment as a gift to oneself. When acting as Protector in 1455, Richard Duke of York appointed himself as Constable of England. This is a highly charged political move designed to ensure that neither himself nor his supporters could be subjected to summary trial.

It also meant that those holding grudges following the battle of St. Albans would need to tread very carefully.

26th May 1465

Elizabeth Woodville is crowned Queen.

It was traditional for a Queen Consort to have her own coronation should the marriage take place after the King had been crowned. So, in May 1465 the coronation of Elizabeth Woodville took place. The year long wait after the secret wedding was unusual, in part because of the secret nature of the marriage at first.

To prepare for her coronation, she spent the night before with her ladies in the Tower of London: note the significance of that in relation to her sons when they went to the Tower.

Newly created Knights of Bath escorted her through the streets of London in a show of pageantry. The bishops of Durham and Salisbury led Elizabeth to the altar.

According to the herald William Ballard, the Queen was wearing 'a mantyll of purpull' robes, exchanged during the ceremony for a 'surcote of purpull', the train held by the Dowager Duchess of Buckingham, and in her hands, she held the sceptre of the realm and the sceptre of St. Edward.

Behind her train followed the ladies of the royal family. The ceremony involved lying prostrate after a symbolic barefoot walk. The bishops prayed as she lay prostrate, and afterwards, she was anointed, crowned, and led to the throne.

After the coronation ceremony, there was a lavish feast, and a tournament was held in her honour.

27th May 1464

John Neville, Lord Montague was created Earl of Northumberland. This promotes him in place of the Lancastrian supporting Percy family.

John Neville was the younger brother of Richard Neville, Earl of Warwick. In the North Eastern campaigns of 1462-4, he had played a significant role in combatting Lancastrian resistance and attacks by the Scots.

It was he who had commanded the Yorkist forces at both the battles of Hedgely Moor and Hexham. These two battles paved the way for a truce with Scotland and the end of any effective Lancastrian resistance in the North East.

As the Earl of Northumberland had fought for the Lancastrians and fled with the Royal party to Scotland. He was stripped of his title. It was duly granted to John Neville on 27th May 1464 to reward his loyalty and military successes.

The creation of John as the Earl of Northumberland gave the Neville family administrative control over the North East, creating a large and powerful power base. For John, it was a natural progression. He had been elevated to the position of Marquess of Montagu the previous year. With the Earldom vacant, he was an obvious candidate to fill the position.

However, when Henry Percy made his peace with King Edward, the title reverted to the traditional Percy landholders. Neville was allocated alternative titles and lands in the south but, feeling slighted, joined his brother fighting for the Lancastrians at the Battle of Barnet, where he died.

28th May 1474

Richard of Shrewsbury is created Duke of York.

Richard of Shrewsbury was the younger of Edward IVs two sons. Born in August of 1473, he was created Duke of York the following year. It was common for the sons of the monarch to be bestowed with titles at an early age. It gave them a basis upon which they could generate an income in later life.

Since this creation, it has been the tradition for the second born son of the monarch to receive the title of Duke of York.

Giving the infant the title was very symbolic. It was the same title that the King's father had held and one that Edward IV himself had a claim to in the short period between his father's death and his taking the throne, and during the Readeption of Henry VI.

The young Richard was made a Knight of the Garter the following year, recognising his importance as a prince of royal blood. As was usual with royal children he was entered into marriage at an early age, to Anne Mowbray. This led to Richard being created Duke of Norfolk and following some legal wrangling's, to the wealth to be had from the extensive Mowbray estates.

Richard was never to see much benefit from these titles. He joined his elder brother, Edward, in the Tower of London to prepare for the coronation. Following his parents' marriage being declared bigamist, the boys gradually faded from public view and their fate remains unproven.

29th May 1500

Death of Thomas Rotherham.

Thomas Rotherham was an important figure during the reign of Edward IV. He had been Edward's chaplain before progressing through ecclesiastical ranks to hold first the bishopric of Rochester before, in 1480, being translated to the see of York.

As well has his significant church role, Rotherham held important administrative positions. In May 1474 he was appointed as Chancellor of England. When King Edward died, Rotherham took a leading part in the funeral.

However, when the young King Edward V was taken to the Tower, it appears that Rotherham was suspicious of Richard's intentions. Thomas More wrote that he handed the Great Seal to Elizabeth Woodville for safekeeping, though no other source corroborates this claim.

True or not, it was clear that Richard III viewed Rotherham with suspicion. He was removed from his office as Chancellor on 13th May 1483, very soon after Richard had been appointed as Protector.

On 10th June he was arrested and sent to the Tower, leading to protests from some quarters. He was released and played a role in Richard IIIs administration, though Russell retained the Chancellorship.

30ᵗʰ May 1445

Coronation of Margaret of Anjou.

King Henry VI's marriage to Margaret of Anjou was arranged by the Duke of Suffolk as part of a peace treaty with France. Once the marriage had been agreed upon, Margaret was escorted in pomp and ceremony from Anjou to Rouen. Here she met the Duke of York, then Lieutenant of France. From Rouen she made her way to the coast and sailed from Normandy to England, landing at Porchester Castle.

Margaret was then taken to meet King Henry. The couple were then married at Titchfield Abbey in a service that was rather quiet by royal standards.

Following their marriage at Titchfield Abbey Margaret made her way to London. Along the route were pageants in her honour, celebrating her as a peacemaker with symbols of doves. Like most royal coronations hers was a lavish affair. In London, the conduits flowed with wine and crowds lined the streets. Her arrival at the City was on a chariot, followed by unnamed ladies in additional chariots. Henry, despite the financial troubles of the time, ensured that she was provided for in a manner fitting her position at his side:

"The Queene most necessaryly have for the Solempnitee of hir Coronation . . . a Pusan of Golde, called Ilkyngton Coler, Garnished with iv Rubees, iv greet Sapphurs, xxxii greet Perles, and liii other Perles. And also a Pectoral of Golde Garnished with Rubees, Perles, and Diamonds, and also with a greet Owche Garnished with Diamondes, Rubees, and Perles, sometyme bought of a Marchant of Couleyn for the Price of Two Thousand Marc." Order made by Henry VI

31st May

Three events merit inclusion for 31st May. Each relates to women of great significance during the period:

31st May 1429

The execution of Joan of Arc. The resurgence of the French during the Hundred Years Wars was largely inspired by this young woman. Her execution by burning at the stake for heresy, later overruled by the church, only served to further inspire the French. The momentum that she had helped create continued and France suffered few setbacks as they gradually reclaimed lands from the English.

31st May 1445

Birth of Margaret Beaufort. An important heiress she was married at an early age, saw that annulled and then was married to the Kings half-brother, Owen Tudor. Though a young bride she soon became pregnant. Widowed during her pregnancy she gave birth to her only son, Henry Tudor, aged just 13. Margaret spent much of the wars protecting her son's interests and in the later stages of the wars played a role in forming the marriage alliance between her son and Elizabeth of York.

31st May 1495

Death of Cecily Neville. Wife of Richard Duke of York. Mother of Kinds Edward IV and Richard III. Grandmother to the Princes in the Tower and Elizabeth of York. She was a Yorkist matriarch who played an important role in court. Cecily was treated handsomely by her sons in their reigns and with respect during the Lancastrian Readeption. Following the death of her son Richard, she devoted herself to a life of holiness and prayer.

June

1st June 1483

Completion of Caxton's translation of "The Book of the Knight in the Towers".

The Book of the Knight in the Towers was authored initially by Geoffrey IV de la Tour Landry in the 14th century. It was one of the first books to be printed in England.

Geoffrey was a noble from Anjou who fought in the Hundred Years Wars and frequented court. Caxton's translation, which states that he completed the work on 1st June 1483, is important because it is one of the earliest books printed using his press.

It is also a significant choice of book as its focus is the correct etiquette for young ladies who are visiting the court and warnings about the ease at which courtiers may manipulate young ladies and bring a noble house into disrepute. The book was written originally as a guide for Landry's own daughter's, so was in effect a guide for their wellbeing when visiting court.

It is an intriguing book on the period's courtly lifestyle and acts in a sense as a feminine version of a chivalric guide.

Landry's original work had been penned in the early 1370s. So whilst it is medieval, society changed between its actual authoring and printing by Caxton. The Hundred Years War, Wars of the Roses, economic depression and diplomatic shifts meant that life at court in the 1480s was possibly quite different from the 1370s: the nature of service to the crown had started to change, for example.

2nd June 1461

Newsletter from Bruges to Milan

The Milanese State Papers provide an interesting insight into how marriages were used to formalise alliances and cement support for campaigns. This example refers to the earlier promise by Margaret of Anjou to exchange Berwick for military aid, along with a suggestion of a marriage treaty.

"King Henry, the Queen, their son, the Duke of Somerset and Lord Roos, his brother, have taken refuge in Scotland. It is said that they are negotiating for a marriage alliance between the sister of the late King of Scotland and the Prince of Wales... They also say that King Henry has given away a castle called Berwick, which is one of the keys of the frontier between England and Scotland".

It is clear from this newsletter that the Lancastrian terms with Scotland were not known in their entirety by the public. Berwick had been gifted to Scotland in exchange for support in the campaigns that followed the Act of Accord. Scottish forces had, therefore, already participated in the march on London. The same arrangement between Margaret of Anjou and Margaret of Guelders led to Scotland supplying Lancastrian castles in the North East of England.

A proposed marriage union between the two families would provide the Scots with greater motivation to aid the Lancastrian cause. If the children married, their wealth and importance would be reliant upon the Yorkist regime being overthrown: so it would make sense to assist King Henry to facilitate improved relationships between England and Scotland in the future.

3rd June 1487

A Proclamation of Henry VII to cities stated that any person found to be spreading rumours is to be put into the pillory.

Henry VII was quite nervous in June of 1487. His grip on the crown was far from secure.

Henry was fully aware that an army had been gathered for the Yorkist cause in Ireland. He would also be uncertain of the loyalty of some key subjects: the Percy family of Northumberland had, after all, fought against him at Bosworth.

With concern over growing support for any Yorkist invasion force in mind, he issued a proclamation that was sent to the larger cities within England. It was aimed at cutting out gossip, rumour and anything that might give rise to Yorkist sympathy.

So, with fear of cities such as York rising against him, he stated that city authorities were to send to the pillory any who:

"feigned, contrived and forged tidings and tales."

Henry's concern was based on previous events. His own invasion of 1485 been bolstered by sympathetic nobles. So too had that of Edward IV in 1471, Margaret of Anjou in 1471 and The Yorkists in 1460.

The fear was that the force gathering in Ireland could gain significant support in the North of England, an area with a considerable history of Yorkist sympathies. Given the Yorkist leaning sympathies of Burgundy, it was possible a second force could land on the East Coast.

The landing that he was expecting happened the very next day.

4th June 1487

Lambert Simnel's army, commanded by the Earl of Lincoln, lands at Piel
Island.

The army gathered by the Earl of Lincoln in 'King Edward's' name landed
at Piel Island, Cumbria.

A force had been assembled that included 2000 Swabian and Swiss
mercenaries, led by Captain Schwarz. Several thousand Irishmen had been
levied into service.

Lincoln, Lovell and Schwartz knew that they now needed to gather
further support. They would also need to strike fast before Henry Tudor
had time to gather the royal army's full might.

The northern landing provided ample opportunity to gain extra men along
the way. Large parts of the North had been supportive of King Richard
III. They had landed in an area where he had held great sway.

From here, they marched south and east, heading towards York, hoping
to benefit from the affection that Richard had been held in within its
walls.

They faced some opposition en route, beating off a force of Baron
Clifford's men, before finding York itself quite unwilling to commit
before any victory had been won.

The army moved on, picking up some additional troops to create a force
of some 10000 men by the time it reached East Stoke, where a battle took
place against King Henry's army.

5th June 1487

King Henry VII and the Yorkist army make plans for supplying their army.

Both sets of commanders in 1487 were eager to ensure that they had the support of the people. One area of particular concern was securing their support in the supply of victuals for their armies.

Anticipating that they may need to camp at, or near, York, both sides addressed the issue in writing to the City of York. On 5th June 1487, King Henry wrote to the City:

"and for that his highness nor his said company in no wise should be destitute of wanting of victuals for man or horse: He strictly chargeth and commandeth every victualer, and all other subjects dwelling in every town or place were his said highness and his said company shall come, to provide and make ready plenty of bread and ale, and of other victuals, as well for horse as for man, at reasonable price in ready money therefor to them: And every of hem truly to be contented and paid."

The commanders of the Yorkist invasion force had a similar concern. On 8th June, they wrote in the same of 'Edward VI' to the City:

"it will like you that we may have Relief and ease of lodging and victuals within our city there and so do depart and truly pay for that We shall take".

On their part, the City of York was also concerned. They did not want to suffer as a result of merchants profiteering. Therefore, they, expecting the arrival of the Royal army of Henry VII, issued edicts that limited food and wine prices: for example, a price limit of 10d per gallon of wine was imposed.

6th June 1450

An inquiry was commissioned in relation to some ringleaders' actions of the Kentish uprising led by Jack Cade.

"It is to be enquired for our Sovereign Lord the King that if John Merfeld of Brightling in the shire of Sussex husbandman and William Merfeld of Brightling the shire foresaid husbandman at Brightling in the open market the Sunday in the feast of St Anne in the 28th year of our said Sovereign Lord falsely said that the King was a natural fool and would oft times hold a staff in his hands with a bird on the end playing therewith as a fool and that another king must be ordained to rule the land saying that the King was no person able to rule the land.

Also, the said John of Brightling the Sunday next afore Saint Luke's day the 29th year of our said Sovereign Lord the King in the open alehouse there…said to William Durford said that the charter that our said Sovereign Lord made of the first insurrection was false…Also the said John at Brightling on St James even the 28th year above said…that he and his fellowship would arise again and when they were up they would leave no gentleman alive but such as them list to have".

Establishing an inquiry into the uprising is a precursor to the trial of those believed to be involved in provoking it. This is a crucial element of the justice system at the time.

The appointment of commissioners to lead the inquiry is also essential. The crown could appoint people based on politics. For example, the crown looked to appoint the Duke of York and other 'loyal opponents' as commissioners. This suited the Queen's favourites as it would force the nobles who the rebels looked to for support at the highest levels to dispense justice. As it happened, the trials were undertaken by the King and many nobles from both factions.

7th June 1467

Richard Earl of Warwick was received like royalty by the French King

In 1467 the court of King Edward IV had opposing factions within it. On one hand, those who sided with the Queen's family, the Woodville's. On the other, the Earl of Warwick and his supporters.

At this time, the King was eager to negotiate a suitable marriage treaty for Margaret of York. As a member of the English Royal family, she would attract suitors of high status. And this meant that the rival factions stood to gain, or lose, from the final decisions made.

The Earl of Warwick was sent to France to negotiate. Meanwhile, the Woodville's worked on wooing their favoured option, a marriage with Charles of Burgundy.

Warwick arrived in France on 7th June. King Louis, fully aware of the political situation in England, set about causing potential problems.

The greeting that Warwick got was not that of an ambassador, no matter how high ranked. Instead, Louis ensured that it was at a level reserved for the most favoured of Kings. He personally greeted Warwick, the Queen was in attendance, lavish banquets and formal boat processions were laid on. Warwick was housed in comfort, next door to Louis.

Louis made numerous visits to Warwick at all times of day and night. He ensured that observers would know precisely when he was holding talks and through the extravagance of reception, hopefully making King Edward jealous. Despite the charade that Louis was playing, Warwick did reach a tentative agreement with the French. The Woodville family eventually won the day with regards to Margaret's marriage.

8th June 1492

Death of Elizabeth Woodville

Elizabeth Woodville lived a remarkable life. Born into a noble family, she married Sir John Grey of Groby, by whom she had two children. Sir John was killed fighting for the Lancastrian army at the 2nd Battle of St. Albans.

Elizabeth soon afterwards encountered King Edward IV. The King was well known for having mistresses. Sources suggest that Elizabeth was beautiful. Legend has it that the King soon became besotted and in love with Elizabeth but that she refused to be his mistress, which led to the couple's secret marriage.

The marriage rocked court and the political world. It was not only a mismatch in terms of the rank, but marriage negotiations had been underway regarding marriages alliances that would improve international relations.

The marriage produced ten children, most famously the Princes in the Tower and Elizabeth of York. It also led to the promotion of many of Elizabeth's family members, causing a rift between the King and Earl of Warwick.

Elizabeth was a very shrewd political operator and she, along with Margaret Beaufort, arranged the match between Elizabeth of York and Henry Tudor. She retired from public life in 1487, taking residency at Bermondsey Abbey, where she passed away.

9th June 1498

Perkin Warbeck and Edward Plantagenet attempt to escape from the Tower of London.

Perkin Warbeck was a pretender to the throne, having claimed to be Richard, Duke of York the younger of the Princes in the Tower. He had received support on the continent from Margaret of Burgundy, sister of Edward IV and Richard III.

His claim led to him marrying Lady Catherine Gordon, cousin of the King of Scotland. These supporters financed several abortive invasions of England. Eventually captured, he confessed to King Henry VII and was placed in custody.

Edward Plantagenet was the Earl of Warwick and son of George, Duke of Clarence. If his father's attainder was set aside, he was the Yorkist with the best claim to the throne.

Unfortunately for Edward, imposters were claiming to be him, which posed problems for the authorities. Both men were therefore sent to the Tower of London.

With a gaoler who appeared to be a Warbeck sympathiser, the pair hatched an escape plan which was to be set into motion on 9th June 1498. The plot was soon discovered. King Henry VII was unwilling to entertain any further attempts or the potential unrest that the pair may cause.

They were shackled and, along with others implicated in the plot, tried for treason. Both were found guilty. Warbeck was executed as befitted his common status, by being hung, on 23rd November. Edward Plantagenet, as a noble, was executed by beheading on Tower Hill on 29th November.

10th June 1483

Richard Duke of Gloucester wrote to the City of York asking for assistance against those who wish him harm.

In a period in which things were changing very quickly in and around court and Government, Richard, then acting as Protector of the Realm, sent an urgent message to the City of York.

It provides a clue as to the insecurities felt by the leading nobles and families at this time. It is sent at a time when members of the Woodville family are imprisoned and shortly before Hastings is arrested, tried, and executed for plotting.

The request holds little back in saying who he believes is plotting against him, making it clear that he believes there is a plot instigated by Elizabeth Woodville against his person.

"Right trusty and well-beloved ... we heartily pray you to come unto us in London as speedily as possible after the sight of this letter with as many well-armed men as possible, to aid and assist us against the Queen, her blood and other adherents and affinity who intend to murder and utterly destroy us and our cousin, the Duke of Buckingham and the old royal blood of this realm".

Richard Duke of Gloucester. 10th June 1483.

Richard's words are open to interpretation. Is he suggesting that the Woodville family are planning to seize power? Or is he making a pre-emptive move for support for his future taking of power? Either is possible at this stage in events.

11th June 1467

Tournament at Smithfield, with the highlight being a bout between Anthony Rivers and 'The Bastard of Burgundy'.

As part of the marriage negotiations between the court of Edward IV and that of Burgundy, for the potential marriage of Margaret of York, a tournament was held at Smithfield.

The tournament was an exercise in propaganda, not only designed to impress the Burgundians but also other foreign powers: remember that Louis of France had very recently set out to wow the Earl of Warwick through a decadent display.

The tournament lasted two days. The highlight being the clashes between Antione, the Bastard son of the Duke of Burgundy and Anthony Woodville, the Queen's brother, who was renowned for his athletic prowess.

The first day saw one single joust with sharpened spears and no tilt. It very nearly ended in disaster as the Bastard of Burgundy was dismounted, and his horse fell on top of him. The following day saw hand to hand combat on foot. The two men fought as though their lives depended on it. So ferocious was the fighting that pieces of armour are said to have been left with large gashes.

King Edward IV then pulled off a masterstroke of diplomacy and made his position as a chivalrous knight and King clear: he, as he alone could, ordered the fight to stop. A draw was the outcome. The men and, therefore, the states they represented were equals. The tournament played a large role in concluded the marriage treaty that was agreed upon between Margaret of York, the King's sister, and the Duke of Burgundy.

12th June 1482

Richard, Duke of Gloucester, was made commander of the English army invading Scotland.

On 11th June, a Treaty was signed at Fotheringay in which the Duke of Albany, Alexander Stuart, declared himself to be King of Scotland and pledged his loyalty to King Edward IV of England.

The problem was that Albany's brother was already crowned as King James III of Scotland and had possession of the major strongholds, including the formidable Edinburgh Castle. English support of Albany's claim had been promised, and so on the 12th, Richard Duke of Gloucester was appointed as commander of an English army to invade Scotland.

The choice of Richard made perfect sense. As Lieutenant-General of the North, he had the right to issue commissions of array across a vast area. He also had administrative oversight of much of the North through the Council of the North. With additional forces and artillery from the royal armouries, he would be at the head of a large and powerful army.

Richard's army swept into Scotland. Men were left to besiege Berwick before marching on Edinburgh. No siege took place, despite much of the surrounding area falling to the English. Albany and his brother settled their differences.

Richard, therefore, turned his attention once more on Berwick. Once the English army's full weight was upon the town, it fell, returning into English hands for the first time since it had been exchanged for military support by Margaret of Anjou in 1461. Berwick has remained an English town and fortress ever since.

13th June 1483

Traditional, though disputed, date of the execution of William Hastings

Hastings had, by the end of Edward IVs reign, become an indispensable right-hand man. Throughout both of Edward's reigns, he served loyally and, despite marital ties to the Earl of Warwick, gone into exile with Edward then levied forces in the Midlands to join the Yorkist army in 1471.

Hastings had followed his father into service for the House of York and fought alongside Edward at Mortimer's Cross and in the Towton Campaign. He was a Captain at both Barnet and Tewkesbury. Hastings held high office being the Lieutenant of Calais and the Chamberlain of the Exchequer.

In 1483 amid rumours of plots and counter plots, Hastings was accused by Richard Duke of Gloucester and the Duke of Buckingham of conspiring against them in collusion with the Woodville family. This accusation was made in Council.

Though precise details are disputed, it is known that Hastings was then tried for high treason and executed by beheading on Tower Hill.

Hastings' involvement in a plot is a possibility but unproven. He had been fiercely loyal to Edward. If plans were being made to put forward the case of the Prince's illegitimacy, he might have proven to be an obstacle and one that needed to be removed. The Woodville family were considered a threat, as they stood to gain or lose much from the Council's decisions on the Prince's future, so it is equally feasible that he was indeed plotting. The date of 13th was noted in contemporary sources; 20th June was suggested as an alternative by Clements R. Markham. Most historians use the 13th.

14th June 1439

Suffolk elicits wardships for himself

One of the longer-term causes of the Wars of the Roses was the way the administration of Government was undertaken. It led to complaints of maladministration from the 'loyal opposition' and charges of 'evil and corrupt' counsellors surrounding King Henry VI.

The charges were not baseless. Following the Duke of Bedford's death, the Council lost the clarity of leadership it needed to be a stable system of governing. As Henry came of age, he had favourites who circumnavigated traditional routes of having matters debated and agreed.

At the forefront of this was the Duke of Suffolk. He was one of the most powerful men in the country, and he ensured that his own followers gained positions within the administration of bodies such as the Duchy of Lancaster. In short, he filled positions with 'yes men' for his own ends. Suffolk also avoided convention by not presenting things to full Council. In 1439 there are repeated incidents of only himself or a few Council members deciding things and having them passed by the King. On 14th June, this was a unilateral decision to place two children into the Duke of Suffolk's care. This allowed him to choose who they married, and that meant that he or his followers will benefit from the inheritances due to the wards (children).

Such matters, for children of magnates, were usually discussed, here it was fait accompli. Over 1439 and 1440, there are at least eleven occasions where council business was conducted either by Suffolk alone or with just one other council member. Stafford, Moleyns and Beauchamp being used as the second council members throughout this period, the latter being the only one to survive the rebellions of 1450 unscathed and untargeted.

15th June 1467

Death of Philip the Good.

Philip the Good had played a pivotal role in the Hundred Years War. As Duke of Burgundy, he had initially forged an alliance with England, signing the Treaty of Troyes. This alliance helped the English to remain a continental power. Burgundian forces captured Joan of Arc and pro-Burgundian clerics who tried her for heresy on behalf of the English.

Philip soon switched allegiances in the conflict, recognising Charles VII as the rightful King of France in the Treaty of Arras and then laying siege, unsuccessfully, to Calais.

Philip's primary concern was the expansion of Burgundy geographically, economically, and culturally. This led to Burgundy becoming renowned for its festivals' splendour; it became a source of trade to and from England and saw Burgundy become the preeminent force in the low countries.

Philip's desire to expand also impacted on the Wars of the Roses. His conflicts with France limiting the French ability to intervene militarily in English affairs.

His death coincided with the early discussions about a suitable marriage for his son to Margaret of York, which was formalised a year later.

The death of Philip, therefore, impacted heavily on English affairs. It brought Charles the Bold to the fore, as the new Duke. He soon became a supporter of the Yorkists and contributed to Edward IVs invasion of 1471. Charles' marriage to Margaret of York later led to support for Pretenders to the English throne.

16th June 1487

Battle of Stoke Field

Stoke Field was the last major battle of the Wars of the Roses. It is often overshadowed by the Battle of Bosworth, but in terms of battlefield strength, this was big: 15000 Lancastrian 8000-10000 Yorkist soldiers.

The Yorkist objective was to oust Henry VII and replace him with the pretender, Lambert Simnel. Though the Yorkists included 2000 Swiss and Swabian forces armed with the best handguns of the day, the Lancastrian longbowmen proved more decisive.

Much of the Yorkist army was Irish, and they wore little armour; they suffered huge losses to the archers. It is estimated that half of the Yorkist force was killed in the battle, including the Earl of Lincoln.

Lambert Simnel was found and taken into custody. King Henry VII took pity on the boy, who was clearly being used, and gave him a job in the King's service.

Though there were further revolts and plots, this marked the end of large-scale warfare.

"For some time the struggle was fought with no advantage to either side, but at last the first line of the King's army (which was alone committed to the fray and sustained the struggle) charged the enemy with such vigour that it at once crushed those of the hostile leaders who were still resisting. Thereupon the remaining enemy troops turned to flight, and while fleeing were either captured or killed". Polydor Virgil

17th June 1483

Richard, Duke of York (of Shrewsbury), joins his elder brother in the Tower of London

In the days that followed the execution of William Hastings, things moved quickly. If there was a plot by the Woodville family, the Duke of Gloucester had a duty to ensure Edward V's safety and that of his younger brother, Richard.

If at this point Richard had set in motion a plan to take the throne, he needed custody of both Princes to secure his position. On 16th June, the Archbishop of Canterbury was dispatched to Westminster Abbey to persuade Elizabeth Woodville that Richard should join his brother in the Tower.

Richard made it clear to Council that the coronation could not occur whilst the heir and the princesses were taking sanctuary. The sanctuary in which the royal children and Dowager Queen were, was surrounded by armed men.

On the 17th, Prince Richard was released to Duke Richard for transfer to the Tower of London. The next day writs (Supersedas) were sent to cities cancelling Parliament: they arrived too late, and Parliament did in fact, sit.

Orders were also sent to the North for Earl Rivers and Sir Richard Grey to be taken to Pontefract Castle, where they and Sir Thomas Vaughan were to be executed at once.

Within a few days of the young Prince Richard joining his brother in the Tower, several key attendants to the young Princes were dismissed. A week later, the boy's legitimacy was called into question.

18th June 1450

The Humphrey Stafford, Duke of Buckingham, was killed during the Cade revolt.

Humphrey Stafford was one of the leading magnates of the time. He was also one of the King's favourites and was singled out as an evil counsellor of King Henry VI. He was killed in a confrontation with the rebels.

The event described in this 1859 text taken from a book by John George Edgar:

"She (the Queen) therefore, deputed the danger of encountering Cade to a gallant knight named Humphrey Stafford... on receiving the Queen's commands, Stafford, and some of the court gallants, put on their rich armour and gorgeous surcoats, mounted their horses, and with a detachment of the royal army, dashed off to engage the insurgents, all eagerness as it seemed, to bring back the leaders head as a trophy. On coming up with the foe, the ardour of the gay warriors rapidly cooled; for, in posting his troops in Sevenoaks Woods the Captain of Kent had made his dispositions with such masterly skill that the insurgents felt high confidence and presented a formidable front. Nevertheless, Stafford did not shrink from an encounter. Boldly dashing onward, he attacked the Kentishmen in their stronghold. His courage, however, was to no avail. At the very onslaught, he fell in front of his soldiers; and they, fighting with n9 good-will, allowed themselves to be easily defeated".

Cade's followers had targeted several high-ranking nobles. It made clear their discontent with the way that the country was being governed. This also determined the way in which the leading rebels were punished.

19th June 1488

James IV of Scotland grants safe passage to Lord Lovell.

Francis Lovell had been one of King Richard IIIs closest friends and advisors. Upon his accession to the throne, King Richard brought Lovell into the higher positions of Government. His closeness to King Richard was such that his influence was ridiculed in a contemporary rhyme:

The Catte, the Ratte and Lovell our dog,
Rulyth England under a Hogge.

The insinuation being that Lovell was King Richard's lapdog.

Lovell was so trusted by Richard that he was placed in command of defences along the south coast to fend off the expected invasion of Henry Tudor. When Tudor landed at Milford Haven, he joined Richard and the royal army. He fought at Bosworth and escaped, though some contemporary accounts had believed him to have died on the field of battle.

In Bosworth's immediate aftermath, Lovell sought sanctuary at Colchester before heading north to Yorkshire, where sympathies for the Yorkist cause were strong. Here he had a plot foiled but was soon alerted to a new plan, that of placing the pretender, Lambert Simnel, on the throne. Lovell joined with the Earl of Lincoln in organising the venture. As one of the army's senior commanders, he helped to recruit and plan for the invasion.

He fought at the Battle of Stoke Field, and reports show that he survived and escaped. Curiously, nobody knows where to. On 19th June 1487, a safe conduct in his name was issued in Scotland. Yet there is no evidence that he ever travelled to Scotland to make use of it. Indeed, he vanishes from the historical record. One legend has it that he lived out his final years as a hermit in a cave.

20th June 1472

Edward IV pardoned the City of Coventry.

In 1471 when King Edward IV returned to reclaim his throne, the two major obstacles were the armies of the Earl of Warwick's and Margaret of Anjou. With Queen Margaret's force being overseas, Edward turned his attention to the force that the Earl of Warwick was gathering at Coventry.

It was a force that was not yet at full strength, so Edward was eager to crush it as quickly as possible. However, the Lancastrian lords refused to take the field of battle and instead readied themselves for a siege. Edward's Yorkist force tried to goad the Earl out of Coventry by briefly, for a week, besieging the Earls nearby castles at Kenilworth and Warwick itself.

The Earl remained within Coventry. When the Duke of Clarence arrived, in support of Edward having changed his allegiance, it was clear that the local area could not provide sufficient supplies for the Kings army, which now numbered some 13000. Frustrated at his inability to lure the Earl from inside Coventry, he reluctantly returned to London for Easter.

This support of the Earl of Warwick went unpunished. Instead, a pardon was given.

"...Edward IV, of his special grace, through mediation of the noble Prince George, Duke of Clarence (grants) his charter of special pardon to the mayor, commonalty and inhabitants: the which charter was delayed because of the heavy grief the King bore to the City and its inhabitants ever since Richard late Earl of Warwick and his company defended the City against his real highness during Lent prior to Barnet field..." From the Coventry Leet Book, ed M. D. Harris

21ˢᵗ June 1481

Aeterni Regis Papal Bull confirms Portuguese right to trade in African slaves.

At first glance, it may strange that a Papal Bull relating to Portuguese slave-trading rights is included in a book about the Wars of the Roses. However, there was a growing merchant connection between England and Portugal, meaning that any alteration in Portuguese trade had a knock-on effect in England.

The fifteenth century work, Instructions for the *Circumnavigation of England,* illustrates this trade's scale and scope. English ships, particularly from Bristol, were making voyages to Lisbon and the Algarve. The economic impact of the Portuguese slave trade was therefore evident to England from the outset.

"Portuguese merchants, benefitting from their new colonies... played a larger part in direct trade between England and Portugal... over the century [greatest in the latter stages] the Portuguese did quite well, shipping movements doubled, Portuguese owned goods increased sixfold..." Wendy R Childs

It was so evident that it caused a diplomatic dispute, settled in favour of the Portuguese. The Principal Navigations, Voyages, Traffiques, and Discoveries of The English Nation noting:

"after the king of England had seene the same, he should giue charge thorow all his kingdomes, that no man should arme or set foorth ships to Ginnee: and also to request him, that it would please him to giue commandement to dissolue a certaine fleet, which one Iohn Tintam and one William Fabian, English men, were making, by commandement of the duke of Medina Sidonia, to goe to the aforesayd parts of Ginnee.".

22nd June 1483

Ralph Shaw preaches a sermon in which he says that Edward IV's marriage was not valid under canon law.

The way Richard of Gloucester was invited to become King has been the subject of a great deal of scrutiny.

Questions over when a move for the throne was planned, who's the idea was, why it was necessary, and whether it was the right thing to do, remain hot topics of debate.

The critical moment in the shift from Edward V being prepared for his coronation to Richard being invited to take the crown is this sermon.

Ralph Shaw states in the sermon that King Edward IV had been contracted to marry Lady Eleanor Butler. Lady Eleanor had passed away by 1483, but, critically, she had been alive when Edward and Elizabeth Woodville had married.

If true, this would mean that the royal marriage was not legitimate, and consequently, the children produced by the relationship would be unable to inherit the titles or crown.

The sermon had an immediate effect. The existence of a previous marriage was confirmed, probably by Bishop Stillington.

The Council and Parliament now faced a dilemma. The preparations for the coronation of Edward V were at an advanced stage. Now there was a strong suggestion that he was illegitimate. This led to days of heated debate, the outcome of which is described in the entry for 25th June.

23rd June 1468

Margaret of York departs for Burgundy.

Margaret of York was the sister of King Edward IV. Her high status meant that her marriage treaty would be of great value to England.

Early discussions, when Margaret was 8, about her future were directed at Charles of Burgundy. However, relations with Burgundy were fragile, and as the relationship between England and Burgundy broke down, Charles' future headed elsewhere.

The Burgundians opted to marry Charles to Isabella of Bourbon. Almost a decade later, a marriage was arranged for Margaret to Peter Constable of Portugal. Peter died before the wedding took place, leaving Margaret unmarried. Meanwhile, in Burgundy, Isabella, wife of Duke Charles, died.

Negotiations soon started between the Woodville dominated court of England and the house of Burgundy. An agreement was made.

Margaret was escorted to Sluys in Burgundy with a significant embassy accompanying her. A party of nobles headed by Lord Scales and Richard Bonville acted as escort for the bride, demonstrating her importance to the English court.

The voyage could have proved dangerous. Not only because crossing the Channel is perilous but also because King Louis of France had ordered his fleet to intercept Margaret's vessel and prevent her from reaching Sluys.

24th June 1441

A commission of Horoscopes is made to try and reassure Henry VI that earlier horoscopes were wrong.

Eleanor Cobham Duchess of Gloucester, was an enthusiastic follower of astrology. This led to her commissioning a horoscope which included predictions about the future of the crown.

As her husband, Duke Humphrey was the heir to the throne in 1440-41, it made her a potential future queen consort.

The horoscope that Eleanor received predicted that the next King's name would begin with G. This provoked outrage in court. In effect, Eleanor's horoscope predicted the death of King Henry VI and, by virtue of the G, the succession of her husband.

At the time, it was treasonable to predict or wish the kings death. Eleanor and the astrologers soon found themselves facing justice, and the Duchess herself faced a trial. She pleaded guilty to 5 out of 25 charges against her but vehemently denied wishing the kings death.

The court found her guilty. Her punishment was a forced divorce from Duke Humphrey, public penance in the form of walking barefoot to churches on 3 successive Sundays and life imprisonment.

Others implicated included the King's physicians. One died in the Tower of London, another was hanged, drawn, and quartered for Necromancy. The woman who had supplied Eleanor Cobham with potions was burned as a witch. King Henry, though, needed reassurance.

As those who had made these predictions were all discredited, a new horoscope was commissioned on 24th June 1441. This carefully written horoscope was presented to the King at Sheen Palace on 14th August 1441. Eleanor was sentenced in October of 1441.

25th June 1483

This date was particularly busy. It was the day on which Richard Duke of Gloucester was invited to become the King of England, which was accompanied by several other events relating to the transfer of the crown.

Edward Vs brief, uncrowned reign ended quite abruptly. In London, Parliament accepted that Edward and his brother, Richard Duke of York, were born illegitimately. This resulted from the sermon that had been preached, and confirmation by a clergyman, stating that Edward IV had a contract of marriage with Eleanor Butler. Therefore the marriage to Elizabeth Woodville was invalid, and their children were illegitimate and consequently unable to inherit the throne.

This decision meant that Richard Duke of Gloucester is now the heir to the throne of England. He was invited to become King of England on this date and assumed King Richard III's title the following day. The decision and reasons were later confirmed by Parliament in Titulus Regius.

The deposed Edward V and his brother remained in the Tower of London, soon to be lost from sight and subject to the debates surrounding the missing Princes in the Tower.

Also, on this date, Earl Rivers, Sir Richard Grey and Sir Thomas Vaughan were executed at Pontefract Castle. This suggests that the sermon's timing, Parliament meeting to discuss the matter, and the removal of key supporters of Edward Vs claim were carefully coordinated.

26th June 1460

The Earls of Salisbury and Warwick land at Sandwich.

The Earls of Warwick, Salisbury, and March sail from Calais land with a force at Sandwich. The port of Sandwich was strategically important at the time. It was one of England's main links to the continent. So much so that in January 1460, Warwick had ordered a raid on the port, causing damage and capturing several notable figures.

Now, having secured Sandwich, the Yorkists had effectively gained control of the English Channel. This gave them a logistical advantage that they were able to press home.

The landing at Sandwich marked the beginning of the Yorkist revival. They had prepared the ground in the South East through propaganda and were able to recruit in the South East before making their way to London.

Along with the men who rallied to their cause, the Calais garrison marched towards the capital. They were aided by ships in the Thames.

Upon arrival, they were admitted into the City of London but not into the Tower of London. This led to the Yorkist siege of the Tower of London, lasting from the 2nd to 19th July.

With the Earl of Salisbury in command of the besieging forces, Warwick and March's men were free to take on the Lancastrian Army. This they did at Northampton on 10th July 1460, resulting in a Yorkist victory.

27th June 1468

The first meeting of Margaret of York and Charles the Bold.

Margaret of York meets Charles the Bold, Duke of Burgundy, for the first time.

Margaret of York was the sister of King Edward IV. A diplomatic marriage was arranged to wed Margaret to Charles the Bold. Burgundy had a long history of involvement in English affairs, and at this time, an alliance suited both parties very well. Charles' previous wife had died in 1465, leaving him a widower with no son to inherit his title. Burgundy was also embroiled in conflict with France and had a particular dislike for Margaret of Anjou. England shared the hostility towards the French, not least because King Charles VII of France was Margaret of Anjou's uncle who had financed landings on the Northern English coast in the years after Towton.

Arranging the marriage had been problematic, though. The French attempted to prevent an Anglo-Burgundian alliance by offering diplomatic marriage alliances of their own liking: to both the English and Burgundians. The fragility of talks led initially to Margaret of York being betrothed to Peter, Constable of Portugal. However, he died on 29th June 1466, and as negotiations with France faltered, the Anglo-Burgundian alliance progressed.

Margaret sailed to Burgundy with Lord Scales and Richard Boyville as her official escorts. She met with her future mother-in-law, Isabella, on 26th June and then the following day met Charles for the first time. The couple married on 3rd July of the same year.

The alliance paid off well for King Edward IV. It was to Burgundy that he fled when faced with the invasion of Warwick. Burgundy supported Edward's invasion and campaign to retake the crown in 1471.

28th June 1461

Coronation of Edward IV.

Following Edward's victory at Towton and the isolation of Lancastrian resistance to a relatively small number of areas of the country, preparations were made for his Coronation.

"King Edward...returned, as conqueror, to London. Here he immediately assembled the Parliament and was crowned at Westminster by the venerable father Thomas, archbishop of Canterbury, and solemnly graced with the diadem of sovereignty." Croyland Chronicle

The ceremony was a lavish affair. It includes the crowning of the King and the preparation of a large and ornate genealogical roll that 'proved' his legitimacy and historical ties to Brutus, Helen of Troy, and the origins of man.

The proceedings included Edward creating 32 men as Knights of the Order of Bath. They then paraded along a carefully prepared route to hold vigil before the enthroning ceremony the next day. Wine was flowing freely from the conduits at the Eleanor Cross and Cornhill. Windows were decorated with gold and silver braid.

Phillipe de Commynes noted:

"I don't recall ever having seen such a fine looking man...".

During this, the Kings Champion, Sir Thomas Dymoke of Skivensby, rode into the hall in his ceremonial armour. He threw down his gauntlet and challenged anyone to assert that Edward was not the legitimate King.

29th June 1509

Death of Margaret Beaufort

Margaret Beaufort, Countess of Richmond, had just the one child, Henry Tudor. It was her lineage that gave Henry the claim to the throne as she descended from Edward III.

Margaret was an important figure throughout her life. She was married twice as a child, the more famous being to Edmund Tudor. Still only 13, Margaret was heavily pregnant when in 1456 Edmund died in captivity of the Plague.

Margaret was cared for by Jasper Tudor, who provided for her and the newly born Henry, and he arranged Margaret's 3rd marriage to Henry Stafford. Margaret then persuaded Jasper Tudor to take Henry into exile. This led to a fourteen-year period in which mother and son did not see one another.

Following Stafford's death, she remarried to Thomas Stanley. As a result, she enjoyed favour at court, and it allowed her to observe the political situation and to ensure that her son's position was safe. This led to her negotiating with King Richard III and conspiring with Elizabeth Woodville.

Margaret Beaufort's most famous political act is undoubtedly the arrangements that she masterminded with Elizabeth Woodville. The agreement to marry Henry Tudor to Elizabeth of York was politically astute.

Following the Battle of Bosworth, Margaret Beaufort became known as "My Lady the King's Mother".

Margaret died the day after King Henry VIIIs 18th birthday and just months after the death of her son, Henry Tudor, King Henry VII. She is buried in Westminster Abbey.

30th June 1484

Richard III inspects the royal fleet

As tension was high and the threat of foreign intervention in English affairs was a very real one, Richard III took a very keen personal interest in the condition of the navy.

Having held the Admiral of England's position, Richard was acutely aware of both the strengths and weaknesses of the naval defences available to the crown. He wrote to the Calais garrison regarding their role in maintaining the security of the channel.

He also personally visited the port of Scarborough on two occasions to inspect the fleet. The second of these occasions began on 30th June 1484, staying until 11th July.

There were several reasons why he visited Scarborough twice. First, he would be very aware of its proximity to Ravenspur, where he had landed as part of his brother's invasion fleet in 1471. If one invasion force could land on the Yorkshire coast, so too could another.

The second was the fact that the French were flexing their naval muscles. They had already attacked the English fleet off Scarborough and captured English vessels, including those of two of England's finest sea captains.

Third, he needed to make sure that the navy would do everything possible to prevent the secreting of important persons, such as his nieces, to the continent.

Fourth, a naval battle had taken place against Scottish ships. This meant that the fleet in the North needed to be well maintained, regularly supplied, and crews ready to sail.

July

1st July 1468

A quitclaim was agreed for a Manor in East Bridgford, Notts.

A quitclaim is a legal agreement to forego rights. In this case, it was an agreement to set aside a right to a small manor in Nottinghamshire. The arrangement was made by Alice, Lady Sudeley and Francis Lovell.

This left the manor in the hands of Ralph Lord Cromwell through his marriage to Margaret Deincourt. This type of arrangement was commonplace. It served all parties well and ensured that the landed society was treated justly on a local level and that there was an element of continuity for the manor in terms of administration.

Upon the death of Lord Cromwell, the manor passed to his niece, Joan Stanhope. Again, this is not unusual. What would typically happen next is that Joan's husband would gain the manor in her stead, or, if unmarried, she would become a much more attractive proposition for a bachelor of similar social rank.

In this case, neither happened. Joan died childless. Whilst it would be possible to identify a next of kin, this route was cut off too. Francis Lovell simply overturned the legal agreement and took possession of the manor. This happened in 1481 and showed failings within the administrative and legal framework of the time: Lovell had ridden roughshod through the law.

It was challenged. Interestingly, though, one of William Hastings's retainers wrote to the Bishop of Winchester about the matter. Hastings himself had sided with Lovell on the case. His retainer quietly complained to the Bishop about the issue. He was, in effect, sitting on the fence so that whatever the outcome, he could benefit. Such was the system of patronage at the time. Loyalties were not as permanent as they had been under earlier forms of the feudal system. Now, the retainers could and did pick sides.

2nd July 1460

Siege of the Tower of London

On 2 July 1460, the Lords of Calais began their blockade of the Tower of London.

Separating their force, the Earls of Warwick and March began to head north, whilst the Earl of Salisbury remained in London and began a blockade of the Tower.

The defenders of the Tower took the unprecedented approach of firing into London from the palace:

"They that were within the Tower cast wildfire into the City, and shot in small guns, and burned and hurt men and women and children in the streets" [Unnamed chronicle cited by D Seward]

This only served to increase the level of support that Salisbury got from London citizens and deployed an armed militia in support of them.

"And then they skirmished together, and much harm was done daily."

Bombards from the Royal Arsenal were taken by London's citizens and used to fire upon the Tower. This resulted in sections of the curtain wall being destroyed, ensure that provisions did not enter the Tower:

"And the Tower was besieged by land and by water, that no victual might come to them that were within."

The plan worked. On 19 July, aware that the Queen's army was defeated and now without food, the Tower surrendered. Lord Scales attempted to escape by boat but was seen, identified, and stabbed to death. His body was unceremoniously thrown into the Thames.

3rd July 1450

Jack Cade crosses London Bridge and declares himself Mayor. The rebels find, try, and summarily execute James Fiennes and William Crowmer.

In rural Kent, the ranks of the rebel army had swollen. Jack Cade then led them to London. Now, it was time for the rebels to force their demands on the authorities. To do this would require force. The Kentish rebels had approached London along the south bank. To have any impact at all, they needed to cross to the northern bank. There was only one realistic way of doing this: crossing London Bridge.

The rebels pressed forward. As advance over the bridge took place, the unpopular Bishop of Salisbury, William Asycough, was discovered by rebels. He was ruthlessly cut down. At the bridge, Cade's men made excellent progress. They made their way across and secured the drawbridge so that it could not be raised.

King Henry VI was quickly being ushered out of London to the safety of Warwickshire. As Cade himself crossed the bridge, he symbolically struck the 'London Stone' and act traditionally done by a new Lord Mayor, which to the delight of his followers he declared himself to be.

The rebels spread out, hunting for the evil counsellors whom they wanted to rid from the government. Many had fled. Not all escaped, though. They found and arrested James Fiennes, Baron Say and Sele, and William Crowmer, sheriff of Kent.

After a brief trial, the men were convicted of treason and executed, their heads then displayed on spikes on London Bridge, as though they were the traitors' heads.

4th July 1475

Edward IV and his army set sail for Calais at the start of the English invasion of France.

Edward led an army into France in 1475. No battles took place as the two sides agreed to terms in the Treaty of Picquardy.

"Edward IV had never been very enthusiastic about this expedition. For even whilst he was still at Dover before boarding ship for the crossing, he had begun negotiations with us. Two reasons made him cross to this side; first, all his kingdom wanted an expedition such as they had been used to in time gone by and the Duke of Burgundy had put pressure on them to do it; secondly, he did it in order to reserve for himself a good fat portion of the money which he had raised in England for this crossing..." Philip Commines

"...The kings being accompanied by certain of their barons, and both with their hosts standing ready armed and apparelled for war a certain distance from the banks of the river... concluded a peace [on 29 August]... The fame of this peace and accord was that the French King yearly, during the peace, deliver to King Edward's assignees within his town of Calais £10,000 in gold crowns." Great Chronicle of London

"...when King Louis understood that Kind Edward was already arrived with an army, he hastily augmented his forces and more danger he saw hung off his neck, so with much more celerity determined to make headway against them...

...the two kings met [at Piqueny] on the bridge over the river Somme, had a long talk together, and finally concluded that King Louis should pay presently unto King Edward, for his expenses in the preparation of this war, 55000 crown and yearly afterwards 50000". Polydor Virgil

5th July 1450

Citizens of London attempted to repel Cade's men.

Until now, the citizens of London had left Cade to his own devices. His men had done little damage, and their actions had been either symbolic or aimed at specific people.

This was to change dramatically. Cade was invited to dine with a citizen of London. After a convivial meal, he suddenly burst into a rage and began plundering the house. His men followed suit. The rebels took their booty to Southwark.

On 5 July, news reached Cade, who was in the White Swan Inn, that the bridge was being barricaded. The violence that had taken place within the City walls was enough to turn the citizens against Cade. Upon hearing of the barricades being constructed, Cade immediately led an advance over the bridge. A fierce, hours long battle was fought.

Eventually, both sides broke from the fight and retired. After careful consideration of how best to deal with the large rebel force at the City's gates, the Council chose to send Bishop Waynflete to speak to the rebels. The Bishop was to offer them a general pardon in return for a peaceful dispersal.

It was a promise that the leaders of both sides had little intention of keeping. Yet, for the time being, Cade agreed to it, and his army withdrew.

6th July 1483

Coronation of King Richard III

The coronation of Richard III and his Queen, Anne Neville, is regarded as one of the most magnificent coronation ceremonies to have been held.

Richard's entourage of 7 men wore gowns of two halves, perhaps resulting from Edward's gowns being altered. The Queen was accompanied by the Duchess of Norfolk, Countess of Richmond, and other ladies-in-waiting.

The ceremony began as the royal couple took their places in the seats of state. A specially prepared service opened the proceedings. Following this was the solemnity of the anointing. They were anointed by Cardinal Bourchier and then dressed in golden robes of state.

As they took their seats, they were blessed with prayers and incense. Richard had the orb and sceptres of state placed into his hands. Leading bishops and nobles made clear their loyalty to the newly crowned King and Queen before a high mass was heard.

A grand procession to Westminster Hall followed the mass, a first chance for the commons to see their newly crowned royal couple. In the hall, a ceremonial banquet was held. The highlight of which was the King's Champion, Sir Robert Dymock, entering on horseback in armour and challenging anyone to question Richard's right to be King. After a brief pause, the hall erupted into cries of 'King Richard'.

The splendour and magnificence of the event did not awe everybody, though. Contemporary chronicler Fabyan noted of the occasion that some lords "now murmered and grudged against him, in such wise that few or none favoured his party except it were for dread or for the great gifts they received from him".

7th July 1461

Grant of liveried apparel to James Damport for life

The court had several Wardrobes. The Great Wardrobe was essentially the clothing and apparel of the King. There was a Privy Wardrobe, and members of the royal family and nobility often had their own.

The task of being Keeper of the Great Wardrobe involved purchasing, tailoring or overseeing tailoring and ensuring that the right garments were available for each type of formal occasion.

Here we see the Keeper of the Great Wardrobe being told that a James Damport has been entered into the King's service as a sergeant-at-arms.

As a member of the King's own household, it was the King, through his great wardrobe, who would provide the correct attire.

You also see how such sergeant-at-arms were remunerated in this extract from the Close Rolls of Edward IV, dated 7 July 1461.

"To the keeper of the great wardrobe for the time being. Order every year to give James Damport during his life livery of one gown of the suit of esquires of the household; as the King has granted to him the office of one of his serjeants at arms for life from 4 March last, on which day he did actually occupy the same, taking therein 12d. a day of the issues, profits and revenues of the lordship, manor and hundred of Odyham co. Southampton, and one gown a year as aforesaid towards Christmas."

8th July 1487

Plumpton Letter: The Earl of Shrewsbury to Sir Robert Plumpton

One consequence of the wars was the seizing of lands from those who had lost. In some cases, this was not done through legal channels. This resulted in good (or bad) lordship being demonstrated, such as the Earl of Shrewsbury's intervention below. It could also lead to legal recourse such as petitions to Parliament.

"I recommend unto you assertions shown to me by my right beloved Dame Joyce Percy, now attending to my wife, how you, contrary to right and conscience have interrupted Dame Joyce of certain lands lying within the lordship of Arkington within the county of York. Which land was purchased of one Robert Percy, knight, her late husband, deceased, and by him granted unto the said Dame Joyce so wherefore, if it be so, I greatly marvel, willing and desiring of you therefore that unto such time as this matter may be had in good and proper examination you will in no ways [indecipherable] or deal with the said land but suffer the said Dame Joyce and her assignees peacefully to occupy the same without any manner of interruption to the contrary... and over this I am informed that one Richard Nicholl late tenant to said Dame Joyce was now in the field against the kings good grace for which cause you have seized his goods.... I will desire you, considering the said Dame Joyce was innocent and [knew] nothing of said misdemeanours you will see that of his said goods such duties may be contested as he owe unto her by reason of any tenures of buildings and that you will tender her in these premises the rather for my sake so as she have not cause to make further suit for her remedy therein, as I trust you".

Earl of Shrewsbury, 8th July 1487.

9th July 1436

Burgundian siege of Calais begins.

In the Hundred Years War, the fortunes of England were intertwined with the success or failure of diplomatic policies'. When England had strong allies in Brittany and Burgundy, things were often in England's favour as the French were fighting or wary on three fronts. When any of these alliances weakened, disintegrated, or one of the continental powers switched allegiance to side with the King of France, it was the English in France and Normandy who were on the defensive.

Burgundy was the most significant of the powers who allied with the English. The Duchy dominated the Low Countries and had been eager to restrict French influence in the region. This resulted in the Franco-Burgundian wars, which resulted in Burgundian forces capturing Joan of Arc.

In 1436, Philip the Good changed his policy. He quickly targeted English held Calais. Had Burgundy succeeded in taking Calais, English hopes of keeping possessions in France would have been shattered.

England reinforced the area via the sea, and after a short siege, the Burgundians withdrew. It reaffirmed the need to ensure diplomacy worked.

In the coming years, it served as a reminder to Council that continental powers could significantly impact English possessions on the continent. This also affected English domestic policy and tax revenues.

Anglo-Burgundian relations from this point onwards were fundamental to how the French Wars were conducted. The links with Burgundy went on to influence the Wars of the Roses, as did English retention of Calais.

10th July 1460

Battle of Northampton

The Yorkist Lords who had fled to Calais had landed at Calais and marched on London.

Upon arriving at the capital, the force is said to have numbered around 20000. The Lancastrian Commander withdrew into the Tower of London. The Yorkists entered London on 2 July. On 4 July, the bulk of the army marched North. The Earl of Salisbury remained in London and besieged the Tower of London.

The Lancastrians knew that the Yorkist army was on the march. They moved from Coventry to Northampton. Here, they built a fortified camp which was surrounded by a small moat. This was defended by cannon and had the River Nene to its rear.

The Yorkists maintained that they had no argument with the King himself. It was the counsellors with whom they claimed to have an issue. Attempts at Parley were made by the Yorkists. After several attempts, Warwick informed the Lancastrians that they would be attacked at 2pm if no agreement had been made.

The Yorkist army assaulted the Lancastrian position. As they reached the barricade, one of the defenders, Lord Grey, switched sides. His men joined the Yorkists, which gave the attacking force a large breach in the defences into which they could advance. With a river behind them and surrounded by their own defensive moat, the Lancastrians could not form up effectively.

Around the Kings quarters, several leading Lancastrian lords were slain. Their number included the Duke of Buckingham, Thomas Percy, the Earl of Shrewsbury, and Lord Beaumont.

11th July 1469

Marriage of George Duke of Clarence to Isabel Neville.

George Duke of Clarence was the younger brother of King Edward IV. Isabel Neville was a daughter of Warwick the Kingmaker. Their marriage was controversial.

At the time, marital laws required dispensation to be granted for marriages where the couple were related within the fourth degree. George and Isabel were related within the fourth degree. And, with the high status of both, they required Papal dispensation. This was not uncommon, many diplomatic marriages or unions of two baronial families required this dispensation, and it was usually granted.

The matter was complicated by the fact that they also needed royal approval because of their rank. King Edward opposed the marriage. This posed a problem, especially as the couple gained Papal Dispensation in March 1469.

Relations between the King and his brother were already strained, and the marriage issue only worsened them. George, however, was determined to press ahead. He and Isabel travelled to Calais, where they were married in a ceremony presided over by Isabel's uncle, the Archbishop of Canterbury.

Accounts of the service itself vary significantly, with one contemporary saying it was extravagant, another saying few attended. The date itself is not definite; most reports saying the 11th though some suggest the 12th.

12th July 1469

A proclamation was made in Calais by the Earl of Warwick, Archbishop of Canterbury, and Duke of Clarence.

In Calais, a proclamation was made on 12 July 1469 by the Duke of Clarence, Earl of Warwick, and Archbishop of Canterbury regarding the state of English politics. The proclamation was similar to the calls made twenty years earlier by the Yorkist faction. They claimed to be the King's true liegemen and identified several seditious and corrupt individuals who were giving the King poor advice. The list of names makes the source of their anger clear, the Queen's family, raised to ranks above their station, dominated it:

"seditious persons, that is to say, the Lord Rivers, the Duchess of Bedford his wife, William Herbert, Earl of Pembroke, Humphrey Stafford, Earl of Devonshire, Lord Scales and Audley, Sir John Woodville and his brothers..." (Warkworth Chronicle)

The proclamation makes the charge against them clear:

"mischeavkus rule, opinion and assent, which have caused our sovereign lord and his realm to fall into great poverty and misery, disturbing the administration of laws, only tending to their own promotion and enrichment". (Warkworth Chronicle)

The proclamation was distributed throughout the South East of England. It also stated that these great lords would be returning to Canterbury. They had set down a challenge that, realistically, was only ever going to end on the battlefield.

13th July 1477

Marriage of Robert Plumpton to Agnes Gascoigne

The Plumpton family were influential merchants operating mainly in London. They were wealthy by the standards of the day and had dealings with Parliament and the nobility. The Gascoigne family were from the gentry, reasonably well off and with channels of communication to the nobility. In modern terms, the families were upper middle class rather than aristocrats.

The wedding contract for the couple was granted on 13 July 1477. Typically, a wedding ceremony could be held straight after such an arrangement was agreed, unless dispensation was also required: it was not in this case.

However, legal proceedings were taken that included representation from the King's treasury which delayed the ceremony. Why?. Robert Plumpton's father had made promises in the marriage contract:

"William Plumpton, knight, shall by the grace of god, shall make of cause to be made unto the said Robert and Agnes a sufficient and lawful estate of lands and tenements to the yearly value of xx over all manner of charges and reprises within the lordship of Kenalton within the county of Nottingham, within a month next after said marriage had... also grants unto William Gascoigne that he nor any other feoffee shall not make use of any feoffee, or lease of any manors, land or tenement..." Plumpton Letters

The case was settled after William Plumpton's death, though the couple married before the legal dispute had been concluded. Land management and the system of enfeoffment could be a complex issue, especially when affected by war and attainders.

14th July 1460

The Earls of March and Salisbury arrive in London after the Battle of Northampton with Henry VI their captive.

John Stone, in his chronicle, describes the aftermath of the Battle of Northampton:

"After the battle, they came to the King and entered with him into the house of monks, Delapre [Abbey], close to Northampton, then into the town of Northampton, with other earls and commoners. After that, the lords returned with Henry VI to the city of London".

The Yorkist victory at Northampton was significant for several reasons. Militarily, it stands out as being an assault on a fortified town. One in which massed gins were used for the first time on English soil. It was also the last time that Parley was attempted in the Wars of the Roses. At the time, the significance was political. The Yorkists had captured the King for a second time and now had the political initiative.

With the Yorkist lords returning to London in triumph the tide had turned in their favour. The Tower of London soon surrendered. The news reached the Duke of York as he readied himself for his return to England.

With Henry in captivity, Richard now chose to press for his hereditary rights. His own return to England was like a royal progress. Upon his arrival in London, he went as far as claiming the throne. This led to the political compromise that was the Act of Accord, which led to all out war between the supporters of Queen Margaret, and those of the Duke of York.

15th July 1483

Henry Stafford Duke of Buckingham appointed as Constable and Chamberlain.

Henry Stafford Duke of Buckingham, initially allied himself with Richard of Gloucester following King Edward IV's death. He was of royal blood, descending from Edward III through the line of John of Gaunt. As such, he was a prominent noble.

Buckingham's rank led to him being appointed as Chamberlain and Constable of England. The former recognises his importance within the court and effectively places him in charge of the King's household. The latter appointment is of more interest to historians.

The Constable of England was the highest of judicial positions, enabling the holder to administer justice on the King's behalf. Such powers had previously seen Richard himself preside over hasty trials and executions following the Battle of Tewkesbury.

Buckingham's tenure was short-lived. He rebelled in the Autumn of 1483 and was executed for treason. However, his time in the position coincides with the period when the Princes in the Tower disappeared.

This has led some historians to speculate that Buckingham may have used his authority as Constable of England to access the Princes and murder them. That suspicion was raised at the time. One Portuguese account observed that:

"...and after the passing away of king Edward in the year of 83, another one of his brothers, the Duke of Gloucester, had in his power the Prince of Wales and the Duke of York, the young sons of the said king his brother, and turned them to the Duke of Buckingham, under whose custody the said Princes were starved to death." Alvaro Lopes de Chaves, Secretary to the King of Portugal

16th July 1460

The Tower of London surrenders to the Yorkists following the Battle of Northampton.

At Northampton, the Yorkist army had won a victory on 10 July. King Henry had been taken by the Yorkists and returned to London with them, in their 'care'. The return:

"was conducted with all outward forms of state and ceremony to London, which he [the King] arrived and where he was affectionately received by all classes, the confederates thereby being constrained to treat him with becoming decorum and reverence." The Chronicles of the White Rose of York

Henry's return to the Capital ended the siege of the Tower of London. The besieged forces, including Lords Hungerford and Scales, were free to leave the Tower unmolested.

Lord Scales, however, was assassinated on the following Sunday by men associated with the Earl of Warwick.

The 'unmolested' clearly only applied to their leaving the tower and gave no assurance f their wellbeing in the days that followed.

Before the end of July, Sir Thomas Blount, John Archer from the Council of the Duke of Exeter and five further members of the Exeter household had faced trial, been found guilty of illegally taking the tower and executed at Tyburn. The Yorkists were making their ascendancy count.

17th July 1453

Battle of Castillon.

In June 1451, the French expelled the English from Gascony. It was the first time in 300 years that the province was not held under English or Angevin rule. It followed hard on the heels of the loss of Normandy and was a shattering blow to English aspirations on the continent.

The French, expecting an assault on Normandy, were surprised when Talbot and an army of 3000 landed to the north of Bordeaux. His son, Viscount Lisle, arrived with a further 2300 men. Local recruitment bolstered the size of the army at Talbots command.

Talbot aimed to take out one army at a time through rapid deployments. When the French lay siege to the town of Castillon, the Gascons pleaded with Talbot to go to the towns rescue. Eventually, he agreed.

At Castillon, the French had formidable defences established, including over 300 guns. Talbot was told that the enemy was in retreat, as clouds of dust were seen

Talbot ordered for the army to form up. The French were not withdrawing; quite the opposite, they were forming up. Nonetheless, the order was given to attack: into the face of 300 guns and hundreds of archers.

The battle was a decisive French victory. Talbot lost his life, as did many under his command. Bordeaux held out for 3 months but, England had now effectively been forced out of Gascony. It is thought by some that the news of the defeat at Castillon brought about King Henry Vis first period of incapacity, thus making it a cause of the Wars of the Roses.

18th July 1455

Parliament absolves the Yorkists of any blame for the 1st Battle of St. Albans.

The Yorkist victory at St. Albans transformed the balance of power within the court, Council and Parliament. This was reflected in the opening addresses of the July 1455 Parliament. Here, the crown acknowledged the Yorkist faction as being faithful lieges whilst also condemning the late Duke of Somerset amongst others for advancing their own interests. The text is intriguing, showing how complete the transformation in fortunes was at this time. It was accompanied by appointment to hear petitions of a predominantly Yorkist group and the exclusion of those affiliated with the defeated faction led by Somerset and Queen Margaret.

"...Lord the King, with the advice and assent of the lords spiritual and temporal, and the commons of his kingdom of England being in the present Parliament, and also by authority of the same Parliament, declared his beloved kinsmen Richard Duke of York, Richard, Earl of Warwick, and Richard, Earl of Salisbury, to be his faithful lieges, in the manner and form presented in a certain schedule in the said Parliament...

... Edmund, late duke of Somerset, Thomas Thorpe and William Joseph, intending, as it is supposed, the hurt and destruction of our true, most trusty and well-beloved cousins Richard Duke of York, Richard, Earl of Warwick, and Richard, Earl of Salisbury, and their heirs, prompted and solicited us by various means to mistrust our said cousins, and to estrange them from our favour and good grace, declaring them not to be our true liegemen, and therefore provoked and incited us to proceed with a great force of people on pretence of our own interest, but in fact to advance their own interests and quarrels".

19th July 1455

Tension runs high in London

Though Parliament had formally absolved the Yorkist Lords of any blame for the Battle of St. Albans, this was not the end of the matter. Having Parliament accept your innocence and honesty is one thing. In politics, making the most of the situation is an entirely different matter. So, despite being acquitted and the main Lords of the Queen's Party condemned in the opening addresses of Parliament, there was still an advantage to press home. So too, was there a perceived threat. To this end, the Earl of Warwick is said to have openly accused Lord Cromwell of being the instigator of the fighting at St. Albans. There are accounts of the Yorkist lords attending matters of state dressed in armour. That may have been precautionary; it may have been to send a chilling message to their foes. The situation was summarised by Henry Windsor in a letter written on 19 July 1455:

"the King our sovereign lord, and all his true lords, are healthy in their bodies but not at ease in their hearts. Two days before the writing of this letter there was a quarrel between Lords Warwick and Cromwell before the King. When Lord Cromwell sought to excuse himself of all responsibility for the battle of St. Albans, Warwick swore he was not telling the truth since it was he who originated all the fighting there. So great is tge ill-will between Lords Cromwell and Warwick at present that, at Cromwell's request, the Earl of Shrewsbury has lodged at the hospital of St, James, for his security. Also, men of Lords Warwick, York and Salisbury proceed in armour daily to Westmknster, having filled their lords barges with weapons..." From the Paston Letters collection. Henry Windsor to John Bocking and William Worcester. 19 July 1455.

20th July 1479

First recorded Wool Fleet

Wool was the backbone of the English economy. Customs duties levied on wool formed a large proportion of national revenue.

The woollen trade had suffered though. War was one factor, but competition had increased, customs duties were being evaded, and raids on lone ships or shipwrecks due to inclement weather had resulted in the trade's profitability being adversely affected.

For most exports of wool, the intention was to sell in Northern Europe. As the Wars of the Roses ebbed and flowed, a series of regulations were introduced to protect English merchants and the interests of the treasury. Most ships leaving England with a cargo of wool had, by law, to sail to Calais.

Newcastle had an exemption, being allowed to sail into more northerly ports in Flanders and to Scotland. The concept of a wool fleet was introduced to address the regular losses and diminish the risk of raiders.

Many vessels would carry goods from many merchants. The cargo shipped by these merchants could be spread over several of the vessels. Therefore, there was safety in numbers, which was easier for the Calais or Sandwich Fleets to protect and, should a vessel sink, the loss per merchant was limited.

The first such fleet set sail on 20 July 1479. It was a fleet of some 38 ships. London customs accounts show that in subsequent days the number of ships departing was, as expected, much lower than previously. The following spring, further wool fleets set sail in a practice that continued beyond the end of the Wars of the Roses.

21st July 1460

William Worcester is executing Sir John Fastolf's will

Sir John Fastolf was an influential member of the gentry. He held lands in East Anglia and positions in London. Fastolf died without natural heirs, and the execution of his will became a long and bitter affair. The arrangements were handled mainly by William Worcester, who on 21 July 1460 was working on the matter in Norwich.

What is particularly interesting about Worcester's work on the execution of the will is its timing. He is travelling as the Wars of the Roses bursts into life.

In the year from May 1460 to May 1461, Worcester travels extensively. He travels to London on 9 May 1460 and stays until 6 June. Then he returns to Norwich via Cambridge and Bury St. Edmunds. Another journey to London takes place in July, arriving on 21 July. He travels through the Midlands to Bristol, taking in Buckingham, Coventry and Withybridge en route from London. He then returns to London briefly before returning to Norwich. He again visits London in January of 1461.

In February 1461, he sent an assistant on a journey, the only time he chooses not to travel. He then travelled again in spring. There are 5 major battles in this period, a siege of London, a destructive advance south by Queen Margaret's army and numerous commissions of array.

The roads are busy with armies marching. And yet Worcester can move freely around the country, with little hindrance to own work. As historian K. B. McFarlane noted, for many people, the Wars of the Roses had minimal impact on their way of life; it went on as usual.

22nd July 1470

Angers Agreement between the Earl of Warwick and Margaret of Anjou.

The Earl of Warwick had tried to control the government when holding King Edward under house arrest. He was thwarted as he did not have enough support from other nobles, meaning his attempts to force things through Council failed.

An attempt to reconcile Warwick and the King was unsuccessful; Warwick remained isolated and disgruntled. Over the years, the Earl of Warwick had favoured a pro-France policy. This now opened an unlikely opportunity for him to regain the initiative. The King of France was eager to have an alliance with England. It would help him in his conflicts with Burgundy. To this end, he suggested an alliance between Queen Margaret and the Earl of Warwick.

This led to Queen Margaret being approached regarding an alliance between those loyal to Henry VI and the Neville's. Given the friction between the Queen and Warwick in earlier years, this was an unusual alliance created out of necessity.

At Angers, the pair agreed on terms. Prince Edward and Warwick's daughter, Anne, would marry. Both parties would muster large armies. They would combine to oust King Edward, reinstate Henry VI as King, and Warwick would act as the chief counsellor.

It was a plan for the readaptation of King Henry VI. The plan was set into motion quite quickly, the alliance being confirmed by Anne Neville's marriage to Prince Edward before Warwick returned to England to begin the process of removing Edward from the throne.

23rd July 1454

Henry Holland Duke of Exeter, was imprisoned by the Duke of York.

In 1450 Henry Holland had been granted livery of his lands and his title. It is thought by some historians that this was in response to the memorandum of the Cade rebels that called for ancient royal blood to be in government.

In 1454 the tension between different factions within the government had reached boiling point. The King was incapacitated, and there had been heated debate over the choice of Protector for the realm. Council had settled the matter by appointing Richard Duke of York to the role. He was the senior Prince of the Blood and heir presumptive.

He was not the only Prince of the blood, though. Henry Holland Duke of Exeter was another. Exeter, who had been granted livery of his lands on this day in 1450, was something of a loose cannon. He had become embroiled in land disputes and used his rank to coerce and violence to force issues. He was also implicated in uprisings. Richard acted decisively against Exeter on 23 July 1454, Benet's Chronicle describing the events:

"[About 19 May] the Duke of York, with a great number of men, rode to York to confront the Duke of Exeter and Lord Egremont who had armed themselves in Yorkshire and rebelled against the King's peace. However, when they heard of the Duke of York's arrival, they fled. On 23 July, the Duke of York seized The Duke of Exeter at Westminster, took him to his house and, later, imprisoned him in Pontefract Castle".

24th July 1465

Henry VI captured by Yorkists and taken to the Tower of London.

Some accounts of King Henry's capture suggest that he was taken prisoner by the Earl of Warwick immediately after the Battle of Hexham. That is the fiction part of historical fiction being dramatised. Henry was not actually at the Battle of Hexham.

He had already moved from the North-East due to the dangers posed by assaults on the remaining Lancastrian castles. By the time of Hexham, Henry was staying at Muncaster. Evidence of his stay there, in the care of Sir John Pennington, can still be seen in the form of a drinking cup that he gifted upon his departure.

From Muncaster, he headed to Bolton-in-Bowland, staying with the Pudsay family. He soon moved to the nearby Waddington Hall. It was here that Henry was betrayed by 'the black monk of Addington'.

Local Yorkists had received the tipoff that Henry was hiding at the hall. On 24 July 1465, Sir James Tempest, Sir James Harrington and others burst in to seize the King.

Henry made an escape, dashing dawn a staircase as the intruders forced entry. He used steppingstones to cross the River Ribble and began to make his way up a path that leads to the moors. The local Yorkists were wise to his movements, though and knew where the trail led.

Henry was soon captured. He was then put on a horse, had his feet tied to the stirrups to prevent escape and began the slow journey to London.

25th July 1474

The Treaty of London

Twenty years of civil war and instability had prevented the English from pursuing their claim for the throne of France. The 'right' had not been forgotten and continued to be a source of displeasure.

Following the decisive victories over the Lancastrian forces at Barnet and Tewkesbury, the situation within England had stabilised. The Lancastrian leadership was dead or incredibly isolated.

This meant that Edward could finally turn his attention to the continent. Firstly he needed to persuade his own Parliament that the campaign was worthwhile: made difficult because he had squandered a previous tax issued for a war with France.

In 1473 Edward managed to persuade the Commons to back an invasion. They stipulated that the money for the expedition would be released after the army had been mustered. Now, he needed continental allies.

Allies against the French were not particularly hard to find in the late 15th century. In Burgundy and Brittany, Edward had two natural bedfellows for war. Both had been sympathetic to the Yorkist cause, and Burgundy had a track record of allying with the English against France.

As is often the case, negotiations over an alliance took some time to agree. Charles the Bold eventually decided to send a Burgundian Army in support of the English invasion. In return, Edward promised to guarantee Burgundy's borders and cede some land from conquests to the Duchy.

The Agreement was signed in London on 25 July 1474.

26th July 1469

Battle of Edgcote. A series of running skirmishes in the days before the main encounter makes the precise dating of this battle one that is not universally agreed. Some historians state the 26th, others, the 24th.

In the summer of 1469, a rebellion had taken place in the north. The revolt, led by Robin of Redesdale, had been orchestrated by the Earl of Warwick. King Edward had moved north to address the problem. As he did so, Warwick and Duke of Clarence declared for the rebels.

A royal army led by the Earls of Pembroke and Devon was marching to Nottingham to bolster the King's army. At the same time, the Earl of Warwick was marching to join with the northern rebels, and the army of Robin of Redesdale was marching south to unite with Warwick. The paths of the royal army and Robin of Redesdale met at Edgcote on 26 July 1469.

The rebels soon realised that they outnumbered the royal army and formed up for battle. The royal army was weakened. The Earls had argued the night before, resulting in the Earl of Devon departing the camp. The Earl of Pembroke had to face the rebel army without any archers and facing odds of two to one.

Nonetheless, Pembroke's men stood firm and gained the upper hand, despite early setbacks. It appeared that they may even have been on the verge of victory. Then an advance party of the Earl of Warwick's army was sighted.

Believing it to be Warwick's full strength, the royal army turned and fled the battlefield. The Earl of Pembroke was captured and executed the following day (see the entry for 27 July). In Nottingham, King Edward had little choice but to acquiesce and became Warwick's prisoner under house arrest.

27th July 1469

The execution of William Herbert.

William Herbert was the Earl of Pembroke. He was created Earl following the attainder of Jasper Tudor in the aftermath of the Battle of Towton.

William had anglicised his name as he progressed through the ranks of York patronage. He grew up in Raglan Castle and saw service in the Hundred Years War, witnessing Le Mans' surrender and being captured and ransomed at Formigny.

Upon his return to Wales, he took up office as a sheriff of Glamorgan in lands held by the Earl of Warwick. As civil war erupted, he remained loyal to the two households he had served and captured Edmund Tudor in 1455, policed the area as civil war broke out in 1459 and fought alongside the Earl of March the Battle of Mortimer's Cross.

During Edward IVs reign, the Earl captured all the Welsh Castles that had been in Lancastrian hands, and once Harlech had fallen, every lordship in Wales was held either by the King or Earl of Pembroke as the chief advisor.

It was this affinity to King Edward that was to prove fatal. Captured following the battle of Edgcote, he was taken to Northampton. The Earl of Warwick disapproved of Pembroke's closeness to the King, accusing him of being one of the evil counsellors. Perhaps through jealousy of William Herbert's power in Wales, anger at the loyalty owed was given to the house of York instead of to him as thanks for his giving if roles in his household, Warwick had the Earl executed.

28th July 1434

Delegation of Staplers to the Duke of Burgundy

One of the long-term causes of the Wars of the Roses was the state of the English economy. Another was England's failure to hold Normandy and France. Failures in foreign policy and customs practices also contributed.

This example, from Burgundy, shows how English fiscal controls impacted upon diplomatic relations. England had introduced several policies relating to the export of Wool. They were designed to boost the treasury and combat to great bullion crisis.

Exports of wool to the continent, except those from the port of Newcastle, had to sail to Calais. At Calais, all trade had to be paid upfront, in coins. This was to increase the amount of bullion within the English economy and ensure that English customs duties were paid.

Whilst being a logical policy fiscally, it caused diplomatic ructions as shown in this letter which was followed by a delegation of Flemish Wool merchants to the Duke of Burgundy:

"We would inform you that the English at Calais enacted several years ago, great, sharp, strict and unjust ordinances concerning wool which are being stiffened from year to year, so that it is impossible to procure English wool save at a heavy cost, which is a great loss not only to the people of Flanders, and likewise to those of Brabant, Hanuit, Holland and Zealand who cannot obtain wool because of its dearness, but also to your merchants of the Hanse who are forced to pay a high price for cloth..."

29th July 1474

English archers took part in the siege of Neuss in support of Burgundian forces.

A component of the alliance system that Edward IV entered with the Burgundians was mutual support. Whilst Burgundy stood to gain from any losses incurred by the French, they had also supported Edward in his bid to reclaim the crown in 1471.

The close ties between the Duchy and England had been solidified once the Kings sister, Margaret, established herself within the court in Burgundy.

Therefore, when Burgundy went to war against Emperor Fredrick of the Holy Roman Empire, England supported the Burgundian army.

Edward's longbowmen were the envy of Europe, so 2000 archers were dispatched to fight under Charles' command.

The siege of Neuss began on 29 July 1474. Though it was an unsuccessful siege (a Papal Legate threatened to excommunicate both sides), it provided the archers with experience on the continental battlefield and how Burgundy operated in military campaigns.

With plans underway for a joint campaign against France, this was a valuable exercise in diplomatic and military relations.

30th July 1447

Richard Duke of York, was appointed Lieutenant of Ireland.

When Richard returned to England to answer a summons to Parliament, it is quite probable that he expected to be reappointed to the position of Lieutenant of France. Government there continued in his name and, in England, he contributed to discussions about policy in France.

Much of his time was taken up addressing the finances of France and Normandy. Ostensibly at least, he was preparing for the proposed visit of Henry VI to his French lands. He also faced criticism from Adam Moleyns, the Keeper of the Privy Seal, a dispute that saw the Duke of York vindicated, though his reputation harmed.

The appointment to the Lieutenancy of Ireland was made on 30 July 1447. On the face of it, his selection was sound. Trouble had flared up between the Talbot and Ormond families, and a man of Richard's stature would be ideally suited to addressing this issue and regaining lands from the Gaelic Irish.

The appointment suited Richard's political opponents too. His ten-year appointment removed from London one of the most vehement opponents of the Duke of Suffolk's policies.

Public opinion at the time certainly saw the appointment as a means of getting Richard out of the way:

"exsylde into Irlonde foe hys rebellyon as thoo a boute the kynge informde hym" Gregory's Chronicle

"banished for certain years" Benet's Chronicle

31st July 1461

Milanese State Paper: The Earl of Warwick

The Milanese State Papers provide many insights into the political arena within England at the time. This Newsletter, written on 31 July 1461, very briefly summarises the situation:

"...they say that every day favours the Earl of Warwick, who seems to me to be everything in this kingdom, and as if anything lacks he has made a brother of his (George) lord chancellor of England."

The Neville family did gain much favour following Edward IV taking the crown. It was only to be expected. The Neville's had committed the most manpower and resources into the campaigns of 1459-61.

George Neville became lord chancellor in 1461. Already the Bishop of Exeter, he was promoted to the role of Archbishop of York in 1464. John Neville, another of the Earl of Warwick's brothers, was created Lord Montagu and acted as Yorkist commander in the north, completing victories at Hexham and Hedgely Moor, which saw him elevated to Earl of Northumberland. Warwick's uncle, William Neville Lord Fauconberg, was created Earl of Kent.

These appointments came with grants of land, enhancing the strength of the Neville household. It led to later marriages of the Earls daughters into the royal family, with Anne marrying first Prince Edward of Westminster and following his death, the future King Richard III. Isabel Neville married George Duke of Clarence, in controversial circumstances.

As the Milanese newsletter suggests, the Neville family were in the ascendancy.

August

1st August 1485

Henry Tudor's invasion fleet embarked for Wales.

Events in England in 1484 transformed the fortunes of Henry Tudor. Now he was the main rival to the crown held by Richard III. To boot, he had acquired substantial backing. This included notable men such as Edward Woodville, brother of the widowed Queen Elizabeth; Thomas Grey, a half-brother to Edward V and Bishops Courtenay and Morton.

Attainders had swollen the number of disgruntled exiles. Henry Tudor had suddenly become a star attraction. That fact had not been lost on the French. Eager as always to meddle in England's affairs, King Charles VII was willing to back the inexperienced Henry Tudor. He financed 2000 French soldiers to campaign for 4 months.

In addition, he provided a fleet to transport the Tudor invasion force across the Channel. A further 50,000 crowns were loaned for the expedition. Mercenaries could be hired. With support from the Bretons, who had been his hosts during exile, a force of 2000 to 3000 men was ready to sail.

The summer had been spent planning and scheming. Family loyalties had been called upon. And on 1st August 1485, the plan was put into motion. Captained by Guillaume de Casemore, the flagship Poulian de Dieppe was made ready to sail.

The various groups boarded under the watchful eye of the experienced French Commander Philibert de Chaudee. They set sail with the tide, with a long and potentially dangerous voyage to the Tudor homelands of South Wales as the destination.

Note: Sources do not agree on numbers.

2nd August 1482

Margaret of Anjou made her final will.

Margaret of Anjou had been Queen consort of England. A woman used to life in court and a role of significance. Even in her childhood, she had become accustomed to riches. Her final years, though, were pitiful by comparison.

Following her surrender to Edward IV in the aftermath of the Battle of Tewkesbury, she had lost all the ranks, grants and splendour. She spent several years under house arrest in the care of her former lady-in-waiting, Alice, Duchess of Suffolk.

When Edward IV agreed on terms with the French in 1475, he insisted that the French pay a ransom for Margaret's return. The French had little choice to accept, and Margaret was transferred into French custody the same year.

She was not taken into the French court though. Nor was she given a warm welcome by her father. Her final years were spent with several loyal ladies living on a modest pension. Her will reflects this change in fortunes.

"...My will is the few goods which God and he [King Louis XI] have given and lent to me be used for this purpose and for the paying of my debts as much to my poor servants to other creditors to whom I am indebted... And should my goods be insufficient to do this, as I believe they are, I implore unto the King to meet and pay my outstanding debts..."

3rd August 1460

James II of Scotland was killed by a fragment of an exploding artillery piece.

The Scottish King, James II, was present at the Siege of Roxburgh when he met his end. Stood close to the artillery bombarding the walls, he was struck by a fragment when one of the bombards exploded. The wound was to kill the King.

James' son, James III, took the throne upon his father's death. However, the new King was a child, and a council was to rule on his behalf during his minority.

The Minority Council was dominated by the Dowager Queen, Mary of Gueldres. Mary chose to continue fighting against the English. It made sense to take advantage of the political turmoil south of the border, with the Yorkists having landed and Henry VIs government in tatters.

So, she not only continued with the Siege of Roxburgh but also that of Wark. Mary also had an eye on seizing the border town of Berwick for the Scots.

Her taking control of the Scottish Council worked very much in favour of those wanting to expand Scotland. As the situation in England worsened, the chances of negotiating with one or other of the factions rose.

This allowed Mary to negotiate with Margaret of Anjou in late 1460. The negotiations resulted in Berwick being ceded to the Scots in return for Scottish support of the Lancastrian army.

4th August 1482

Richard Duke of Gloucester agreed on a truce with the Scots.

On 2nd August, an agreement had tentatively been made between Richard Duke of Gloucester and the leading Scottish lords and bishops.

Richard's army was encamped at Edinburgh. James III was in Edinburgh Castle, refusing to come out. It was a stalemate situation. James could sit out a long siege, proving to be costly for the English.

Richard had several objectives at this point.

If Edward Hall was correct in his chronicle, he would promote the Duke of Albany's interests.

He had also been charged with addressing the issue of the advance payment made for the proposed marriage of Cecily of York to the then Prince James of Scotland.

Lastly, the border town of Berwick and most particularly its Castle was wanted by the English.

Richard had the upper hand over the Scottish lords. They could not challenge the army that had swept into Scotland. Negotiations soon led to an agreement that satisfied most of the objectives that Richard, and the Duke of Albany, had.

The Scots agreed to repay monies that had previously been sent to Scotland as an advance dower payment for the marriage of James IIII to Cecily of York, a union that never happened. The Duke of Albany was also granted control of Edinburgh Castle. The English then withdrew, returning to England via Berwick, where a portion of the army was left to retake the Castle.

5th August 1469

Richard Neville Earl of Warwick, was in Calais preparing to invade England.

His plans were being hampered by organisational difficulties and a blockade instigated by Charles the Bold of Burgundy.

The fall out between the King and the Earl of Warwick had already boiled over in the rebellions of 1469.

Warwick, now confident of Lancastrian support, was ready to make his move.

Sir John Paston wrote, on the 5th August 1470 that:

"There may be many folks up in the north, so that Percy is not able to resist them: and so the King has sent for his feedmen to come to him, for he will go to put them down. And some say that the King should come again to London, and that in haste, and, it is said the Courtenay's will land in Devon, and there rule... [and that Clarence and Warwick] will essay to land in England every day as folks fear."

The inevitability of a resumption of the wars was apparent. It was merely a matter of time before Warwick's forces were mobilised and ready to force the readeption of King Henry VI.

What was less clear was where the Lancastrians would land. As the source shows, there was a threat of a landing in the South West. Warwick would most likely land in the South East, though he could land anywhere on the east coast. Furthermore, there was the prospect of Scottish involvement in any invasion and Edward IV would be wary of French involvement.

6th August 1463

On 6th August 1463 at Westminster, a case was brought against John Halle, a merchant from Salisbury.

Halle was found to have illegally captured, boarded, and stolen from a Breton merchant vessel, 'le Johan'. Put simply, piracy.

Perhaps unluckily for Halle, the Breton vessel was travelling under the Kings protection and with the Kings seal.

The cargo of le Johan was woollen cloth, potentially highly valuable at the time depending on the quality. The gravity of Halle's crime was such that he had to return the vessel, its cargo, make good all damages and pay a bond of recognises to the King of 400/.

Additionally, he was to cover the expenses of the merchants whose vessel he had captured. Halle was given two weeks report directly to an official, John Delarigge, who answered to the Chancellor of the Exchequer or a commissioner appointed as his deputy.

In an age where thefts of property could result in the punishment of being hanged, this seems to be an incredibly lenient sentence. Especially so given that the case was heard at Westminster.

Why so lenient? Brittany was harbouring Lancastrian exiles, which may have led to an element of tokenistic 'justice' being meted out. Second, the Close Roll opens with the fact that Halle is a merchant to the King, so perhaps he had a working relationship with the royal household that was valued. Whatever the reason, it seems a light sentence for piracy against a vessel sailing under the King's protection.

7th August 1485

Henry Tudor lands at Milford Haven.

Henry Tudor's small fleet docked at Mill Bay. Legend has it that Henry dropped to his knees on the beach and recited from the psalms:

"Judge me, O God, and favour my cause"

This secluded location at Mill Bay offered him an opportunity to land undetected. As it happened, there was no need to fear detection by local troops. The garrison of the nearby Dale Castle offered no resistance to Tudor whatsoever. His year of letter writing and propaganda appeared to have paid off. To the relief of Henry, local landowner and Richard's primary Lieutenant in southern Wales, Rhys ap Thomas, offered no resistance: and following Henry's disembarking ap Thomas shadowed Tudor before opting to side with him.

Tudor moved fast. He needed to gather troops to face Richard.

"From thence departing in the breake of day he went to Haverforde, which vs a towne not xne. myles from Dalley, wher he was receavyd with great goodwill of all men, and the same he dyd with suche celerytie as that he was present and spoken of all at once." Polydor Virgil

So once his French mercenaries were convinced that it was safe to leave the ships, they offloaded their supplies and artillery and headed north, towards Haverford West. Tudor is thought to have endeared himself to South Wales people through references to his own heritage. Born at Pembroke Castle, this was easy to do by suggesting a 'homecoming'.

8th August 1483

Richard III receives an ambassador from Queen Isabella of Castile.

Both the instructions of the Spanish Ambassador and Richard's subsequent letter to the Lords of his Council refer to the diplomatic problems caused by the marriage of his brother to Elizabeth Woodville:

"Besides these instructions given in writing by this Orator, he showed to the Kings Grace by mouth, that the Queen of Castile was turned in her heart from England, in time past for the unkindness which she took against the King last deceased, whom god pardon, for his refusing of her, and taking to his wife a widow of England..."

The context of this is straightforward. Richard was recently crowned, and it was diplomatically important to recognise him as being a just and righteous king.

The ambassador was meeting with English officials to discuss trade agreements; the negotiations would be far easier if Richard was flattered and his brother's flaws made clear.

Further to trade, the ambassador also noted that:

"...if it were his intention to go to war with Louis, King of France, for the recovery of possessions pertaining to the crown of England, she [the Queen] would open her ports to his army and supply them with arms and provisions at a reasonable price: she also promised to raise a force... in sufficient number, the king paying their wages". Harl MSS 433 fol.235

9th August 1468

Court of Common Pleas hears a trespass (force and arms) case that is prosecuted as Assault; Trespass (Chattels)

The legal system in the late medieval period allowed commoners to raise cases against each other. In much the same way as a claim could be made today, there was the ability to sue for damages against wrongdoers.

These cases were heard at the Court of Common Pleas. The court's findings were binding, and each party would be able to be represented by an Attorney.

This case stands out due to the value of damages claimed. The record for the hearing states:

"Pleading: George Hyde states that on 9th August 1466, Roger Tygo forcibly assaulted him at Throcking, and on 29th August 1465 RT forcibly depastured his grass worth £20 with his animals, against the peace and to his damage of £40".

This is probably a substantial amount of land. A baronial income was typically under £500 per annum: The Duke of Exeter was valued at £300 when granted livery of his lands.

The court heard attorneys for both parties and gave imparl to octave [time to discuss and reach an out of court settlement] initially on one count, until the following court sessions, then later for 9 counts, again until the subsequent sessions of court.

No outcome is recorded, so it can be assumed that the sides agreed on a settlement.

10th August 1453

"On or about" this date, Henry VI had his mental breakdown.

On or about 10th August, King Henry VI fell into a catatonic state. At the palace of Clarendon, he suddenly became unresponsive.

It is widely believed that Henry had inherited a condition from his grandfather, Charles VI of France. Another popular theory is that the news of Talbot's death and the catastrophe at the Battle of Castillon was simply too much for him to bear.

Henry was attended to by the best surgeons in England with no success. He remained unresponsive even when presented with his son, Prince Edward. His incapability lasted over a year. He became responsive again at Christmas of 1454, recovering as quickly as he had fallen into his period of illness.

His incapacity led to political change and increased tensions. Queen Margaret pressed for her to be made Regent in his stead. Though not unprecedented, having a female regent was not popular amongst the magnates and bishops who made up the Council.

Instead, they turned to the heir presumptive, Richard Duke of York. This was controversial because of the factionalism that had emerged.

The Duke of Somerset found himself imprisoned under the Protectorship of Richard, though in most aspects of rule, York was balanced and aimed at improving the way that government was managed.

11th August 1482

Richard Duke of Gloucester's army began the siege of Berwick.

The Scots, encouraged by the French, had made increasing numbers of raids over the border in 1480/1. King Edward IV was determined to put an end to it. Sovereignty within Scotland had been a long-standing issue in which the English staked a claim.

This was to be Edward's justification for an invasion. The brother of the King of Scotland was, rather conveniently, living in exile at Fotheringay Castle. A secret pact was made. Lord Bothwell was to claim that his brother was illegitimate and take the throne. England would support him with military backing. In return, Lord Bothwell promised the return to England of Berwick, a Scottish possession since Margaret of Anjou's Treaty of 1461.

An army of 20,000 English soldiers marched north under the command of Richard Duke of Gloucester. 11 ships from the navy sailed north to support a siege of Berwick. Some 2000 sheaves of arrows and artillery pieces were moved by 120 carts from Newcastle-upon-Tyne. This force faced the town of Berwick-upon-Tweed and the rather more formidable obstacle of Berwick Castle, defended by some 500 Scots.

The town quickly surrendered; the castle refused to surrender. Richard moved the main body of his army on to Edinburgh in support of Bothwell's claim. The Earl of Northumberland was deployed to attack smaller castles, fortified houses and to destroy Scottish property and crops. Richard soon returned to Berwick from Edinburgh as the political situation there had changed. The garrison at Berwick, faced with the full might of Richard's army and the navy, soon surrendered. Berwick-upon-Tweed has remained an English possession ever since.

12th August 1469

Execution at Kenilworth of Richard Woodville, 1st Earl Rivers and his son John Woodville

"The Queens father and brother were taken, probably at Chepstow, and executed outside Coventry."

Richard Woodville, 1st Earl Rivers and his son were captured shortly after the Battle of Edgcote. They became prisoners of the Earl of Warwick. River and the Woodville family were a source of annoyance for Warwick. They had received patronage because of favour shown to the Queen's family, perceived to be at the expense of Warwick and the Neville family. Warwick had the King in his custody. Government was in the King's name but, overall, by Warwick's word. In this position of strength, Warwick executed several leading opponents. Rivers and his son, John Woodville, were executed at Gosford Green, Kenilworth, on 12th August 1469.

"Some days afterwards Edward was captured at Honiley or Olney, near Kenilworth, and brought by Archbishop Neville to Coventry, there to meet the Archbishop's "brother of Warwick." He was detained in the city as a prisoner until 9th August. But even then his humiliation was not complete. Three days later, when the King was certainly no further removed from the city than Warwick, the father and brother of Edward's Queen, Lord Rivers and his son, John Woodville, who had been captured by rioters at Chepstow, fell into Warwick's hands, and were beheaded on Gosford Green by his order. ".
The story of Coventry, Mary Dormer Harris

13th August 1485

Henry Tudor's army arrived at Machynlleth.

Tudor had landed on 1st August 1485 at Mill Bay. After camping at Dale, his army had begun the march northwards. Henry's correspondence shows the route quite clearly. He chose initially to march northwards, along the coast.

This route would maintain distance between himself and Richard III, useful whilst his own army grew in size, and his heralds went to and fro in their quest to raise further support. This route took in Haverfordwest, Cardigan and Llwyn Dafydd.

This was an area known to Jasper Tudor and one where Henry could begin to use his Welsh ancestry to full effect. Already using Welsh heraldry on his banners, he was also referred to as the Prince of Wales. After Llwyn Dafydd, Henry moved to Aberystwyth, where the garrison of the Castle offered no resistance.

With his messengers bringing him positive news about troops being raised, he then turned inland. From Aberystwyth, he marched to Machynlleth, where he spent the night of 13th August. The following morning, he would march on to Dolarddun.

Tudor was now marching toward Rhys ap Thomas, who had agreed to join him with a force of over a thousand men. It was also bringing him closer to the English border.

From this point, the castles would be harder to persuade to submit, towns may bar entry, and the King of England would, somewhere, be waiting.

14th August 1468

The siege of Harlech comes to an end as the garrison surrender. The siege began in 1461, making it the longest siege of the Wars of the Roses.

Following the defeat of the Lancastrian army at the Battle of Towton, the Yorkists were dominant. They did not have total control, though. A large pocket of resistance existed in the North-East of England, which saw the Neville brothers engaging in battles and sieges for several years until the region was secured. In Wales, there was also opposition.

Much of Wales was loyal to King Henry due to the Tudor family's lordship. William Herbert was granted the Earldom of Pembroke in South Wales and given the task of flushing out opposition throughout Wales as Edward's chief official in the principality.

Most castles in the south surrendered reasonably quickly. Jasper Tudor's army was defeated at Twt Hill. Tudor sailed to exile in Ireland, leaving garrisons in his northern castles. One by one, the castles surrendered. Harlech refused.

In the 15th century, Harlech was coastal, and the Lancastrians resupplied the castle via the sea. It became the site from which plots and even a small, attempted invasion of Northern Wales would take place over the course of 7 years.

The siege was not one of continuous warfare. For much of the time, the Yorkists were content to simply isolate the castle and rely on poor weather disrupting supplies. After seven years of intermittent attacks, Harlech finally surrendered on 14th August 1468. To date, it is the longest siege to have taken place in the British Isles.

15th August 1485

Word reaches Richard III that Henry Tudor has taken Shrewsbury. The implication is clear, loyalty to the crown in Wales had not been as strong as anticipated. Jasper Tudor had previously struggled to raise troops, so the expectation may have been that Tudor's advance would have been severely hampered by forces under Rhys ap Thomas and William Thomas's command.

Lord Stanley's failure to respond to the summons also meant that a hurdle to Tudor's advance had been effectively removed. Richard, meanwhile, is continuing to raise forces for his own army. Upon hearing of the landing, urgent requests for assistance had been sent out. Sir Henry Vernon of Derbyshire received a demand to "come with such number as ye have promised... sufficiently horsed and harnessed" with an implication that land rights would be forfeited if he failed to respond also in the message.

The Duke of Norfolk received his summons to arms on 14th August. John Paston was instructed to be at Bury St. Edmunds with his men by 16th. Messages to the north would arrive later. York exchanged messages with Richard and only decided to send men on the 19th.

Dates are unknown for other magnates or towns, but it can be surmised that many supporters heard between the 15th and 18th of August and would have needed to travel on horseback to join with the King in all haste.

Richard, knowing that messages and mustering would also take time, is said, by Polydor Virgil, to have "begin with grief to be in fervent rage" as a consequence of the news. Yet Henry Tudor was cautious. He was yet to have any English lord declare for his side.

16th August 1469

Earl Rivers' execution had left the Treasurer's position, one of the Great Offices of State, vacant. Warwick sought to sure up support for his policies at the highest level by appointing a long-term supporter, Sir John Longstrother, to the role.

When the Earl of Warwick and Duke of Clarence wrestled control of Edward IV's government, several changes were made. Key positions were filled with men who had an affinity for Warwick.

Sir John Longstrother was a supporter of Warwick's cause. He was also well known and well respected within government. Longstrother was a councillor for King Edward in 1463, so in some ways, his elevation to the position of Treasurer was a natural progression for him. He had also been unanimously elected as head of the Knights of St. John of Jerusalem in the March of 1469, meaning he had support within the highly influential crusading organisations.

His tenure, though, was brief. As a replacement for Edward's own Treasurer, he found himself replaced very quickly once Edward was released from the captivity that Warwick had held him in. Upon Henry VIs readeption, Longstrother was once more given the role of Treasurer.

When Edward IV returned from exile in 1471, Longstrother joined with the Lancastrian army in the South West. He fought at the Battle of Tewkesbury. Having survived the battle, he joined senior officials and senior members of the nobility in seeking refuge within Tewkesbury Abbey. He was one of the men who were dragged from the Abbey days after the battle. Like his more famous counterparts, he was tried at Tewkesbury by Richard Duke of Gloucester and sentenced to be executed. His remains were taken to the church of St. John in Clerkenwell for burial.

17th August 1469

Humphrey Stafford Earl of Devon was lynched in Bridgewater by the citizens on their own initiative.

Humphrey Stafford came from a cadet branch of the Stafford family. He was distantly related to the Earl of Wiltshire and the Dukes of Buckingham, one of whom he shares the same forename.

Humphrey Stafford had inherited a substantial amount of land from his father, which was added to through inheritances from his mother's family. It made him the largest landholder in the South West. His power in the region was to grow to unprecedented heights because of the Wars of the Roses.

Having fought at Mortimer's Cross and Towton, he was awarded the Duchy of Cornwall's stewardship, became constable of Bristol, and was granted much of the land forfeited by Thomas Courtenay's attainder.

Stafford then played a role in the trial for treason of another Courtenay, Henry. This proved unpopular in some parts of the South West. In 1469 Stafford and the Earl of Pembroke were called upon to march north to aid in crushing the Robin of Redesdale rebellion. Stafford survived the battle.

On his way back to his lands, a mob identified him in Bridgwater. The crowd summarily executed Stafford.

It remains unclear what the motive was, but it seems most likely that they were either supporters of the Earl of Warwick or angry at the treason trial of Henry Courtenay.

18ᵗʰ August 1466

It was not just the nobility who needed to go to the Chancery to have land rights formalised. The lower levels of the gentry, too, had to register any changes to claims on the land. On 18ᵗʰ August 1466, such an amendment was entered by Walter Sunnyng.

He entered a quitclaim in favour of his mother, her new husband, and their heirs. The land was a farm or smallholding with a watermill, woods, and fishing. A substantial amount by the standards of the day.

The quitclaim removes William's rights to the land as his father's heir. Instead, he passes his claim to his mother, who, unlike today, would not ordinarily be the next of kin in terms of inheritance.

The quitclaim also mentions hedges among the fields, suggesting that parts of it may have been enclosed. Access to fishing and woodland would be very beneficial. A water mill's existence indicates that the land and property associated with it could have generated a reasonable income.

"William Sunnyng of London… to the said Juliana and John Dey, their heirs and assigns. Quitclaim with warranty of a messuage and water mill in the 'Brookende' of Pychelesthorn co. Buckingham, with a curtilage and croft adjacent, stanks, rivers, stews, hedges, ditches, woods, rents etc. in that parish thereto pertaining, which were of his said father, and which they had jointly by feoffment… 18th August, 27 Henry VI, to him and the said Juliana, and of all the lands, rents, reversions and services in Aston and Pychelesthorn late of his father, which the said Walter and… Quitclaim with warranty of a messuage and water mill in the 'Brookende' of Pychelesthorn co. Buckingham, with a curtilage and croft adjacent, stanks, rivers, stews, hedges, ditches, woods, rents etc. in that parish..."
Close Rolls of Edward IV

19th August 1485

Henry Tudor spends the night in Litchfield.

Henry Tudor's army had begun the march from the relative safety of
Wales into England. Henry Tudor will have been buoyed by the arrival
and declaration to his cause of Rhys ap Thomas. Thomas was one of the
lords who Richard III had charged with Wales's defence against a Tudor
invasion.

Having shadowed the Tudor army up the coast and across central Wales,
he had now made his move to join with the invading army.

Behind the Tudor force was another army. Thomas Stanley was 'keeping
an eye' on the invader. This is subject to lots of debate given events that
unfolded at Bosworth, coupled with the fact that William Stanley had
persuaded Shrewsbury to open its gates to the Tudor force.

Henry's force also picked up its first English supporters as it headed in a
southeasterly direction.

Still, his army would be outnumbered, and he needed to ensure that his
strategy was correct in the coming days.

It is most likely that he had news of Richard preparing to head south.
There was no question as to whether a battle for the crown would take
place. Both sides were on the march. The King and the invader were both
growing in strength.

Now it was simply a matter of where and when that battle for the crown
would take place.

20th August 1463

The Close Rolls of Edward IV record the crime of piracy. This example has a punishment to be carried out no later than 20th August 1463.

One John Halle had taken a Breton vessel in the Channel. The ship had a cargo of cloth and, unfortunately for Halle, was sailing under the English King's protection. His punishment is relatively lenient.

He was to return the vessel to its rightful owner, make right any damages, and pay recognises of 400 marks. The reparation to the owners would be checked by named English officials or their representatives.

Why did Halle receive a lenient punishment? Quite possibly because he had represented Salisbury at four Parliaments and was known to the government's inner circles. It is also most probable that he hired a crew rather than he himself who decided to seize the Breton ship.

John Halle of Salysbury co. Wiltshire 'marchaunt,' to the King. Recognisance for 400*l.*, to be levied etc. in Wiltshire.

Condition that before 20th August instant he shall deliver to John Delarigge one of the merchants thereof, or to his deputy, a ship called '*le Johan*' of Garrand, in Brittany, by him lately taken at sea while under safe conduct of the King, with all the gear therof, and all the woollen cloths therein at the time of capture, specified in a coket under the King's seal which is with John Delarigge, and if ship, gear or cloth be damaged while in his hands, shall content John Delarigge or his deputy for the same at the discretion of commissioners appointed by George bishop of Exeter the chancellor, and content the merchants for their costs and expenses by reason of the capture and the value of the victuals in the ship at the discretion of the said commissioners.

21st August 1484

John de la Pole Earl of Lincoln, was appointed Lieutenant of Ireland.

John de la Pole, Earl of Lincoln, was one of the House of York's senior members. He had served Richard III well since his accession to the throne.

Lincoln had already been made president of the Council of the North, which gave him a degree of authority. It was far from as extensive a remit as had been held by Richard through his Ducal council.

The appointment as Lieutenant of Ireland was the highest rank outside of the 6 great roles of state that could be bestowed onto somebody. A Lieutenant acted on behalf of the King and exercised monarchical powers in his name.

Some historians believe that in naming the Earl of Lincoln as Lieutenant, Richard was effectively marking him as heir presumptive.

The Irish connection proved to be useful to the Earl once he chose to join the 1487 rebellion against Henry Tudor. It was to Ireland that he, Lovell and the pretender, Lambert Simnel travelled.

They crowned the pretender as King and used the Irish affinity with the House of York to recruit an army. It was that army that landed at Piel Island and fought and lost the Battle of Stoke Field, in which John de la Pole was killed.

22nd August 1485

Battle of Bosworth.

The armies of Richard III and Henry Tudor came face to face at Bosworth on 22nd August 1485.

The royal army was the larger one, commanded by Richard III, the Duke of Norfolk, and the Earl of Northumberland. Henry Tudor's smaller force had himself, Jasper Tudor, and the Earl of Oxford.

Early exchanges in the battle included the use of artillery against the Earl of Oxford's men. This battle was vulnerable. The Duke of Norfolk's battle advanced on them in superior numbers. In doing so, a weakness was opened in the Yorkist line. The Earl of Northumberland was called upon to bring his men forward. Contemporary accounts suggest that Henry Percy Earl of Northumberland, did nothing.

Richard chose to take a direct approach. Henry Tudor, too was in a weakened position. Richard led a charge on his position. It was intended to kill Henry Tudor and win the day by eliminating the very reason that there was an invading army.

The plan did not work, the account of Edward Hall describing events as follows:

"The earl of Northumberland… ought to have charged the French, but did nothing except to flee, both he and his company, to abandon his King RIchard, for he had an undertaking with the earl of Richmond.. The King bore himself valiantly according to his destiny, and wore the crown on his head; but… found himself alone on the field he thought to run after the others… One of the Welshmen then came after him, and struck him dead with a halberd, and another took his body and put it before him on his horse and carried it, hair hanging as one would bear a sheep".

23rd August 1461

King Edward IV visits Lewes and East Meon in Hampshire as part of a determined effort to be seen in public. He listens to complaints and recommends raising some issues as petitions to Parliament.

Winning the Battle of Towton may have made Edward king, but it did not mean that his position was secure. The Lancastrian leadership had moved to the North East where they were fending off assaults from the Neville brothers, and resistance was met in Wales, where Henry's half-brother, Jasper Tudor, had held many lordships.

In the south, there had been a threat of intervention from France. The French threat waned somewhat following the death of King Charles in July of 1461. The south, though, needed to be secured and thanked for its support for the Yorkist cause. With that in mind, Edward made a tour of the south in August of 1461.

He made initially for the port of Sandwich, stopping at Sittingbourne and Canterbury on the way. From Sandwich, he moved to Ashford, which he departed on the 20th. By the 22nd, he had reached Battle, where he attended a service at the Abbey.

On 23rd August, Edward was in Lewes. Here he listened to the concerns of the people. In some instances, he gave advice and advised some to petition Parliament about specific situations. This charm offensive was especially important. It had been the South where uprisings had begun against Henry and his council. The south that faced the possible invasion from France, and the south, where Yorkists gained support in 1460 and 1461.

From Lewes, Edward returned to Westminster via Arundel. He was soon on the move again, travelling to South Wales to discuss the Welsh campaign with William Herbert.

24th August 1483

Edward of Middleham was created Prince of Wales.

The rank of Prince of Wales is traditionally held by the eldest son of the reigning monarch. Until recent legislation, this would always be the heir presumptive.

Richard, having only just been crowned himself, was keen to enhance the legitimacy of his rule. A strong visual message, accompanied by festivities, would do just that. Following the elaborate coronation of himself and his queen, Anne Neville, Richard went on a progress.

Naturally, he spent time in York, a city where he had many supporters from his days running the Ducal Council. Richard chose, therefore, to create his son Prince of Wales at an early stage. He did so on 24th August 1483, before leaving London.

This is intelligent timing, ensuring that London's citizens hear the proclamations but allowing his northern subjects to enjoy the festivities that accompany the investiture ceremony. That ceremony occurred on 8th September and is covered in this book.

Another reason to create his son as Prince of Wales is to make the line of succession clear. Edward's children's possible existence, with the history of their titles, presented potential problems in the future. So too, the presence of Edward Plantagenet.

By creating his own son as Prince of Wales, Richard asserts his rights and those of his heirs as per the statements of his legitimacy and those of Edward's children's illegitimacy as made by Parliament. It quickly removes any doubts over the matter, and as investitures were accompanied by festivals and tournaments, it was an ideal opportunity to allow a period of eager anticipation.

25th August 1485

Richard III buried without ceremony at Greyfriars, Leicester.

Richard III was killed, leading a charge towards Henry Tudor during the Battle of Bosworth on 22nd August 1485.

Following the battle, his body was identified by the Tudors and taken to Leicester. As was customary for significant individuals at that time, his body was washed and laid out for public viewing: there would be no doubt that King Richard III had been killed in the battle.

On 25th August, the body was laid to rest. The burial had little in the way of ceremony. Richard's remains were buried in consecrated within the grounds of Greyfriars Monastery, Leicester. The site of his grave was well known at the time. Some ten years after his death, Henry VII paid for a modest gravestone to mark his resting place.

That grave became lost following the Dissolution of the Monasteries. As the church at Greyfriars was demolished and construction works were undertaken over the centuries, his grave's location gradually became lost from common knowledge.

Some literature suggested, disingenuously, that his corpse had simply been thrown into the River Soar. In 1993 a local historian gathered much of the documentary evidence about Richard's resting place.

Later, that evidence and further research were undertaken by the Finding Richard project. This project, led by Phillipa Langley and John Ashdown-Hill on behalf of the Richard III Society in partnership with the University of Leicester, rediscovered Richard's remains in 2012. Permission was granted to exhume his remains, and DNA testing confirmed the identity. He was reburied in a ceremony at Leicester Cathedral in 2015.

26th August 1488

Appointment of Richard Cholmley to positions in the North.

One of the concerns facing the new Tudor regime was the administration of the regions. As had been seen in 1461 and 1483, changes of the monarch could lead to resistance to new methods of governing.

Henry Tudor was aware of this. He would also have been very aware of the areas most loyal to the Yorkist regime.

Many of these were in the north of the country. While the Percy family remained in post, their loyalty could not be relied upon yet. Henry needed his own men in administrative roles, and they needed to be good.

On 26th August, an appointment was made. Richard Chomley, a Cheshire man thought to have served Margaret Beaufort, was appointed to several positions: chamberlain of Berwick; treasurer of war at Berwick; receiver-general of all the crown's lands in Durham and Yorkshire; the receiver of Middleham and after the death of the Earl of Northumberland receiver of numerous other estates.

Henry Tudor was ensuring that the unruly north had a steady hand overseeing it. This would enable him to focus on central government and uprisings against his rule, such as the invasion in 1487.

Henry Tudor, as King, gained a reputation as a good administrator. Much of this reputation was acquired due to the careful selection of people for roles such as those to which Chomley was appointed.

27th August 1471

William Herbert 2nd Earl of Pembroke commissioned

Following his reinstatement on the throne, Edward IV needed to restore law and order throughout his realm. From 1468 to this time, there had been a succession of uprisings and the upheaval of the return of civil war.

The battles of Barnet and Tewkesbury had all but eliminated any risk of an all-out civil war breaking out again. The Lancastrian leadership was dead, or in the case of Margaret of Anjou, under house arrest and with nothing left to fight for.

King Edward now needed to reassert his authority, particularly in South Wales, where Jasper Tudor had gained lots of support for the Lancastrian cause. Edward visited the region himself. He also needed the management of the area to be administered on a day-to-day basis.

He turned to the young William Herbert, 2nd Earl of Pembroke. On 27th August, he was appointed to administer the South of Wales, a role his father had managed with a great deal of success.

The younger William Herbert was not as accomplished as his father. He showed little interest in the role. In 1479 he was forced to relinquish his title. They were subsequently granted to the Prince of Wales.

28th August 1463

English fleet receiving victuals for a campaign against Scotland

The English fleet and the army had been preparing for an invasion of Scotland for some time. 28th August 1463 is the last known record of victuals being provided for this purpose.

The intention had been to crush Scottish support for the Lancastrians once and for all. It was upon Scottish, and to a lesser extent t, French, aid that the Lancastrians in the northeast relied upon.

Large sums of money were allocated to the task of dealing with the Scots. In June 1463, King Edward had asked Parliament for £37000 for defence against the Scots. He had intended to lead an army against them in person. A further £4800 was requested to finance a fleet under the command of the Earl of Worcester.

The continued problem of castles in the north changing hands needed stopping: they changed hands 3 times due to defections and sieges.

The invasion never happened, though. He travelled as far north as York, but Edward turned his attention to diplomatic affairs with Burgundy and France. This led to consternation among the taxpaying commons.

"there was ordained a great navy and a great army both by water and by land... all was lost and in vain and came to no purpose by water or by land" Gregory's Chronicle

29th August 1475

Treaty of Picquigny

King Edward IV had sailed to Calais at the head of the English army. The intention was to assault France alongside allies from Brittany and Burgundy.

Upon marching into France, it became evident that the Bretons were not going to commit whilst the Burgundians were still busy fighting elsewhere, and towns under their control had barred the English entry.

King Louis of France had a substantially larger army than the English but saw an opportunity to take diplomatic advantage of the situation. He sent messages to King Edward to say that he was willing to discuss terms.

The two kings met on a specially built bridge at Picquigny. Louis agreed to pay Edward a sum of 75000 crowns at once, followed by an annual pension of 50000 crowns. Several leading English nobles also received an annual pension from France. It was agreed that the King's daughter, Elizabeth of York, would marry the Dauphin of France. Furthermore, the French would pay a ransom for the return of Margaret of Anjou.

In military matters, both sides agreed to go to the other's aid if attacked, and a committee comprising of 2 bishops from each country would arbitrate over any claims to territories and titles.

Edward left with a great deal of much needed money. He had not spent all of the funds granted by Parliament and had potentially tied his family to that of the French royal family.

30th August 1461

On 30th August 1461, an Italian ambassador wrote to Fransceco Sforza to outline the situation in England at the time. He paints a picture of support for the House of Lancaster fading away. Indeed, he cites Lord Rivers, who was a recent convert to the Yorkist regime. Most telling is that he states that the cause of Henry VI is 'lost irretrievably'. Such views being spread throughout Europe would have a damaging impact on Queen Margaret's ability to gain financial or military support for continued resistance to Edward's rule.

Letter from Count Ludovico Dollugo to Fransceco Sforza.

"The lords' adherent to King Henry are all quitting him, and come to tender obedience to this King, and at this present one of the chief of them has come, by name Lord de Rivers, with one of his sons, men of very great valour. I held several conversations with this Lord de Rivers about King Henry's cause, and what he thought of it, and he answered me that the cause was lost irretrievably.

King Henry has withdrawn to a country called Wales, belonging to a brother of his by right of his mother. This country is on the borders of England towards Scotland, a sterile place and but little productive. Had it abounded in provisions, King Edward would have marched to drive him out, but he has now determined to wait until after the harvest, as it will supply him with victuals".

That such news is being sent via ambassadorial memos shows that the situation in England was, by the end of August 1461, seen as a total Yorkist victory. The ambassador all but writes off the chances of a Lancastrian recovery and, interestingly, cites Earl Rivers as a source well before the King and Elizabeth Woodville's secret marriage.

31st August 1422

Death of King Henry V.

On 31st August 1422, King Henry V died. He was succeeded, without contest, by his 9-month-old son, Henry VI. Henry V had been a warrior king, winning a great victory over the French at Agincourt and regaining lands in Normandy and France. Furthermore, he had forced an agreement on the French that would see the French crown pass to himself or his heirs upon the King of France's death.

As an infant, his son required a regency council to rule on his behalf until he reached his majority. This created a long period of uncertainty over policies on the continent and occurred when the economy required experienced and sound leadership.

That leadership came through a council of senior magnates and bishops. The nominal head of the council was the young King's eldest uncle, John Duke of Bedford. Bedford spent much of his time dealing with matters in France.

As a result, the King's other uncle, Humphrey Duke of Gloucester, acted as Protector in England when Bedford was in France. The council was to rule based on majority views being accepted.

Cliques formed around the dominant figures, Bishop Beaufort in particularly attracted followers as it was loans from his estates that enabled England to continue the defence of her continental possessions. This led to conflicts between Beaufort and the enigmatic Duke Humphrey.

The Council oversaw policy until the King came of age. It was an incredibly long time for a minority council to hold power and saw its head, the Duke of Bedford, pass away before the King was an adult.

September

1st September 1458

A warrant is issued calling for additional ordnance for the Royal Arsenal and fitting a new gun at Calais.

Such warrants were issued when there was a need to strengthen London's fortifications and the south coast. At the time, there was a perceived threat from France. Following the loss of French and Norman lands, it was feared that there would be French intervention in England.

Additionally, it calls for the transfer of military equipment from Kenilworth to London. The warrant, therefore, reflects the growing schism between the Lancastrian and Yorkist factions within court. London was controlled by the Yorkists, as was Calais. Kenilworth was the seat of power of the Royal Court.

In issuing the warrant, the Yorkists responded to the increasingly partisan financial policies emanating from the Coventry regime dominated by Margaret of Anjou and attempting to strengthen their own hand.

This is a clear example of how tensions were growing, and relatively simple matters become ones that serve to widen the divide between the two factions in court.

Having so much royal ordnance outside of London or the Cinque ports was quite unprecedented. Along with the increased issuing of the Prince of Wales' livery, it was one of the reasons that suspicion of the Queen's intentions increased in the Yorkist camp.

2nd September 1469

A proclamation is issued in London against riots or affrays, particularly those opposing the alliance with Burgundy.

International diplomacy had a large impact on London merchants and those who had employment directly tied to trade with the continent. Any policy change could make or break people's livelihoods.

Throughout the reign of Henry VI and Edward IV, there had been policies relating to the sale of goods on the continent that intended to improve England's supply of bullion, secure tonnage and poundage duties and ensure that the mercantile classes could continue to prosper.

Because of the wars with France, the primary source of continental trade had been with merchants from Burgundy. They used high quality English wool to produce cloth which in turn was of high value. The relationship with Burgundy was sometimes problematic. The Dukes of Burgundy and the English court had a rather unpredictable relationship, leading to periods of harmony and trade agreements followed by, usually short, periods where relations were strained.

In 1469 the changes to policy provoked outrage in some quarters. It was a politically tumultuous time, with the King effectively the prisoner of the Earl of Warwick. This was reflected in policy, the uncertainties frustrating trade and ultimately leading to rioting in London.

As a result, a proclamation was made on 2nd September 1469 about the affrays and riots. Citizens were warned not to say or do anything against the Burgundian trade agreements.

3rd September 1485

The State Entry of Henry Tudor into the City of London.

Two days after the Battle of Bosworth the Common Council of London met at the Guildhall to consider its response to the Tudor victory over Richard III.

In 1461 and 1471, the city of London acted as a kind of kingmaker, determining which claimant it would support, Yorkist on both occasions, and backing them with finance, manpower, and simple refusal to let the Lancastrians into the city.

In 1485 the situation was different. The memory of 1483 and 3 kings in 3 months was fresh in the memory. So too was the rebellion against Richard's rule and the plantation of northern lords into southern estates.

Henry Tudor offered a fresh start, one backed by influential nobles and merchants. So, the Council agreed to greet Henry Tudor as their King. The Mayor, aldermen and others dressed in the City of London livery met the new King outside London and escorted him triumphantly into the city.

This is not to say that Henry Tudor was warmly welcomed or secure. Keith Dockray noted that Tudor was less secure than his predecessor had been in 1483. There was hope though, DeLoyd Guth noted that 'normalcy would return to the realm' and a feeling that 'the city could now begin to relax'.

For Henry, the ceremonial entry was important. He needed to be seen and seen to be a fair and just monarch. He followed this entry up with a carefully staged coronation then, the following year, his marriage to Elizabeth of York.

4th September 1461

King Edward arrives in Bristol

Having already undertaken a progress around the coastline of Kent and Suffolk, the King, after a short stay in Westminster, moved his attention elsewhere.

The Welsh Marches were an area he was very familiar with. The Yorkist stronghold at Ludlow was in the vicinity, and loyal support for the Yorkist cause came from William Herbert, a powerful presence in the area. Edward chose to take a royal progress through the area with the destination being Bristol.

From Bristol, which he reached on 4th September 1461, he could assess the progress made by William Herbert and Sir Walter Devereux in crushing Lancastrian support in Wales. He could also take a personal look at the fleet assembled to support Yorkist campaigns in Wales.

He would then move to Hereford from Bristol, where the royal army had been summoned to muster by 8th September. Whilst in Bristol the King also took personal control of several trials. Men of rank who had fought against him at Mortimer's Cross or on the Towton campaign had by now had ample opportunity to pledge their allegiance to him.

Some had not, and they received little mercy. At Bristol, Sir Baldwin Fulford was tried by the King for treason, found guilty and beheaded. His head was placed on a spike in Bristol where it remained until 1463 when it was removed due to complaints that it regularly fell off the spike and ended up amongst the feet of the locals going about their daily business.

5th September 1451

Birth of Isabel Neville

Isabel Neville was the eldest daughter of Richard Neville, 16th Earl of Warwick. She was co-heiress to his wealth, along with her sister Anne.

Isabel became the centre of political controversy surrounding her betrothal and marriage to George Duke of Clarence. Her father was keen to ensure that his daughters married into the highest of circles. To this end, he arranged for Isabel to marry George, who at the time was heir presumptive.

His other daughter was married to Edward of Westminster, Prince of Wales in the Lancastrian rule and then to Richard Duke of Gloucester. The match between Isabel and George was problematic. Firstly, it required papal dispensation as the couple were related within the fourth degree; Second, King Edward opposed the match. In theory, permission was needed from him for the marriage to go ahead.

The marriage took place in Calais on 11th July and is covered in this book. Isabel and George had four children. The first died at sea in infancy. Margaret became Countess of Salisbury. Edward became the Earl of Warwick and, following Richard III's death, had the best bloodline claim to the throne from a Yorkist perspective: for which he was eventually executed, and finally, Richard, who died in infancy.

Isabel herself died just two and a half months after the death of Richard. George, consumed with grief, blamed a nurse, Ankarette Twynyho and committed what can only be described as judicial murder.

6th September 1459

Payment of 40 Shillings is agreed for the services of a Tallow Chandler.

"Elyas Wymond, tallow chandler of Shordich co. Middlesex, to William Kebyll of the King's household. 40 shillings to be paid on the feast of St. John Baptist. Dated Westminster, 6th September." Close Roll of Henry VI.

A tallow chandler is a candle maker. Elyas Wymond was the provider of candles for the royal household in 1459. Typically, debts of this nature were billed and paid quarterly in medieval times, so this most likely relates to the 3 months up to Michaelmas.

40 shillings for candles is a substantial amount. Relatively speaking a candle would have more value in 1459 than it does today. The National Archives currency converter suggests the value of 40s in 1460 would be in the region of £1300 in 2017. It was the equivalent of 64 days' pay for an average labourer. This would be enough to buy 4 cows or 12 stone of wool.

Many homes relied on rushlights, candles were a luxury item that was typically found in wealthier churches and the homes of the nobility. They were made from a mixture of oils and fats. The limited use was because of restrictions on earnings for labourers; also, the Tallow Chandlers had apprentices and masters, ensuring a high standard of craftsmanship that pushes prices up.

Tallow Chandlers were recognised by Henry VI in 1456. He awarded them the right to have a coat of arms for their association. In 1462 they were permitted to become one of the livery companies of London, The Worshipful Company of Tallow Chandlers remains active today.

7th September 1450

Richard Duke of York returns from Ireland, landing in Wales on his way to London.

The exact location where Richard Duke of York landed on his return from Ireland, though we know it was on 7th September. He had been made aware of the political situation so knew of the murders of the Duke of Suffolk, Adam Moleyns and the revolts of Thomas Cheyne and Jack Cade.

He was evidently also aware that rumours persisted that he intended to mount a challenge for the crown. King Henry had been told by a sailor that, 'the Duke of Yorke then in Ireland should lyke manner fight with traytours at Leicester parliament' (the sailor was executed for this).

That Richard was aware and concerned is evidenced in several ways.

He stated in one bill that he was a loyal subject and refuted rumours spread about him.

In a second bill, he was quite direct. He had been barred from entry to several ports, and his bill bemoaned this and the execution of good men and wrongful imprisonment of others.

In these two bills, Richard had effectively become the head of the loyal opposition to the King's favourites, in particular, the Duke of Somerset.

This is a turning point in Richard's political methods. Following his return, he was proactive in his approach to politics. It led at first to the standoff at Dartford, then clashes with the Duke of Somerset Duke of Exeter, and later his claiming of right to the throne.

8th September 1483

Investiture of Edward of Middleham as Prince of Wales.

Edward of Middleham is the only known son of Richard III and Anne Neville. Little is known of his childhood, and he only entered the public eye upon his father becoming King.

The decision to create Edward as Prince of Wales was made on 24th August. Richard sent messengers to London with orders for regal robes for the investiture ceremony.

The ceremony was held in York. It was presided over not by the Archbishop of York but by the Bishop of Durham. The ceremony itself consisted of a solemn mass.

After the mass, the Royal party paraded in full regalia to the Archbishop of York's home. Here, the investiture itself took place, this consisted of Richard crowning his son as Prince of Wales.

Edward of Middleham returned to the Royal castles held in Yorkshire after his investiture, most probably Middleham. Richard had his son formally recognised as heir to the throne by Parliament in February 1484 and took the precaution of having the nobility swear their allegiance to the young Prince.

The measures being taken to secure the Prince's future were in vain, though. He died quite suddenly in March 1484. The location of his grave is subject to debate.

9th September 1460

Richard Duke of York landed in England and began a monarchical style of progress towards London.

Following the rout at Ludlow Richard Duke of York had travelled to Ireland. The other great Yorkist lords had travelled to Calais. Whilst in exile, they were attained at the Parliament of Devils.

With the Earl of Warwick retaining control of the Calais fleet, the lords could communicate and even meet. This allowed them the opportunity to plan for a return to England.

The plan was for dual forces to land and force the Council and Parliament to make changes to the way that England was being governed.

The Earls of Warwick, Salisbury, and March set sail from Calais, landing at Sandwich They advanced on London and then engaged the royal army at Northampton. Having defeated the Lancastrians, captured Henry VI, and secured the Tower of London, the Yorkist party was again ascendancy.

Richard returned to England on 9th September 1460. The other lords had promised that they simply wanted good governance and reiterated their loyal opposition. Richard, on his return, made a progress style march to London.

When he arrived in the capital, he placed his hand on the throne and stated his right to the crown. In doing so, he surprised most of the nobility. His argument was debated and whilst his claim to the throne was accepted, the nobles were unwilling to overthrow an anointed king, Henry VI.

The compromise was the Act of Accord, which named Richard as heir.

10th September 1469

Edward IV was freed from the virtual captivity that the Earl of Warwick had held him in.

In July 1469, the Duke of Clarence, the King's brother, the Earl of Warwick and George Neville, formerly Chancellor, issued a remonstrance against the King's Council. From Calais, they called for the removal of the Kings' evil councillors' and a return to good governance.

The three men meant the Woodville family who had risen in prominence since Edward IVs marriage to Elizabeth Woodville.

Angered at their loss of influence, the 3 had decided that enough was enough. They sailed to England, raised an army, and with Edward in the North, set about attaining their goal.

At Edgcote on 26th July they defeated the royal army. Soon after, Edward found himself King in name, but a puppet in practice as the Neville's held him in Middleham Castle.

The Earl of Warwick attempted to rule in the kings' name. It was a plan that received little support from other nobles though. Without sufficient support for his policies or enough men loyal to him personally, Warwick was forced to free the King.

Free again, Edward began to assert his authority, triggering the sequence of events that led to the readeption of Henry VI and later, Edward's own successful reclaiming of the throne.

11th September 1472

Treaty of Chateaugiron

The Treaty of Chateaugiron was an agreement made between England and Brittany. The two parties agreed to combine forces for an attack on France or into parts of Gascony that the French held.

The treaty was the result of negotiations undertaken by Anthony Woodville, Earl Rivers. In 1472 the Bretons had sent a request for England to come to their aid. Under attack from the French, they had requested that Edward send 6000 archers.

Instead, they found a band of 30 archers and a small personal entourage accompanying Anthony Woodville, Earl Rivers. Woodville did persuade the King to allow further men to be sent to Brittany. King Edward permitted a further 1000 archers, at Woodville's expense, to sail to Brittany.

It was at this time that Woodville opened talks with the Bretons about an alliance treaty.

Similarly, Edward had opened talks with Burgundy on the same matter. Woodville was successful, as was Edward, and as a result, the Treaty of Chateaugiron was signed on 11th September 1472.

These agreements helped King Edward negotiate with the Bretons and Burgundians as he formulated his plan to invade France. These plans took some time to come to fruition due to concerns held by members of the English Commons. In the meantime though, the Treaty acted as a warning to France not to interfere with the autonomy enjoyed by England's continental allies.

12th September 1440

Eton College founded by King Henry VI.

King Henry VI founded Eton College as a Charity School for poor boys. It was intended that the boys would then progress to Kings College, Cambridge, also founded by Henry.

The King employed the headmaster from Winchester College to establish his new school and brought some boys from Winchester to Eton to establish classes. Eton was incredibly fortunate to have a dedicated founder. The King made substantial grants of land to the new school, ensuring that it had ample land and an income.

Some lands held by alien priories were forfeited to the crown, and Henry used these as the basis of Eton's income. He appointed men of high status to act as feoffees of the endowment. This included Archbishop Chichele, the Duke of Suffolk and John Somerset the Chancellor of the Exchequer and other bishops and members of the King's household.

Henry intended for the buildings to be grand, the nave of the chapel was initially intended to be the longest in Europe. The pope was petitioned, successfully, to grant the school special religious rights.

The school was allowed to provide indulgences to penitents, and it acquired holy relics, including a piece of the True Cross. Building Eton was a long process, and it had not been completed by Henry's fall from power in 1461.

Edward IV had less interest in the project and fewer funds. So much of the intended building plan was reigned in, resulting in the buildings as we see them today.

13th September 1470

The Duke of Clarence and Earl of Warwick landed at Plymouth.

In July of 1470, the Earl of Warwick had met with Margaret of Anjou, resulting in an unlikely alliance between the two former foes.

Both Margaret and the Earl of Warwick now found themselves in exile. They retained supporters in England and had backers on the continent. Individually, however, neither had the resources to change things in their favour in England. Combined, they did.

Warwick had wealth and could call upon his own large retinue. Margaret and the Prince of Wales retained the allegiance of many nobles, who remained loyal to the crowned King Henry VI. Margaret lacked funds though and her armies had been defeated by the Yorkist King.

Allying themselves brought together both sets of armies and secured the funding for two expeditions to England. Warwick and Clarence would sail first and raise armies in the Midlands. Margaret and the Prince of Wales would follow mustering forces in the South-West and from Wales.

A declaration was sent by the Duke of Clarence and Earl of Warwick to the people to garner support. An extract is below:

"Wherefore we entend, by the grace of God, and the helpe of every well disposed man, in right short tyme, to put us in deboure to the uttermost of our powers, to subdwe and put undar falshod and oppression; chastice and punishe the seyde covetows persons in perpetuall example to all other; and to set right and justice to theyr places, to se them equally ministred and indifferently, without mede or drede, as owght to be, and to reduce and redeme for evar the said Realme from thraldome of all outward natyons, and make it as fre within it self as evar it was heretofore"

14th September 1435

John Duke of Bedford dies.

John Duke of Bedford was King Henry V's brother and the eldest uncle of King Henry VI. When Henry V died, Bedford was nominally in charge of the Minority Council appointed to manage state affairs until the infant king reached his majority.

Bedford spent much of his time in France managing English affairs there. It was a period when the French were beginning to recover some ground in the Hundred Years War with their army being inspired by Joan of Arc. Therefore, most of the time, the political and military priority was to counter resurgent France through arms and diplomacy.

This led to some problems at Council as its head, Bedford, was rarely in attendance. This left the Duke of Gloucester as the senior royal on Council and whilst he is remembered as Good Duke Humphrey, he was a rather divisive figure.

Bedford's diplomatic judgement could be called into question with regards to his choice of a second wife. His first wife was Anne of Burgundy. Anne died in 1432, but their marriage had helped bind England and Burgundy together against the French: vital if France were to be defeated.

When Anne died, Bedford took Jacquetta of Luxembourg as his second wife. This infuriated Philip the Good of Burgundy as Luxembourg was an area into which Burgundy had expansionist designs. The alliance became strained as a result and contributed to it breaking down. However, Bedford was a figure of stability within English politics, and his death left a void that needed a strong and capable figure to fill.

15th September 1485

Henry VII issued writs for his first Parliament

Henry Tudor had defeated Richard III at the Battle of Bosworth on 22nd August 1485. News of his victory had reached London quickly, and the city council had met and agreed to meet Henry as King, which they did in a formal state entry to the city on 3rd September.

Henry now needed to establish himself as King. To do this, he needed the nobility, Parliament and the commons to accept his rule. The commons in London were wholly unfamiliar with their new monarch, before his state entry he had visited London just once, as a teenager. They would get several opportunities to see the new King in ceremonies in the coming months.

Parliament and the nobility were the immediate priority, their acceptance would ensure that governance could be effective. So, on 15th September 1485, just weeks after his victory, Henry issued writs summoning members of Parliament to meet on 7th November at Westminster.

This was part of a very hectic schedule for Henry. His coronation was scheduled for 30th October, deliberately before Parliament met so that he was not beholden to them. He was putting things into place in a calculated order to enhance his position.

16th September 1451

William Oldhall, the speaker of the commons, was indicted for plotting to seize the King on this date.

In 1452 an allegation was made to the King that Sir William Oldhall had plotted to seize the King on 16th September of the previous year. The allegation stated that the plot had been stated in no less a place than at the King's Bench. Furthermore, allegations were added that once the 16th September date had been and gone, Sir William had plotted the death of the King whilst at Hunsdon on 3rd November.

Additional suggestions stated that persons associated with the plot received treasonable letters from Richard Duke of York. These were incredibly serious charges against people of great influence: Sir William was Speaker of the Commons. Sir William entered sanctuary at St. Martins Chapel on 23rd November 1451, following an accusation of theft of the Duke of Somerset's goods made by an esquire of the King's house.

His decision to seek sanctuary sealed a guilty verdict at his trial, in his absence, for treason. Sir William was outlawed and attained for his crimes. He remained in sanctuary until July of 1455 when his attainder was reversed by the pro-Yorkist regime.

The mention of the Duke of York in allegations did little to ease tensions. As these allegations were being made, York was at the head of an army of 2000 enforcing peace in a private feud in the south west: one with national ramifications.

The Oldhall affair was one of a series of incidents that led to the standoff between York and the royal party at Dartford in 1452.

17th September 1451

There is a standoff involving the Earl of Devon and Lords Moleyn and Cobham.

As seen in yesterday's entry, tensions were running high in 1451. On 17th September, an argument in the South West threatened to break out into private war. Benet's Chronicle describes the situation:

"On 17th September the Earl of Devon, Lord Moleyns and Lord Cobham on one side, the Earl of Wiltshire and Lord Bonville on the other, with many men, threatened to do battle. The Duke of York, however, despatched 2000 men to prevent hostilities and harm. The King, nevertheless, much angered by these disturbances, sent for the participants, imprisoned the Earl of Wiltshire snd Lord Bonville in Berkhamstead castle, and Lords Moleyns and Cobham in Wallingford castle, even if only for a month. York and Devon, despite several summonses, failed to respond..."

The rivalry in the south west was part of the ongoing feud between the Courtenay and Bonville families. It illustrates the lack of authority that the crown had over the nobility in parts of the country. The Duke of Exeter too had been admonished for his behaviour in the region.

The Duke of York's involvement was in support of his allies in the region, whose support he was to call on when he called for reform and made a challenge to the crown and Parliament at Dartford the following year.

18th September 1467

Thomas Bourchier was created Cardinal*.

Thomas Bourchier had been educated at the University of Oxford before embarking on an ecclesiastical and administrative career. His first senior position was that of Bishop of Worcester to which he was appointed in 1434.

He transferred bishoprics to that of Ely in 1443, whilst also being the Chancellor of the University of Oxford. In 1455 he was translated to Canterbury as a bishop. Bourchier quickly gained a reputation as an able administrator, leading to his appointment as Lord Chancellor in May 1455.

He did not last long in this role as he was one of the people who was replaced during Richard Duke of York's tenure as Protector. However, he remained influential and was one of the people who set about organising the Loveday Parade intended to ease tensions between the rival factions in 1458.

In 1459 he took the side of the Yorkists as conflict broke out. It was Bourchier who crowned Edward IV in 1461. During Edward's reign, Thomas Bourchier became close to the King and royal family. He held trusteeships of royal estates, acted on the King's behalf in proroguing and dissolving Parliament and in 1462 acted as the King's locum for a period.

His loyalty and dependability were rewarded in 1465 by the King petitioning for Bourchier to be created a Cardinal. This was confirmed on 18th September 1467.

*The necessary ceremonies and a Cardinals hat were not in place until 1473.

19th September 1465

Land rights played a major role in the governance of the land and regularly resulted in claims and counterclaims for manors or smallholdings.

The frequency of such contests is one reason why so many enfeoffments were recorded on the Close Rolls in the Chancery records: that was a clear and binding record of the enfeoffment, removing any doubt.

The claims often resulted in the nobility stepping in and acting as arbitrators. Here we see the Earl of Warwick asking (telling) Sir William Plumpton that he is enfeoffed onto lands that Sir William is claiming and that he should do nothing concerning those lands until the rights are determined, presumably by a court.

The Earl of Warwick wrote to Sir William Plumpton.

"Right trustie and well beloued I grete you well. And whereas I am enformed ye pretend claim and title to a close called Spencer Close belonging to my wellbeloved Thomas Scarborough, whearin with others I stand infeoffed. I therefore desire and you that you will suffer the said Thomas the ssid close in peaceable wise to haue and occupie without vexation or trouble vunto time that, by such persons therevpon by your both assets being elect and chosen, the matter be thouroughly determined whether of you the same owth to have right. And our Lord haue you in his keeping. Written at Topcliffe the nineteenth day of September. Therle of Warwick and Salisbury, grete chamberlaine of England and captain of Calais. R. Warwick

Endorsed: to my right trustie and wellbeloved Sir William Plompton. Knight"

20th September 1435

Treaty of Arras

In 1435 the English and French agreed to negotiate. At a conference held in Arras, the Hundred Years War's combatant nations sought a mutual understanding that would secure a lasting peace.

Both countries sent delegations that were led and staffed by nobles of high standing. The English delegation included Cardinal Beaufort, John Kemp the Archbishop of York, and the Duke of Suffolk. The French delegation was led by the King's brother-in-law, Charles Duke of Bourbon. Regnault de Chartres the Constable of France and Archbishop of Reims and the Constable of France, Arthur de Richemont also attended.

The conference did not go well for the English. The French wanted England to renounce the claim to the French crown. The English delegation refused. Two French captains began raiding English held towns as the conference was held.

English delegates had little choice but to go and address this problem. Whilst the English were dealing with the French attacks, the French contacted Philip the Good of Burgundy and offered to punish the men who had murdered Philip's father, adding that the Duke of Burgundy would no longer need to pay homage to the King of France.

The English returned to the talks to find that France had made an agreement with Burgundy.

Furthermore, the only diplomatic tie to Burgundy had been John Duke of Bedford. He had died just a week earlier. England had gone to Arras with high hopes of an agreeable peace. They left with no continental allies. The coming months proved incredibly hard for English forces in France and Normandy and draining on the English treasury.

21st September 1474

Commission of over and terminer held at Pontefract Castle

On 21st September 1474 Richard Duke of Gloucester, acting to preserve his control of the region, opened a commission of oyer and terminer.

The commission, which lasted until 25th September 1474, was intended to bring a peaceful solution to a feud. Two of the north's most powerful lords, Sir John Saville, and Sir John Pilkington had become embroiled in a bitter feud. It had become violent and was threatening the stability of the north.

Richard's intervention had limited impact, clashes continued until the death of Sir John Pilkington in 1479.

It is often said that the north was stable and peaceful under the lordship of Richard. Whilst administratively it was much better managed, and the great northern magnates remained at peace with one another, that was not always the case within the lower nobility and gentry.

The ducal Council was also asked to intervene in a dispute between Gerald Salvin of Croxdale and Thomas Fishburn. Additionally, arbitration was needed to settle matters between Richard Clervaux and Roland Place. The chief difference between Richard Duke of Gloucester's tenure as 'Lord of the North' and earlier means of dealing with problems was that the issues could be, and were, dealt with at an early stage. This limited the risk of the great magnates being drawn into feuds and, whilst not perfect, improved the prospects of peace and prosperity in the region.

22nd September 1411

Birth of Richard, who became Duke of York

Richard had a troubled infancy. His mother died shortly after his birth. His father, Richard, Earl of Cambridge was implicated in the Southampton Plot in 1415 and executed for treason.

Richard's future looked uncertain. It became complicated following his uncle's death, Edmund Duke of York at the Battle of Agincourt, to whom the infant Richard was heir, coupled with the posthumous attainder of his father.

Fortunately for Richard, Henry V did not extend his father's attainder to his heirs, the young Richard now stood to inherit the titles and estates of both his father and his uncle. His upbringing was placed initially under Sir Robert Waterton's care until 1423 when Ralph Neville bought his wardship for 3000 marks.

In 1425 Richard's worth rose again as he was the sole heir to the Mortimer inheritance. The boy was now in line to be one of the country's largest landholders when he reached his majority.

Following Ralph Neville's death, his guardianship passed to Joan Beaufort, who betrothed Richard to Cecily Neville. The couple married before October 1429.

Richard's inheritance was complex due to the number of estates and types of landholding that they had been. Nonetheless, by the time he was granted livery of the estates, the income that was due from them exceeded £17000 per annum: he needed to take legal action to recover some £6000 of this from his inherited wealth.

23rd September 1459

The Battle of Blore Heath

Tension had been rising between the rival factions in court. Both sides had begun to strengthen their retinues and were jostling for strategic advantage. Amid this mutual suspicion, the Duke of York called for his supporters to join him at his stronghold at Ludlow.

Queen Margaret had been doing similar in the Midlands, an area that the Earl of Salisbury would need to pass through to rendezvous with the Duke of York. The gathering of large armies would have made the likelihood of war seem high. Queen Margaret decided to land the first blow.

She ordered Lord Audley to intercept Salisbury's force to devastate the Yorkist hopes before they had combined. Audley chose a strong defensive position at Blore Heath to meet the Yorkist army.

At 10000 strong, Audley's force outnumbered Salisbury's by 2 to 1. Plus, the Yorkists would have to traverse a beck before making an assault. Following the traditional exchange of arrows, Salisbury opted to use a ruse.

The centre of the Yorkist line drew back as if in retreat. Upon seeing this, the Lancastrian cavalry charged, trying to rout their foes. However, the Yorkists, instead of fleeing, simply returned to their original positions and used the beck against the Lancastrians.

Many were killed and a second assault was launched, in which Audley was killed. Lord Dudley then ordered an assault by foot soldiers. This too failed and saw many Lancastrians change sides. The Lancastrian army then fled, being chased down by the Yorkists for several miles. Salisbury quickly regrouped and made for Ludlow, aware that other Lancastrian armies were in the area.

24th September 1459

Sir Thomas Stanley writes to Queen Margaret making his apologies for not arriving at Blore Heath in time. He also writes to the Earl of Salisbury, congratulating him on his victory. In fact, Sir Thomas had been with his men just some two miles from the battle and prevaricated over which side to join.

The Stanley family gained something of a reputation during the Wars of the Roses for avoiding fighting unless there was a definite gain in it for them. The first such example of this sitting on the fence approach was at Blore Heath.

Sir Thomas had a force of 2000 men, whom he chose to keep at roughly 2 miles from the battlefield. He had found himself in an awkward situation. The Queen had given him direct orders; however, his wife was the Earl of Salisbury's daughter.

As a result of his family ties, Stanley had been corresponding with the Earl of Salisbury. Assurances had been made to him but also to the Queen. Having sat out the battle, he wrote to the Queen to apologise for having not turned up for the battle. To the Earl of Salisbury, he sent his congratulations on the battlefield victory and the way he then evaded other Lancastrian forces.

Stanley's reputation for ensuring that they were always on the winning side grew as the wars rumbled on. He failed to support the Earl of Warwick, his brother-in-law, in his rebellion of 1470. Then he gave the appearance of supportiing the readeption but failed to intervene when Edward landed at Ravenspur. He took no part in the Battle of Tewkesbury, even though it was possible for him to have participated. He also sat out the Battle of Bosworth.

25th September 1472

Inquest Post Mortem into the estate of Robert Watton.

This Inquest was called for by letters patent. The investigation, therefore, was requested by the crown. This was later the subject of a court of common pleas hearing, in 1480, at the request of Cardinal Thomas Bourchier.

Robert Watton was a knight. The Inquisition Post Mortem him found to have held a half share in several manors during his lifetime: Palstre, valued at £8 per annum; Crongbery, valued at 10m per annum; Boughton Monchelsea, valued at 10m per annum; a fee tail in the Manor of Addington, valued at 10m per annum. These were held in Kent, from the Duchesses of Buckingham or York.

In Court in 1480 the Cardinal stated that Watton's daughter and sole heir, Katherine, was abducted by a Hugh C. Katherine was underage and held in the Cardinal's care.

The jury found that at the time of Watton's death the estates should have returned to the crown, as the King himself was tenant-in-chief of each of the manors for which Watton held a share. Further, they found that Katherine, who had been aged 4 at the time of her father's death, was the sole beneficiary of her father's wealth.

The Chancery confirmed that following the death of Watton, the manors in question had, through letters patent, been assigned to the Cardinal. So too had custody of Katherine and with that, her marriage rights until she came of age.

It was alleged that Hugh C abducted Katherine in 1472 and failed to hand her over as required by the letters patent until 1477. The jury found in the Cardinal's favour and awarded a sum of 230m. This illustrates how wardships were sources of income for nobles and bishops.

26th September 1469

On 21st August 1469, the Duke of Norfolk moved on Caister Castle, held by the Paston family. This was a local dispute that escalated because of the wider conflict.

The Paston Letters suggest a force of 3000 was brought to bear upon the castle, though this is probably an exaggeration. The Duke did bring with him artillery and is known to have requested more to be brought from Lynn. Inside the castle, the defenders too had use of firearms, an earlier castle inventory refers to hand cannons.

The 30 or so defenders were a mixture of men with fighting experience and locals levied into service. Margaret Paston attempted to improve the castle's defences, writing to one son imploring him to go to the aid of the other son.

We also know that legal efforts were, unsuccessfully, made to halt the Duke's assault. The continued siege wore the defenders down. Food was in short supply. Some of the defenders had been killed. Gunpowder was running low.

An exchange of letters from Paston family members who were not inside the castle illustrates the gravity of the situation. And so, they petitioned George Duke of Clarence.

Clarence appears to have played a significant role in bringing the siege to an end. Terms were agreed that enabled John Paston III and the surviving defenders to leave the castle unmolested.

The Duke of Norfolk would then take possession of the castle. According to historian John Ashdown Hill, the defenders left on 26th September 1469 with the Duke of Norfolk making it clear that they had the Duke of Clarence to thank for the peaceful outcome. The legal wrangling over this private feud was to drag on well into the 1470s.

27th September 1470

Edward IV departs England for the safety of Burgundy. His brother Richard, the Duke of Gloucester, joins him in seeking Burgundian aid.

The events of 1469 and 1470 were tumultuous. Many of the great lords changed allegiances as first the Robin of Redesdale revolt, and then that of the Duke of Clarence and Earl of Warwick shook the country.

King Edward had already suffered the humiliation of being kept as a puppet leader under house arrest. On his resumption of control, he faced problems. His brother, George Duke of Clarence and the Earl of Warwick remained disgruntled.

In restoring the Percy family to their title, he gained an ally. However, in taking that title from John Neville, he created animosity. Instead of halting the army of the Duke of Clarence, Neville (Lord Montagu) joined it. The Warkworth Chronicle describes the events as:

"But Montagu… declared to the people there gathered with him, how the King had first given him the earldom of Northumberland, and how he took it from him and gave it to Harry Percy made him Marquis Montagu and gave him a magpies nest to maintain his estate with... King Edward was not strong enough to give battle to Marquis Montagu, so sailed over the sea to Flanders."

Edward had found himself outwitted and outnumbered. He fled to the east where he and his loyal supporters set sail to Burgundy, where his sister Margaret was Duchess. His welcome there was not initially as warm as he would have hoped Duke Charles not greeting him or meeting him until Burgundian politics made an English (Yorkist) alliance favourable.

28th September 1422

An interim council for the minority government of the infant King Henry VI was established.

As Henry became King as an infant, his government was managed by a minority regency council. This Council ruled in his name, theoretically based on majority decisions being accepted.

The Council was nominally headed by the elder of King Henry's uncles, John Duke of Bedford. As Bedford spent much of the time managing English affairs in France, the King's other uncle, Humphrey Duke of Gloucester acted as Lord Protector.

The main area of concern for the minority council was the Hundred Years War. At the time of Henry's accession, England was in the ascendancy. Soon they faced a resurgent France, inspired by Joan of Arc.

The Council became split over the policy that should be adopted over the French campaigns, with some Lords wanting an aggressive policy and others a defensive one. War in France also led to severe shortages of funds. This led to the rise in importance of Bishop, later Cardinal, Henry Beaufort. Loans from Henry Beaufort funded many of the campaigns fought in France which led to a faction in court developing. He frequently clashed with Duke Humphrey throughout the war.

John Duke of Bedford, died shortly before the King came of age. He left a precarious situation. England had lost favour with Burgundy, partly due to Bedford's second marriage and had seen the French making gains. Bedford was replaced in France by Richard Duke of York.

29th September 1464

Sheriffs were sworn in by the City of London

On 29th September 1464, the City of London swore in John Tate and John Stone as sheriffs. Tate had been selected by the Lord Mayor of London; Stone had been elected by the commons of London.

The role of the two sheriffs was administrative. In terms of justice, they were responsible for the imprisonment of those accused of serious crimes until such time as a judge was available for a trial. For lesser crimes, it was the Sheriff who organised the county or city courts. They were also responsible for collecting local taxes and fines and ensuring these revenues got to the treasury. Furthermore, if a commission of array was issued, it would be the Sheriff who was responsible for overseeing the muster of men. The record of the election reads as follows:

"The Feast of St Matthew 4 Edward IV. [A.D. 1464], in the presence of [many officials], and very many Commoners summoned to the Guildhall for the election of Sheriffs—John Tate was elected one of the Sheriffs of London and Middlesex by the Mayor, and John Stone, tailor, was elected the other Sheriff by the Commonalty.

The same day, Robert Colwich, tailor, was elected Chamberlain for the year ensuing; Peter Alfold and Peter Calcot were elected Wardens of London Bridge; Ralph Josselyn, Ralph Verney, Aldermen, John Aleyn, goldsmith, William Persone, "taillour," John Stone, "taillour," and Richard Frome, skinner, Commoners, were elected Auditors of the accounts of the Chamber and of the Wardens of London Bridge in arrear.

Afterwards, viz., on the eve of St Michael [29th September], the said Sheriffs were sworn at the Guildhall, and on the morrow of the said Feast were presented and admitted before the Barons of the Exchequer".

30th September 1473

The beginning of the siege of St. Michael's Mount.

On 30th September 1473, the Earl of Oxford and Lord Beaumont landed at St. Michael's Mount, Cornwall with a force of 397 men. They took the castle by surprise, capturing it seemingly without a struggle. There followed a siege of 22 weeks.

The Earl of Oxford and Lord Beaumont had fled to the safety of Scotland after the Battle of Barnet before sailing to France where they received a sympathetic ear from King Louis XI.

After a period of engaging in piracy, Oxford and Beaumont decided to take St. Michael's Mount. It was a target that would not be expecting an attack. Defensively it held many advantages, and it was accessible from the sea, allowing supply and potentially an escape route.

They landed on 30th September 1473. The island fortress fell, as expected, with ease. Initially, Edward opted for a blockade of the castle and island. However, supplies got to the castle, and the siege began to frustrate the King.

In December of 1473, King Edward sent John Fortesque with 6000 men to take charge of proceedings. He also sent John Wode, master of ordnance at the Royal Armouries. Ships from Edward's fleet enforced a naval blockade.

Pardons were offered to any defenders who left the castle. The stranglehold that the royal forces had around the island soon worked. In February of 1474, the remaining defenders, including the Earl of Oxford and Lord Beaumont, surrendered.

Oxford and Beaumont were imprisoned. Oxford famously escaped from Calais in 1485 and was one of Henry Tudor's commanders at the Battle of Bosworth.

October

1st October 1449

Loans to the state made by Lords Sudeley and the Earl of Arundel.

In 1449 the country was on the verge of bankruptcy. It became clear to nobles when only 3 months of salaries were offered to head an army in France. The standard was 12 months. John Watts in Henry VI and the Politics of Kingship notes that:

"...during 1449-50 no one higher than Lord Powys was prepared to go.."

A Great Council was called, which met in September 1449. Following this, a Parliament was summoned, which, unusually, was accompanied by requests of loans.

Lord Sudeley and the Earl of Arundel made loans of 100 marks each on *1st October 1449*. The Earl of Wiltshire, Grey of Ruthin, Earl of Devon and the Duke of Norfolk soon followed suit.

The financial situation was the first political matter addressed in the November 1449 Parliament, although an outbreak of the Plague had seen Parliament prorogued until spring of 1450. Taxation was set:

And thus for every whole 20 s . arising from the said annual value of 20 s . from any of the foregoing, over and above the annual charges thereof, to and at the sum of £20, 6 d

And;

persons have any such estate, possession or occupation, up to any annual value exceeding the sum of £20 and up to the sum of £200, over and above the annual charge thereof, for every 20s . of such value, 12d

Translations of Parliamentary Roll, British History Online

2nd October 1452

Birth at Fotheringay of Richard, later King Richard III.

"The women cried,
'O Jesus bless us, he is born with teeth!'
And so I was, which plainly signified
That I should snarl and bite and play the dog"

Henry VI Part 3, Act 5, Scene 6

Richard, son of Richard Duke of York and Cecily Neville, was born on 2nd October 1452 at Fotheringay Castle. There are limited sources on Richard's birth and first months. This is hardly surprising. As a younger son of the Duke of York, he would be expected to have status within the court, but it was improbable that he would ever rise to the kingship itself.

Indeed, the earliest accounts of his birth are written with a Tudor audience in mind. John Rous wrote that Richard was born with teeth and hair down to his shoulders: both slurs.

"Richard was…retained within his mother's womb for two years and emerging with teeth and hair to his shoulders. … like a scorpion he combined a smooth front with a stinging tail".

Antiquarian, Mr Hutton, spent 18 years researching the childhood of Richard III. He noted that there are many 'idle tales' that he suggests are 'beneath the notice of history'. More tellingly, he summarises his findings of Richard's early years by saying that 'infancy was spent in his father's house, where he cuckt his ball and shoot his taw with the same delight as other lads'. In other words, he was a perfectly normal baby and infant.

3rd October 1390

Birth of Duke Humphrey

Though Humphrey Duke of Gloucester had died prior to the Wars of the Roses, his life and actions impacted upon the longer-term causes of the conflict.

Humphrey was the younger of Henry Vs brothers. When the King died prematurely in 1422, Humphrey was one of two uncles of the infant Henry VI. Humphrey's role has been subject to debate.

Nonetheless, when his elder brother, the Duke of Bedford, was managing English affairs in France or Normandy, Humphrey had nominal charge of affairs in England. As the French wars began to favour the French, Humphrey became quite outspoken about the policy in France.

A divide emerged between those favouring an aggressive policy and those who wanted a more conservative approach towards the French. His views were not shared by the majority on Council but made him a popular figure among the Commons.

Humphrey fell from grace when his second wife, Eleanor Cobham, was found guilty of necromancy at the King's expense. A forced divorce was imposed, and Humphrey retired as far as possible from national politics.

His popularity did not wane, though. In 1447 Humphrey was accused of treason. Whilst under arrest, he died. The timing of his death led many to believe that foul play was involved. The modern theory is that he most likely died of a stroke. Humphrey left behind a sizeable cultural legacy. He had been a sponsor of the arts and had amassed an extensive library.

4th October 1461

Henry Windsor writes of the situation in Wales.

Henry Windsor wrote to John Paston on 4th October 1461 to update him on the military situation. Within the letter he provides details of how the Welsh Campaign was progressing.

His account demonstrates that news reaching the capital was not always entirely accurate. Not all Welsh Castles and strongholds had yielded, Harlech would not fall for a further 7 years.

"...all the castles and strongholds in south Wales and north Wales are given and yielded up into the King's hand. And the Duke of Exeter and the Earl of Pembroke are flown and taken to the mountains, and several lords with great power are after them; and the most part of gentlemen and men of worship are come unto the King, and have grace, all of Wales." Henry Windsor to John Paston 4th October 1461

Windsor was incorrect in his assertion that all the castles in the south and north Wales had fallen. Many had had, but there remained a strong pocket of Lancastrian resistance, mainly in Snowdonia.

Indeed, just 2 weeks later, the Lancastrians fought the battle of Twt Hill, led by the Earl of Exeter and Jasper Tudor. Though defeated, the leaders managed to escape capture and sailed to Ireland.

They retained control of Harlech Castle for another 7 years. During this time, Harlech was supplied by sea and used as a base from which incursions into Northern Wales could take place. This meant that while the siege was usually one of containment, the Yorkists did need to maintain a force in the area which was costly and reduced their ability to react to events elsewhere.

5th October 1459

King Henry VI appoints the Duke of Somerset as Captain of Calais.

1459 saw the Wars of the Roses burst into life. The Battle of Blore Heath and the rout at Ludford Bridge made it inevitable that war was to follow.

So too did it make changes to essential appointments inevitable. One of the most important positions that the crown appointed was that of the Captaincy of Calais. Calais was England's gateway into the continent. It had military significance as the home of a fleet that protected English interests in the Channel.

Calais was the port to which most English exports had to sail and where imported goods entered. Control of Calais was a priority for the Treasury and Crown. So, when the conflict between Yorkists and Lancastrians flared up, it stood to reason that the Captaincy of Calais would be stripped from the Earl of Warwick and handed to a loyal Lancastrian.

On 5th October 1459, that change was enacted. King Henry VI appointed the Duke of Somerset to the prestigious position. There was one significant drawback to the appointment, though: The Earl of Warwick, Earl of Salisbury and Earl of March were all in Calais, and the garrison and their followers remained loyal to them.

The Duke of Somerset was going to have to oust them from Calais to take up his position. Calais is sited in a strong defensive position. To access Medieval Calais, an attack would have to come from the sea or across one narrow strip of land. The Duke of Somerset attempted this in April of 1460. The Battle of Newnham Bridge was a resounding Yorkist victory as the Lancastrian artillery became waterlogged and could not fire.

6th October 1486

John Morton is appointed as Archbishop of Canterbury.

John Morton's career is remarkable in many ways, culminating in his appointment as Archbishop of Canterbury, which led to his being created Cardinal and concurrently holding the position of Lord Chancellor.

Morton did not have an easy journey to these high-ranking positions. Though he was a graduate of Baliol College, Oxford, his first positions were as Rector, then archdeacon at Norwich Cathedral. He made more of a name for himself as a lawyer, being the person who drafted the 1459 attainder of Richard Duke of York.

That Act and his association with the House of Lancaster led to him joining Queen Margaret in exile. He remained in France until 1469 when Warwick was in the ascendancy.

His stock rose as a result of making his peace with Edward IV. He gained both government and ecclesiastical roles, as Master of the Rolls and Archdeacon of Winchester, then Berkshire and finally Norfolk. This led to his elevation to the bishopric of Ely in 1478, consecrated the following year.

Morton was a political opponent of Richard III and was imprisoned for a period as a result. This did mean that he could resume high office under Henry VII, being translated to Archbishop of Canterbury and appointed Lord Chancellor.

Morton's reforms played a large role in ensuring that the Treasury balanced its books. He died in 1500.

7th October 1460

Parliament repealed all legislation passed at the Coventry parliament of 1459.

With the Yorkists now in control of the government, the previous Parliament's acts, heavily dominated by Margaret of Anjou, could be set aside.

The 'Parliament of Devils' as the 1459 sittings are known, had attained all of the leading Yorkists and consolidated the power base around Queen Margaret. The new Parliament, once formalities were dealt with, opened with a powerful statement of intent:

"To the king our sovereign lord, the commons assembled in this present parliament pray that various seditious and ill-disposed persons, having no regard for the fear of God, or for the harm of the prosperous estate of your most noble person, or of this your realm, in a malicious and importunate manner urged your highness to summon and call a parliament to be held at your city of Coventry, on 20th November, in the thirty-eighth year of your noble reign [1459], with the sole intention of destroying certain of the great, noble and faithful true lords and estates of your blood, and others of your true liege people of this your realm, because of the great rancour, hatred and malice that the said seditious persons had long felt towards them, and because of their insatiable greed for the lands, hereditaments, possessions, offices and goods of the said lords and true lieges; by which urging, certain acts, statutes and ordinances were made in the said last parliament against all good faith and conscience, to completely destroy your said true lords, estates and liege people..." Translation of the Parliamentary Roll for the October 1460 Parliament.

8th October 1453

The Council ordered the Neville and Percy families to bring an end to their warlike behaviour.

The conflict between the Neville and Percy families had been ongoing for some time. Matters had only got worse as both families built up a large base of retainers. Younger members of each family were eager to press home claims.

Hostility was open and regular. Lord Egremont was recruiting and distributing Livery in May of 1453, an act usually only done in war. He then ignored royal summonses.

The Neville's attacked Topcliffe, a Percy base, because of this. July saw clashes at Sandholme, Halton and Swinden. In August 1453, a servant of the Earl of Salisbury had been kidnapped and imprisoned by the Percy's.

A house believed to be that of Lord Egremont was ransacked by Sir John Neville and his men. The King had already been ignored by the hot-headed Lord Egremont, and now Henry VI was unwell. Council intervened. A letter in the King's name stated to the Earls of Salisbury and Northumberland that they were aware of the pairs:

'...greatest assembly of liegemen, and thereto had appointed time and place, that ever was made within this land at any time that man can think...'

Consequences for the pair were also mentioned. The feuding needed to stop. It was not just Council that intervened to keep the peace. Extant letters show that the Earls were in contact with the Archbishop of York, who acted as a mediator. The feuding did not, however, come to an end.

9th October 1459

Writs of Summons were issued for a Parliament to be held at Coventry.

No writ was sent to the Duke of York or his sons or to the Earls of Salisbury and Warwick.

Queen Margaret was presenting a fait accompli to which the Yorkists could only respond through force of arms or exile, either of which reinforce the Lancastrians' image as the true defenders of the people.

The intentions were clear. Tension had risen throughout the late 1450s. It had exploded into life at Blore Heath when armies of the rival factions clashed. Queen Margaret had attempted and failed to inflict a devastating blow to the Yorkist cause in that battle.

The differences between the two sides had got to breaking point and broken. Already, the King had announced the appointment of the Duke of Somerset to the Captaincy of Calais. A parliament in the heart of lands loyal to Margaret, despite Warwick itself being very close, could force through punitive legislation against the Yorkist leadership. The lack of summons made the intention all the more clearer.

The Yorkists, therefore, opted to face the King's army and prepared for battle. The subsequent meeting of the two armies is covered in this book on 12th October.

10th October 1460

Richard Duke of York entered Parliament brandishing a sword. He walked to the throne and placed his hand upon it, claiming it as his own.

The events of October 1460 are among the most unusual in England's history. Following his arrival back in England, the Duke of York had progressed southwards, meeting with men who asked him to take the crown. York met with the Earl of Warwick in the midlands before continuing towards the capital. He was acting like a king.

The Yorkists who had been in Calais, on the other hand, had issued a manifesto that pledged allegiance to Henry and called for reforms. A letter to the Earl of Worcester, who was in Venice at the time, describes events:

"...The kyng whith lordes spiritualle and temporalle as the archbusshoppis of Cant and York, bishop is of Excetter Ely Lincoln London Worcestre and Chicestre, the Duke of Northefolk Erlyss of Marche Warwick Salisbury with many abbats and Baronys sittying in the parlement chambre except the kyng the commyens beyng in ther place accustomed in Westm' ther cam my lorde of york with viij hundred horse and men harneysed atte x of the clok, and entred the paleis with his swerde born uppe right by him for thorowe the halle and parleament chambre. And under the cloth of estaye stondyng he gave them knowlich that he purposed nat to ley daune his swerde but to challenge his right and so toke his loggyng in the qwenys chambre... purposed no man shuld have denyed tge croune fro his hed."

Richard was persuaded to delay his intended coronation of the next day. The baronial Council met. They agreed that the claim to the throne was valid. However, they did not agree that it was necessary to remove Henry VI.

11th October 1483

"traitororiously turned against us".

Richard III was made aware of the Duke of Buckingham's involvement in the plots and rebellions that were breaking out.

The Duke of Buckingham had been one of Richard IIIs most trusted and loyal subjects. He had been with the Duke of Gloucester to arrest Anthony Woodville and had been instrumental in helping Richard through the period in which he became King.

Buckingham had been given several significant positions by Richard. He was appointed Chief Justice over Wales and in August was commissioned to investigate treasons in London. He is sometimes accused of having been responsible for the murder of the Princes in the Tower.

During Edward IVs reign Buckingham stood to inherit 38 Manors from the estate of Henry Bohun. Edward, however, kept the estates for the crown. This possible motivation for rebelling is confused by the fact that this matter was being tackled.

A letter sealed by signet ring had transferred the estate to Buckingham in July, pending Parliamentary process. It is plausible that Buckingham was being opportunistic. He was descended from Edward III and possibly saw an opportunity to take the kingship for himself. However, there is only circumstantial evidence to go on.

The only certainty is that the Duke did rebel. The rebellion often bears his name as he was the most senior figure within the revolt but again, it is not clear whether he had masterminded the uprising or joined once it was already underway. He was captured by men loyal to Richard and executed for treason on 2nd November 1483.

12th October 1459

The Battle of Ludford

Following Loveday, the Lancastrian faction had armed itself and prepared for war. In 1455 they had been caught relatively unprepared for a Yorkist attack. The Queen was not willing to risk this happening again. A Great Council had been called and, in their absence, charged York, Salisbury and Warwick with treason.

With further conflict likely and writs of summons to Parliament excluding the Yorkist lords, those leader forces combined at Ludlow to ready themselves for whatever was to happen next.

Ludlow was well defended by the Yorkists. They had cannon at the head of their forces defending the southern bank at Ludford Bridge. Experienced men from the garrison at Calais had been brought to Ludlow by the Earl of Warwick. The Earl of Salisbury's men, fresh from their victory at Blore Heath, were also present, along with the loyal local forces of the Duke of York.

The two sides met each other at Ludford Bridge, outside the town. York's men took a defensive position on the south bank of the river. Parley was attempted. The King offered a pardon to all except those responsible for Lord Audley's death: this would not have pardoned the Earl of Salisbury. Throughout the night of 12th/13th October, cannon were fired toward the Royal lines.

The Parley demonstrated to some of the Yorkist troops that the King himself was present. The Royal Standard was clearly visible. The Calais Garrison was not willing to fight the King himself. During the night, the men from Calais switched sides.

13th October 1453

Birth of Edward of Westminster.

The birth of Edward of Westminster came as King Henry VI was suffering from a mental breakdown. That the King was incapacitated at the time of the Prince's birth led to scurrilous gossip about the paternity of the young Prince, with rumours that the true father of the boy was the Duke of Somerset or Earl of Ormonde who both were politically close to the Queen.

Such rumours were never taken too seriously by Henry VI whilst he was well, and he acknowledged Edward as his son. Edward was created Prince of Wales in the summer of 1454.

This may appear to be early in the boy's life. Symbolically and politically, his legitimacy as a royal prince and heir presumptive was essential and were sensitive political issues.

In the short term, Edward's birth settled the matter of inheritance and potentially diffused that aspect of clashes between factions. In the medium term, his rights were overlooked in favour of the Duke of York and his heirs under the Act of Accord.

That triggered the busiest period of campaigning in the Wars of the Roses, resulting in the Lancastrian loss at Towton. Prince Edward lost his life fighting for the Lancastrian cause, being killed at the Battle of Tewkesbury.

14th October 1404

Birth of Marie of Anjou.

Marie married her second cousin, at the time Dauphin of France. As Queen Consort, she acted as Regent within France on occasions.

Her involvement in state affairs is said to have contributed to her husband's ability to concentrate his efforts on removing the English from France.

Marie was also related to Margaret of Anjou. The formers' involvement in matters of state is an excellent example of the expectations that Margaret may have had of a role as consort in England.

This is a consideration that is often overlooked when appraising the approach of Margaret of Anjou towards Queenship. It was quite normal in France for females of noble birth to act as regents, as had been seen under the earlier Plantagenet rulers when Eleanor of Aquitaine assumed such a role.

The involvement of foreign powers in the Wars of the Roses and the way they facilitated this is often overlooked. However, affairs in England were closely monitored in France, Burgundy, Brittany, and the Hanseatic League as it directly impacted their economies. For the French, it also affected England's ability to, or intent to reignite the claim to their crown.

As such, the role of Marie of Anjou is quite significant in terms of English affairs. Her relationship with Margaret would influence the French willingness to support the Lancastrian cause, which had longevity into the Tudor claim.

15th October 1470

Henry VI leaves the Tower of London

With Edward fleeing into exile, the restoration of King Henry VI could take place. It was done in some pomp with leading members of the new regime riding to the Tower to ceremoniously free Henry from his incarceration.

They immediately took the King to St. Paul's to have his kingship confirmed before god. And as they were celebrating the readeption of Henry VI, they tried, sentenced, and executed the Earl of Worcester for his role in the Yorkist regime. Worcester's execution took place on 18th October and is covered within this book.

"[On 15th October 1470 the Duke of Clarence] accompanied by the Earls of Warwick, Derby and Shrewsbury, Lord Stanley, and many other noble men, rode to the Tower and fetched thence King Henry, and conveyed him through the streets of the city, riding in a long gown of blue velvet to St. Paul's... And thus was this ghostly and virtuous prince King Henry VI, after long imprisonment and many injuries, derisions and scorns sustained by him patiently of many of his subjects, restored to his right and regality...

The Earl of Worcester was arraigned in the White Hall at Westminster, and there indicted of treason, [and sentenced] to go forth from thence upon his feet to Tower Hill and there have his head struck off..."

Great Chronicle of London

16th October 1461

Battle of Towt Hill

Following the Lancastrian defeat at the Battle of Towton, pockets of resistance to the Yorkists existed in several parts of England and Wales.

Those fortunate enough to escape the rout fled in several directions, to the North, following the King and Queen to Northumberland, to the West into areas of modern-day Cumbria, Lancashire and Cheshire that were ambivalent towards the new rulers, or further West, into Wales.

In Wales, there was the potential of long and protracted conflict. King Henry's half-brother, Jasper Tudor, was the Earl of Pembroke. He held lordships and castles throughout Wales and commanded the loyalty of many men.

Jasper Tudor also had the support of the Duke of Exeter, who had made his way from Towton to Wales to fight alongside Pembroke.

Edward charged William Herbert and Walter Deveraux with the task of eliminating Lancastrian resistance.

The Lancastrians used the mountainous North to gather a force. The two sides met near Caernarvon, at Twt Hill, on 16th October 1461.

Little is known of the battle, except it was a decisive Yorkist victory.

Pembroke and Exeter fled to Ireland. Soon the Lancastrian Castles were capitulating. By mid-1462, only Harlech remained in Lancastrian hands.

17th October 1469

Richard Duke of Gloucester, appointed Constable of England

As King Edward IV sought to shore up his government, he took steps to appoint people he could trust to the land's highest positions. His youngest brother, Richard, had remained loyal to Edward throughout and was not tarnished by any of the wars previous ebbs and flows.

Though only 17, Richard of Gloucester had grown up seeing the workings of the state, the politics at play and the nature of justice, and injustice, being meted out.

Edward decided that this was ample training for a senior position. As a prince of the blood, he would command respect and, most importantly, he would protect the King's interests.

Edward made Richard the Constable of England on this day in 1469. This role, one that Richard would use decisively in 1471, was the most senior judicial position in the country.

The Constable was responsible for the administration of feudal law, and cases of many serious crimes in the land would be referred to the Constable court.

In normal circumstances, only treason by a magnate would be heard by a higher authority, though the Constable could, and Richard did after the Battle of Tewkesbury, hear these cases.

18th October 1470

Execution of John Tiptoft Earl of Worcester

John Tiptoft Earl of Worcester, was known as 'the butcher of England'. Already a wealthy Earl, he was recalled from the Holy Land upon Edward IV's accession and appointed initially as chief justice of North Wales, where he was a substantial landholder.

He was made Constable of the Tower of London in December 1461 and then, in February 1462, was appointed as Constable of England. It was this role that gained Worcester a reputation as being a 'butcher'. His remit was to try cases of treason on inspection of fact. That meant no jury, just himself examining the evidence and determining guilt or innocence, with sentencing also in his hands.

This made him a despised figure among the Lancastrian cause. It was Worcester who tried the Earl of Oxford and his eldest son shortly after being appointed.

He fought in the North East in the bid to remove Lancastrian resistance from the area and was thus on hand to administer judicial proceedings should prisoners be taken. This was the case after the Battle of Hexham and upon the taking of Bamburgh Castle.

In 1467 he was sent to Ireland to replace the deputy governor, Thomas Fitzgerald, who was not trusted by Edward IV. Worcester duly removed him from office, tried him for treason and had him executed along with the Earl of Desmond.

When Henry VI was restored to the throne, Worcester had been found and detained by Lancastrians. His record of condemning so many Lancastrian loyalists sealed his own fate. After a brief imprisonment in the Tower of London, he was executed by beheading at Tower Hill on 18th October 1470.

19th October 1470

Debts of Anthony Woodville

Anthony Woodville was in temporary exile with Edward IV on this date. This presented debtors with a problem. Debts were paid at set times, here at 'Christmas next', but with the readeption of Henry VI, it was likely seen as inevitable that Woodville, like other leading Yorkists, would be attained.

Here we see a move to secure payment of monies due to Geoffrey Gate. The claim, dated 19th October 1470, intends to hold the debt against Woodville's land, presumably believing that it would remain tied to the estates should it be forfeit.

In the event, Woodville's exile was relatively short, returning with Edward as he reclaimed the crown.

"Henry VI, a writ of record was delivered to the sheriff of Northampton, ordering him to arrest Anthony Wydeville knight, lord Scales and de Neusels, who on the last day of October, 6 Edward IV, before Ralph Verney, mayor of the staple of Westminster for the admission of debtors, acknowledged that he owed Geoffrey Gate knight the sum of two thousand pounds payable at Christmas next following, but as yet undischarged: and to hold the said lord in prison, causing a valuation to be made of his lands and chattels by the oath of good and lawful men, whereby this debt may be discharged, and informing the King in chancery, wherever he may be found, on the morrow of All Souls next, of the manner in which is command has been executed. Dated 19th October, 49 Henry VI"

20th October 1445

Richard Duke of York returned from France at the end of his term as Lieutenant.

Richard Duke of York had initially been given the Lieutenancy of France as a temporary measure following the Duke of Bedford's death. It had then been extended to run until 1445.

At the expiry of his tenure, it was presumed that Richard would be reappointed. Letters from King Henry VI written at Woodstock on 17th September intimated that Richard's input was required into meetings in England in October but that he would be back in Rouen by 6th November.

The Council, perhaps at Suffolk's suggestion, had also suggested to Richard that he begin negotiations for his son Edward to be married to a daughter of the French King. It was a proposal welcomed by York and one that only made diplomatic sense if the intention were to retain Richard as Lieutenant.

It was not to be, though. Truce extensions and Henry's personal policies regarding France led to delays, followed by Richard being appointed as Lieutenant of Ireland. Richard's record in France is regarded as being good. With limited resources, he restored law and order, reintroduced effective administration and ensured that Normandy would not be taken by France without a fight.

The Duchy's defensibility was compromised, though, by lack of funds forthcoming for soldiers pay and improved defences. That was a political and fiscal issue beyond Richard's control.

21st October 1449

Birth of George Plantagenet, later Duke of Clarence

George was the 3rd eldest of Richard Duke of York and Cecily Neville to survive infancy. He was born in Ireland but spent much of his childhood was spent at Ludlow.

George was created Duke of Clarence by his brother, Edward. He was then created a Knight of the Garter and was made Lord Lieutenant of Ireland for life in 1462.

During the 1460s, George spent lots of time at Middleham Castle. Despite King Edward wanting a diplomatic marriage for George, he sought Papal Dispensation to marry Isabel Neville, which was granted and whom he wed against his brother's wishes in Calais in 1469.

This was when George had allied himself with the Earl of Warwick against his brother. He made his peace with Edward and when his father-in-law, Richard Neville, was killed in the Battle of Barnet. He then became Earl of Warwick by his wife's inheritance. As this was by right of his wife, the title was passed to his son upon George being executed.

A dispute over the Warwick and Salisbury estates broke out with his brother, Richard, who was married to another of the Kingmakers daughters, Anne. Edward had to intervene to split the inheritance.

George and Isabel had 4 children, 2 of whom died in infancy. In 1476 Isabel died, shortly after childbirth. A grief-stricken George then committed several acts that further tarnished his reputation.

Finally, he sent an ex-Lancastrian to protest the innocence of a retainer at Parliament. This resulted in George being arrested, tried, and executed, reputedly drowning in a vat of Malmsey wine.

22nd October 1465

Debt recovery

One of the tests of any legal system is its ability to efficiently manage issues relating to credit and outstanding debts. In the modern world, we can apply for county court judgements.

The medieval world had a manageable system too. On 22nd October 1465, a memorandum was dispatched to the Sheriff of Middlesex relating to an outstanding debt. One Hugh Brice, a goldsmith, had failed to adhere to a recognisance made the previous November.

The method of ensuring payment is simple and straightforward. If payment is not made, Brice would be imprisoned until payment is made, the court could seize his lands and use them to recoup the debt. To ensure that the debt is fully recovered, the same memorandum is sent to all the neighbouring sheriffs.

The memorandum, from the Close Rolls of Edward IV, is as follows:

Memorandum of delivery to the sheriff of Middlesex, 5th February this year, of a writ (text follows), tested at Westminster, 22nd October, 4 Edward IV, reciting a recognisance made 19th November then last, before Geoffrey Feldynge mayor of the staple of Westminster by John lord Straunge knight, lord of Knokyn and Mowghune, to Hugh Brice citizen and goldsmith of London for 56l. payable at Easter then next and not yet paid it is said, and directing the sheriff to take and imprison the said John until the same be paid, to cause his lands and chattels to be extended and appraised and to be seized into the King's hand for livery to the said Hugh, and to certify the execution of the same in chancery; the King having given like command to the sheriffs of Buckingham, Southampton, Warwick, Oxford, Northampton, Salop and Devon.

23rd October 1455

Thomas Radford, a Justice of the King's Peace, was murdered on this day in 1455.

The murder was associated with the Courtenay-Bonnville dispute, which saw two powerful landowners in the South West engage in a private and violent feud.

Involving a Justice of the Peace, appointed by the King, is risky, even for a senior magnate.

The petition regarding the murder of Radford reads:

"...Radford was at his place called Uppecote in Cadleleigh and was in the King's peace, and   Thomas Courtenay came with others bearing arms and attacked Radford's place and set the gates of the place on fire. Radford came and admitted them after Courtenay (said) that he and his goods would be preserved. While Courtenay distracted Radford, the men stripped the place, turning Radford's sick wife out of bed and carrying all away. Afterwards Courtenay said that he had to take Radford to his father and then departed. Philip and the others then struck Radford on the head with a glaive so that his brain fell out and cut his throat. Afterwards at his burial when his body lay in his chapel, Henry Courtenay came with others and took upon him the office of coroner and held an inquest without authority. Afterwards they cast his body from the coffin into the grave and threw the stones conveyed there for Radford's tomb onto the body crushing it. Justice is requested for the ... so that an example is not set if the murder, felony and robbery pass unpunished".

24th October 1474

Treaty between King Edward IV of England and King James III of Scotland.

For the intended invasion of France to go ahead, England needed to make her peace with any who may intervene. This meant peace treaties with some nations and affirmations of trade deals, and mutual trust with others.

The most pressing of these deals was that with Scotland. If the bulk of the nobility and retainers were on campaign in France, the Scots could cause many problems through raids of an invasion of northern England. So, king Edward made terms with James III of Scotland.

"Forasmuch as this noble isle, called Great Britain, cannot be kept and maintained better in wealth and prosperity than that such things should be practiced and concluded between both the realms of Scotland and England, whereby they and their subjects might be encouraged to live in peace, love and tenderness, concluded that, considering the long continued troubles, dissensions and debates between the two realms, with great and mortal war that has followed therefrom, a nearer and more special way is to be found than merely the assurance of the present truce... The most convenient and direct road to this is to conclude a marriage between James, first born son and heir of James III and Cecily, youngest daughter of Edward IV... During the time of the truce neither shall favour or give assistance to traitors or rebels of the other..."

Treaty of Edward IV and James III of Scotland, 24th October 1474.

25th October 1460

Act of Accord.

On 10th October, Richard Duke of York had entered Parliament brandishing a sword.

Richard put forward his claim to the throne, a scenario that remains unique in English parliamentary history. The stunned Parliament had to quickly diffuse the situation.

A delegation had persuaded Richard not to proceed with an immediate coronation. The baronial Council considered Richard's claim. They accepted that he did have a better claim to the throne than King Henry VI but also agreed that it was not right to use the legal process to remove Henry in favour of Richard.

The compromise that the barons came up with was the Act of Accord.

This Act retained Henry as King until his death. It then stated that succession would pass not to the Prince of Wales but to Richard or his heirs.

Richard and his eldest son, the Earl of March, agreed to the compromise.

The Act of Accord was duly passed on 25th October 1460. It led to an immediate call to arms from Queen Margaret, who was willing to fight for her sons right to succeed.

On 31st October, the Act of Accord was extended and created Richard the Prince of Wales, Earl of Chester, Duke of Cornwall and Lord Protector of England.

26th October 1440

The Duke of Suffolk and Lord Moleyns are the only council members present with the King as a series of grants are awarded.

This was repeated on 2nd and 3rd November when Suffolk was alone with the King. It repeated a method utilised on 5th December 1439.

Such lack of openness led to a view that the King had favourites, was easily influenced and that errors were due to these evil counsellors. It was a view that would gather apace through Henry's reign.

These councillors were the ones who gained a negative reputation because of their influence over the King and underhand methods. They were not alone, though. The Duke of Gloucester was championed by some elements of the commons as being 'Good Duke Humphrey', the man who stood up for openness and fairness. Yet he also acted on his own initiative, using his office as Lord Chamberlain to endorse royal grants and, as an officer of the state, to provide one to one advice to the King: i.e. had precisely the same level of influence as those who were criticised.

There are examples of orders being taken directly to Moleyns to be placed and funded, along with petitions heard in private rather than by the appointed triers of petitions.

The usual method for awards to be granted was for Council to debate them. After which, the King would approve or decline, usually in line with the majority view. For petitions, there were several members of the commons who were appointed as triers. They were tasked with determining the merits of a petition. If it had merit, it could be taken to Parliament for debate or passed to the government's relevant administrative department. Bypassing either structure leaves officials open to charges of corruption.

27th October 1479

Letter of Archbishop Booth forbids veneration of Henry VI at York Minster.

Following the death of Henry VI in 1471, a cult emerged based on his holiness. The cult was primarily based around his, and it became hugely popular in the years after the Kings death: as a pilgrim site, it was second only to that of Thomas Becket.

In 1475 a new rood screen was installed at York Minster. Remarkably, the screen included a statue of King Henry VI. The screen and statue became a source of adoration of the King.

Soon the popularity of the statue posed a problem. It was fast becoming a shrine to the deceased Lancastrian monarch. The Yorkist regime chose to limit the reverence in which the former King was held in the City of York.

The Fabric Rolls of York Minster contain the response, and notes made by Raine, a Victorian antiquarian, who says:

"In Yorkshire, the Lancastrians were a very numerous body… In the Minsters of Ripon and York I find that there were images of him [King Henry VI] erected, to which adoration was doubtless paid… The feeling of veneration towards the royal sufferer was not extinguished, as in 1479 we find an order from Archbishop Booth, that no worship should be paid to his image".

The reason given was that there was no Papal permission for such veneration and that the King had not been laid to rest in the Minster. Such removal of the right to venerate Henry VI was not nationwide, though. It was permitted for pilgrims to visit his tomb, though this was moved during Richard IIIs reign to its present site, in Windsor.

28th October 1484

Richard III orders the Earl of Oxford's transfer from imprisonment in Calais to the more secure gaol at the Tower of London. By the time the order reaches Calais, the Earl has already escaped.

John de Vere Earl of Oxford, had been a thorn in the side of the Yorkists. He was a proven and capable commander in battle. In 1471, the Earl of Oxford prevented Edward IV from landing in Norfolk, which could quite easily have been catastrophic for the Yorkist cause.

At the battle of Barnet, his battle was, if anything, too successful. His men superbly forced Lord Hastings' men into retreat, but in the fog, were then mistaken for King Edward's force and attacked by archers from their own army. Oxford, his brothers, and Lord Beaumont escaped Barnet. They went to France where Oxford orchestrated raids, on Calais and the Essex coast, before capturing and holding St. Michael's Mount for 22 months.

He was imprisoned for this in 1474 and attained in 1475. His place of imprisonment was Hammes Castle, part of the English held Calais Pale.

The risk of an invasion under the banner of Henry Tudor made Oxford a critical prisoner. He could be an asset for the Tudors, so on 28th October 1484, King Richard III ordered his immediate transfer to the Tower of London.

However, Oxford had heard of the invasion plan and persuaded his gaoler to change his allegiance to the Lancastrian cause. By the time the message to transfer the Earl reached Calais, he had already escaped, joining Henry Tudor. Oxford went on to command part of the Tudor army at the Battle of Bosworth.

29th October 1480

Scottish attacks

On 29th October 1480, the Milanese embassy in France made an entry into their regular newsletter that Scotland had attacked England.

Such attacks were not uncommon. They had been a feature of border conflicts between the two nations throughout the medieval era. This one stands out, though. It was only 6 years earlier that Kings Edward and James had agreed a treaty that included the proposed marriage of royal children.

England had even sent an advance on the dowry of Princess Cecily. It led to a worsening of relations that later resulted in Edward's willingness to intervene in Scottish internal politics through the use of force, as agreed with the Earl of Bothwell in the Treaty of Fotheringay.

It also influences diplomatic and trade discussions, which subsequently seek to further isolate France economically.

The following is from the Milanese State Papers archive, sent from Tours to Milan on 29th October 1480:

"...the Scots have attacked the English and I think it is the handiwork of the king here (France)... I am confirmed in this opinion because I chance to have seen a letter of the King of Scotland to the king here, in which he advises him that the English made an incursion into his country, but his people had forthwith cast them out, and they had done but little harm and gone away with the worst of it... [I am] practically certain that the king here has a hand in it, since he asks him for help against the English, who are in league and close affinity with his majesty."

30th October 1485

Coronation of King Henry VII

Unusually for an event of such magnitude, there are no contemporary accounts that survive describing the coronation of Henry VII.

It is known that the legal 'device' used for the coronation ceremony, that is, the document asserting his right to be King and list of supporters, was quite simply the document that Richard had used in 1483 with names changed.

Henry is also known to have had his coronation deliberately before the opening of his first Parliament. This is because he did not want to be accountable to Parliament for his right to be King. It is an assertion of his authority over them.

One of the earliest accounts of the coronation comes in the mid 16th century. This is written by chronicler Raphael Hollingshed:

...[Henry] with great pompe... rowed unto Westminster, & there the thirtith daie of October he was with all ceremonies accustomed, anointed & crowned King, by the whole assent as well of the commons as of the nobilitie, & called Henrie the seaventh of that name... in the fortie and sixt yeare of Frederike the third then emperour of Almaine, Maximillian his sonne being newlie elected King of the Romans, in the second yeare of Charles the eight then King of France, and in fiue and twentith of king James then ruling the realme of Scotland."

31st October 1460

Battle of Stamford Bridge between the retinues of the houses of Neville and Percy.

The Neville and Percy families were the primary landholders in the North East and Yorkshire. Following the rebellion of 1405, the Percy's had been attained and their land forfeit. When the attainder was overturned, the Percy's regained their title and most, but not all, of their lands. The lands that they did not recover were now held by the Neville family. This led to animosity between the two families and their retainers.

The disagreements became increasingly violent, and law and order in the region broke down. In 1454 the most violent of these clashes occurred against the backdrop of the wider national divisions, in which the two families were firmly in opposite camps. In 1453 a clash had taken place at Heworth, as the Percy's attempted to block the Neville's attending a wedding. When Richard Duke of York became Protector, the Percy family had a problem: York was allied to the Neville family, they could now face the wrath of the government.

So, they looked for support and gained it in the form of the Duke of Exeter. Buoyed by their improved standing, some 200 men of Percy retainers and their retinues assaulted a Neville manor at Stamford Bridge, near York, on 31st October 1454.

The Neville's intercepted the force, and Lord Egremont, a Percy, was captured. He was taken to trial and found guilty, with a liability of more than £11000 against him. Lord Egremont was not a wealthy baron; his income was in the region of £100 per year, and so as he was unable to pay his debt, he was imprisoned until such time as the debt was paid on his behalf. He escaped custody in 1456 and went on to play a significant role in the conflict in the North.

November

1st November 1483

The Duke of Buckingham is brought to court following his betrayal. Legend has it that he was armed with a knife with which to kill Richard III. However, Richard refused to see him.

Henry Stafford 2nd Duke of Buckingham had risen in rebellion against Richard III in October of 1483. Buckingham had raised his standard in Brecon, assured of the support of his retainers and other nobles. At the same time, Henry Tudor had been formulating a plan to land in the South West.

Buckingham's plot soon faced problems. Many of the men who he believed would rally to his cause failed to materialise. One of the retainers, Sir Robert Vaughan, waited for Buckingham to leave Breckon Castle and promptly ransacked it as he despised the Tudors as his father had been executed by them.

Soon, King Richard heard of the revolt. A royal muster was called. Buckingham's force was already smaller than intended, so the odds were against him. Things got worse. Heavy rain demoralised his men, and many deserted. The Duke now stood no chance of winning any pitched battle. He went into hiding.

A £1000 reward on the Duke's head was enough for him to be betrayed by Ralph Bannaster, the retainer whose home he was hiding in. Buckingham was duly arrested by the Sheriff of Shropshire. From there, he was taken to London. Legend has it that he was armed with a knife as he sought an audience with the King. Whether or not that is true is immaterial. Richard refused to see him. The following day, Buckingham suffered the ignominy of being taken into Leicester's marketplace and, without any trial, beheaded outside the Blue Boar Inn.

2nd November 1470

Edward, the future Edward V, is born

Edward was born in Westminster Abbey, where his mother, Elizabeth Woodville, had taken sanctuary following King Edward's need to go into exile. Following his fathers return to the throne, he was created Prince of Wales and Earl of Chester on 26th June 1471. The lords spiritual and temporal pledged their allegiance to the young prince the following week.

His land interests were managed by a council and gradually were added to over the 1470s, granted the Earldom of Pembroke and his fathers' earlier title of Earl of March. His upbringing was dominated by his mother's family, the Woodville's. This posed problems when King Edward IV died as it was believed that they would wield too much influence and act in their own interests rather than the young kings own.

The Kings uncle, Richard, had Earl Rivers arrested and imprisoned. Soon the planned coronation of Edward was postponed. His brother joined him in the Tower of London to prepare for that coronation. The Tower was a palace as well as a gaol at that time. The coronation never happened. A sermon was made proclaiming that King Edward IV had been contracted to marry Eleanor Talbot before his marriage to Elizabeth Woodville. It was confirmed by a member of the clergy.

Edward V was soon found to be illegitimate by Parliament. He was in effect, the King that never was. He and his brother remained in the Tower. Sightings of the pair gradually reduced. Soon rumours spread about the possible fate of the boys, known now as the Princes in the Tower.

3rd November 1456

Edmund Tudor died of the Plague

Edmund Tudor was stepbrother to King Henry VI and the brother of Jasper Tudor. Edmund was created Earl of Richmond in 1452 on the same day that Jasper was created Earl of Pembroke.

Margaret Beaufort, then ten years old, was placed in Edmunds wardship. She was a wealthy heiress and descended from Edward III through John of Gaunt. Edmund and Margaret married soon afterwards. Remarkably at the age of ten, this being Margaret's second marriage, her first one having been annulled.

The Tudor brothers managed to avoid lots of the early tensions between factions at court. They had good relationships with the House of York on a regional level until after the First Battle of St. Albans. At that point, Edmund seized the opportunity to assert his authority in Wales, taking Carmarthen Castle from Gruffudd ap Nicholas.

This provoked a response from Yorkists. As soon as news of the Castle being taken reached the Welsh Marches, William Herbert and Sir Walter Deveraux assembled an army of 2000 men and set about quickly retaking the Castle.

Edmund was imprisoned. His imprisonment did not last long, but whilst in captivity, he had contracted the plague. He died of it on 3rd November 1456. His wife, Margaret Beaufort, was pregnant when Edmund died. The couple's son was named Henry and later became the first of the Tudor monarchs.

4th November 1461

A series of attainders are issued.

An attainder is a legal device used by Parliament to strip somebody of their rights, titles, or lands, or all of those. They could be applied solely to the person in question, who would be a traitor to the realm, or have it applied to their heirs as well. The latter was usually reserved for the most serious offenders, where they held a position or title of considerable significance, such as a claim to the crown.

In the November 1461 Parliament, such a set of attainders were issued for the leading Lancastrians. It was unusual for any noblewoman to be attained, but Margaret of Anjou's actions were considered worthy of such. A separate document of attainder was drawn up for lesser nobles, knights and gentry who had fought against Edward.

Margaret, in consideration of her transgressions and offences... [be] convicted and attainted of high treason. And that the same Margaret and also the said Edward her son shall be legally unable, and taken, held, deemed and considered unable and unworthy, to have, occupy, hold, inherit or enjoy any estate, name of dignity, pre-eminence or possessions ... the same Margaret and Edward her son shall forfeit to our said liege lord King Edward IV all the castles, manors, lordships, honours, lands and tenements... And also that the said Henry, Duke of Somerset, Thomas Courtenay, late earl of Devon, Henry, late earl of Northumberland, Thomas, Lord Roos, John, late Lord Clifford, and John, late Lord Neville, shall be legally unable forever henceforth to have, hold, inherit or enjoy any name of dignity, estate or pre-eminence within the same realm...

5th November 1484

A Commission of Array issued in Bridgport enables William Herbert to muster men to tackle rebels against Richard's rule.

William Herbert and his brother Walter were both issued with Commissions of Array in the November of 1484. The invasion of Henry Tudor was expected. It was known that there were sympathisers to the Tudor cause in Wales, particularly the south, where the Herbert brothers held lands and titles that had previously been held by the Tudor family.

The Herbert's muster and their actions have led to a debate about their allegiances. Charged with stopping the rebels, Herbert did not engage them. It could be said that his role was merely to prevent the Tudor invasion force marching directly east through his lands. Two counter-arguments have been put forward to suggest that he was actually in collusion with Tudor.

First, once it was apparent that Tudor was marching north with his full army, Herbert could quite easily have engaged the relatively small invasion force, he did not. Second, he was granted a full and unusually detailed pardon by Henry VII as early as 1486.

Furthermore, Herbert was granted titles by Henry VII at an early stage in his reign. The Earldom of Pembroke was removed from him as it was traditionally a Tudor title. That of Earl of Huntingdon is used in parliamentary records in 1486, in his pardon, and in reconfirming his rights in 1488.

Herbert may well have stuck fastidiously to a command from Richard III in the build-up to Bosworth. He may have opted to sit out the battle for the crown, hoping for the favour of the victor. Or he may, like Rhys ap Thomas, have determined to aid a fellow Welshman in his cause.

6th November 1461

Death of John Mowbray, 3rd Duke of Norfolk

John Mowbray 3rd Duke of Norfolk, is perhaps best remembered for his decisive role at the Battle of Towton. His force was marching to catch up with the Yorkist army. It did so as the battle raged and where the outcome was far from certain. His battle entered the fray and though weary from marching, were fresh compared to those who had fought all day.

The intervention saw the collapse of the Lancastrian line and many men's subsequent slaughter as they fled down the slope towards Cock Beck.

Norfolk's life before the Wars of the Roses had been eventful. A significant power within East Anglia, he had regularly clashed with neighbours over land rights.

In the 1430s, he became involved in feuds with William de la Pole that became quite violent. Twice this led to his imprisonment in the Tower of London before being bound over with large bonds secured against hh8s future conduct.

His aggressive streak did serve him and the country well, though. Norfolk fought in the Anglo-Scottish wars in Normandy and served from Calais.

As court became, factionalised Norfolk had initially been loyal to the Court Party. His allegiance drifted towards the Yorkists over the course of the 1450s, and by the events of 1460, he was a firm supporter of the Duke of York.

7th November 1485

Attainder of Richard III

The first Parliament of Henry VII soon set about the task of delegitimising the reign of Richard III.

It also dated Richard's attainder to 21st August, meaning that those who fought for him had committed treason against King Henry VII.

This is incredibly savvy politically. Those who had fought against Henry Tudor would now need to consider their positions very carefully, as not submitting to Henry would now result in the full weight of law being used against them.

The attainder reads:

"Therefore, our sovereign lord, calling to his blessed remembrance this high and great charge enjoined on his royal majesty and estate, not oblivious or unmindful of the unnatural, wicked and great perjuries, treasons, homicides and murders, in shedding infants' blood, with many other wrongs, odious offences and abominations against God and man, and in particular against our said sovereign lord, committed and done by Richard, late duke of Gloucester, calling and naming himself, by usurpation, King Richard III; who... on 21st August in the first year of the reign of our said sovereign lord [1485], gathered a great host at Leicester.. traitorously intending, plotting and conspiring the destruction of the royal person of the king, our sovereign liege lord... from the said 21st August until the following 22nd August, when they led them to a field within the said county of Leicester, and there by premeditated intent traitorously levied war against our said sovereign lord and his true subjects present in his service and assistance under the banner of our said sovereign lord, to the overthrow of this realm and its common weal".

8th November 1476

Governance of the north

Richard Duke of Gloucester is considered to have established personal dominance in the North East of England. He held sway in large tracts of the region, the Earl of Northumberland in other areas and the two worked in tandem to establish fair and just administration of the region.

Richard, as an overlord, was establishing structures that later became enshrined in his Council of the North. Not everything was quite as fair and transparent as it seemed, though.

Whilst Gloucester and Northumberland had spheres of influence, there were cases of manors being held within each other's areas. This could lead to low-level disagreement, as illustrated in this letter written on 8th November 1476 by Godfrey Green to Sir William Plumpton:

"...contained in your writing to inform you the lords and their counsel of the misgovernances of Gascoigne and his affinity [in Knaresborough], it is thought by your council here that it would be disworshipful to my Lord of Northumberland who was the chief rule there under the king... [As] for the message to my lord chamberlain (Hastings), when I laboured to him that you might be justice of the peace [in West Yorkshire], he answered thus: that it seemed your labour and mine that we would make a jealousy between my Lord of Northumberland and him..., Sir, I took that for a watchword fir meddling between lords..."

9th November 1458

Attempted assassination of the Earl of Warwick

Tensions between the rival factions at court built even after the Loveday procession. The kings attempt at reconciling the different parties had a short-term effect.

Compensation orders were made against the Yorkists, and both factions had agreed to maintain the peace. It was a hollow promise. In the north, it served only to encourage the feud. In London, the large retinues accompanying the magnates continued to be ever present. At some point, those retinues would clash.

That happened on 9th November 1458. The English Chronicle states:

"[On 9th November], the King and Queen being at Westminster, there occurred a great quarrel between Richard Earl of Warwick and men of the King's household, so much so that they would have slain the earl [had he not] escaped to his barge and went soon after to Calais, of which he had been made Captain shortly before by authority of Parliament. Soon afterwards the young Duke of Somerset, by canvassing those who hated the Earl of Warwick, became captain of Calais, and a privy seal was directed to the earl in discharge to him of the captainship; however the earl, for asmuch as he had been made captain by authority of Parliament, would not obey the privy seal but continued exercising the office for many years after…"

The Earl of Warwick evaded harm and made his way to Calais. It was a stark reminder to him and the other Yorkist Lords that the political differences between themselves and the court party could quite easily prove to be fatal.

10th November 1433

Birth of Charles the Bold

Charles the Bold of Burgundy played a key role in the Wars of the Roses. Charles' influence over English affairs was significant. In 1468 he married Margaret of York, sister of King Edward IV. This led to Edward, the Duke of Gloucester and many of their supporters seeking refuge in Burgundy as Warwick forced the Readeption of Henry VI.

Though Charles was initially reluctant to become involved in English wars, the French's actions made it beneficial for him to have a strong Yorkist government in England. In 1471 he supported the invasion of England by Edward IV with finances fleet and soldiers.

This led to a close relationship between England and Burgundy for much of the reign of Edward IV. English archers fought alongside Burgundian forces on the continent during the quieter periods of the 1470s. Charles agreed to join England and Brittany in an invasion of France. In the event, Burgundy did not participate in that expedition as they were engaged in conflict with the Holy Roman Empire. However, the alliance was a crucial part in securing a deal that was beneficial to England.

Charles also oversaw Burgundy's economic policies, and these saw the trade in wool and cloth between England and Calais prosper. Via the port of Calais, merchants from both states enjoyed increasingly peaceful travel across the channel and customs arrangements were introduced to boost Burgundian trade.

Charles the Bold died in January of 1477. His wife Margaret continued to be influential, and Burgundy financed Yorkist pretenders and rebellions against the Tudors long after Charles' death.

11th November 1430

Marriage of William de la Pole to Alice Chaucer

Alice Chaucer was the granddaughter of the famous writer, Geoffrey. She was a wealthy heiress who had been married twice before. William de la Pole was the Duke of Suffolk, who became one of the kings leading ministers.

The union of Alice and William came at a time when both were enjoying a rise in influence. William received positions in France in 1430, Alice became a Lady of the Garter in 1432. Both retained this level of influence as the young King came of age.

In 1444 it was William who oversaw negotiations for King Henry VI's marriage to Margaret of Anjou. Alice was one of the Ladies dispatched to France to escort the King's bride to England. Alice and Queen Margaret became close friends, and Alice remained a Lady in waiting until the outbreak of war.

William's stock also rose. He became increasingly important to the King and became seen by the commons as one of the corrupt counsellors responsible for the failings of government. The same charge was laid against him in Parliament, which impeached William in 1450.

Found guilty, William de la Pole was forced into exile. However, he was murdered as he sailed to Calais. Alice continued to play a role in court following the death of her husband. Their son married Elizabeth of York, sister of Edward, George, and Richard.

Following the collapse of Lancastrian resistance following King Henry VI and Prince Edward's deaths, the former Queen Margret was placed into the care of her former Lady in waiting. Alice Chaucer died in 1475.

12th November 1472

Anne of York secures an annulment

Anne of York was the eldest daughter of Richard Duke of York and Cecily Neville. Aged eight, she had married the seventeen-year-old Henry Holland, Duke of Exeter, in 1447.

Exeter was an ideal marriage match for Anne. At the time, England had few Dukes of Royal Blood, so a union with Henry was as good a match as possible without marrying a lord from overseas. With Anne having parents from the two most powerful families in the land, it also potentially had enormous benefits for Exeter.

The marriage, however, did not work out very well. As England descended into war, the spouses found themselves supporting opposing sides in the conflict. Anne made it clear that she was supportive first of her father and Edward, her brother and later King.

Exeter had gained a reputation as a violent hot-headed young noble. He had been rebuked on several occasions for his methods in the South West and became known for his cruelty as Constable of the Tower of London.

He fought for the Lancastrians at Towton, fled to Wales, where he fought alongside Jasper Tudor, then went into exile in Ireland. He and Anne spent many years apart as a result and only produced one child.

In 1471 Exeter was severely injured and left for dead on the battlefield at Barnet. Once her brother had secured the crown once more, Anne petitioned her brother to have the marriage annulled.

The formalities of the process were completed on 12th November 1472. Anne went on to marry Thomas St. Ledger of her brother's household.

13th November 1462

Margaret of Anjou and King Henry VI sail from Northumbria to the safety of Scotland

In November of 1462, King Edward IV was determined to extinguish Lancastrian resistance in the North East. A short-term truce had been negotiated with Scotland earlier in the year. The fleet had been readied for war. Edward planned and, in November, made for the north. He issued commissions of array as he marched on the pocket of resistance.

With just a few castles holding out for Henry VI, supported by a severely depleted armed force, the situation looked quite desperate for the Lancastrians. Some support had come from France, and there was sympathy and some military aid from Scotland. It was not enough to survive a siege from Edward's army. The Yorkist fleet was being loaded with artillery from the royal arsenals. It was only a matter of time before Margaret, Henry, and Prince Edward would be captured.

Faced with these odds, Queen Margaret saw that the royal family had little choice but to go into exile. Symbolically it was important to have a foothold in England. Pragmatically, they needed to be able to fight another day.

So, Margaret set about organising for the royal party to be secreted to Scotland. It would be a difficult task. Edward had ordered the Earl of Douglas to use the Newcastle Fleet to harass the Lancastrian held castles in the region. The weather, too, would make even a short journey to Scotland arduous.

On 13th November 1462, the escape from the northeast took place. The weather did hinder the short voyage, the royal party being lucky to reach Berwick unscathed.

14th November 1468

Execution of Richard Stairs

November 1468 was a period of plotting. Many people were implicated as the machinations of Warwick, and Clarence began to undermine the regime. Sir William Plumpton was:

'committed to the Tower, and, it [was] said, kept in irons, and [had] confessed many things' but faced no further punishment. Others were less fortunate. Richard Stairs, described as being 'one of the cunningest players at tennis in England' was, on 14th November, 'drawn through the city [of London] and beheaded at Tower Hill… And upon the morrow following were drawn through the city to Tyburn two gentlemen named [William] Alford and [John] Poynings to be executed. But then when they came thither, and the hangman had fastened the cords to the gallows, their pardon was shown, and they were saved…' (Great Chronicle of London).

Historian Charles Ross suggests that Alford and Poynings were executed. Further to this, another source also claims that Alford and Poynings were executed, on a different date. There is a suggestion that the executions went ahead on 28th November.

The crime though, is not disputed. Each of the men was accused of passing treasonable correspondence. This was to the Lancastrians and to rebels in Calais. Others implicated in the plots, according to the Croyland Chronicle, were:

'…many nobles and great men of the kingdom, as well as very many bishops and abbots, were accused before the King of treason.'

15th November 1460

The Gates of Durham are reinforced

Following the Battle of Northampton, Queen Margaret had fled to Wales before moving north to Scotland. A call to arms was sent to those followers who remained loyal to her cause. The call was answered by the Earl of Northumberland and Earl of Westmoreland.

Both Earls issued arrays throughout their lands. As the area was so used to being arrays due to the wardenship of the marches, the Earls raised a sizeable army in a short amount of time. The armies mustered to the north of Durham. Once the full complement of men had arrived, the Earls marched to York and Pomfret (Pontefract).

Wary of the Scots taking advantage of their march south, the Earls ordered that Durham's gates be closed and reinforced once they had passed through. This took place on 15th November 1460.

The significance of this rapid array and deployment is enormous. Pontefract is adjacent to the Duke of York's lands, in which Sandal Castle can be found. News of the large army appearing so close to his own lands must have startled the Yorkist lords.

Such a large force put the Yorkists control of Government and the Act of Accord at risk. The only practical solution to the problem was to face the Queen's army.

The Duke of York gathered an army and marched to Sandal. This led directly to the Battle of Wakefield, in which he, his son Edmund and the Earl of Salisbury fell.

In the event, reinforcing the gates of Durham was unnecessary. The scots formed an alliance with Queen Margaret and sent an army to support her campaign.

16th November 1485

Henry VIIs first Parliament discusses the validity of the Yorkist Kings actions.

The Colchester Roll provides a summary of the events of the first Parliament of King Henry VII. On 16th November 1485, the roll states that:

'there ware qwestionns moved for the comenwell of thise false persons which hath reyned many dayes amongs us and non conclusion.'

The motives behind this are open to interpretation. The comenwell is the common people, in the form of petitions to Parliament. It also relates in some contexts to false coinage, common wealth.. 'thise false persons' are undoubtedly the two Yorkist Kings, Edward IV and Richard III. The non conclusion part of the statement suggests that a move was made to draw a line under the policies of Richard III and therefore the question was: what happens now? Do the actions and laws of the previous two kings remain intact, or are they void?

This would have been a difficult issue for Henry VII to address. He could not simply void everything done by the Yorkist Kings, yet at the same time he had to assert both his own authority. It was further complicated by the fact that some of his own supporters had been in Edward IVs household, and he was due to marry Elizabeth of York.

If such a petition was discussed, little came of it. Henry retained the elements of Yorkist governance that appealed to him and amended those that did not. This can be seen in the way in which the restoration of lands was administered. No longer could the restored lord claim compensation for the revenues paid to another lord in the period in which they had been held by another lord.

17th November 1485

Bill of the Countess of Warwick heard in Parliament

The Dowager Countess of Warwick had been the wife of Warwick the Kingmaker. Upon his death, there was a period in which there was fiery debate over what should happen to this inheritance: complicated by the Kingmakers daughters' marriages to George duke of Clarence and Richard Duke of Gloucester.

An Act of Parliament settled the matter in 1474, granting the lands not to the Countess but to the two Dukes by right of their wives. On 17th November 1485, she sought to overturn the 1474 Act of Parliament that had formalised that forfeiture. The Countess's argument was:

And that the same Isabell and Anne, the doughters, shuld be heires of blode to the seid countesse, and so be reputed and taken frothensforth, and to have, sue and take all maner of accions, sutes, entres, particions, avauntegez, profites and commodites as heires of the seid countesse, and to all other their auncestres, in like wyse and forme as yf the seid countesse had ben then naturally ded. Source: Parliamentary Roll, Henry VII, November 1485 Parliament.

In effect, the argument is that the inheritance was unlawfully passed to the two Yorkist princes. Given that Richard had become the King whom Henry VII had defeated in battle, you may think that there would be a sympathetic ear. There was not. Richard's lands had become forfeit to Henry VII upon Tudor's accession to the throne; restoring the lands would cost him personally dearly.

Instead, Henry agreed to pay the Countess an annuity of 500 marks a year. At Henry's next Parliament, the 1474 Act was repealed as part of a settlement that saw the Countess hand back all lands except one manor, which she retained for her own upkeep.

18th November 1477

William Caxton prints Anthony Woodville, Earl Rivers translation of 'Dictes and Sayings of the Philosophers'

In 1473 Anthony Woodville, Earl Rivers was lent a copy of an Arabic book's French translation. It was a compilation of sayings from philosophers from across the ancient world. It contained words of wisdom from prophets, philosophers and even from myths and legends. Earl Rivers took the book with him on a pilgrimage to Santiago de Compostela. Whilst on pilgrimage, he translated it into English.

At around the same time, William Caxton established a printing press in Bruges from where he produced the first ever printed book in English: The Recuyell of the Historyes of Troye [The history of Troy]. Successful in Bruges, Caxton then moved to Westminster in 1476 to establish himself in England.

Caxton had possibly already printed a book in Westminster before becoming aware of the Earls work. However, a man as influential as Rivers was an ideal candidate for his first printed publications. Therefore, he took the manuscript and set about making it ready for print.

He added an epilogue to the Earls manuscript and made two firsts in the history of the English language. Firstly, he dated the book. All of Caxton's earlier works were undated. Secondly, he included a Colophon. This is the printer's imprint on a book which we would recognise today as a publisher's logo.

The book was printed on 18th November 1477. It was reproduced on several occasions using Caxton's press.

19th November 1455

Richard Duke of York appointed protector and defender of the realm

With King Henry VI once again unable to rule, a protector was required. The Yorkists, having been victorious at the First Battle of St. Albans, were in the ascendancy. Therefore, the commons petitioned for Richard Duke of York to be appointed to the role. The Chancery Patent Rolls record the event:

'Appointment, on petition of the Commons in the present Parliament, of Richard Duke of York as protector and defender of the realm and church, and the king's principal councillor, until he be discharged by the king in Parliament by the advice and assent of the lords spiritual and temporal, [the duke's] authority ceasing when Edward, the king's first-born son, comes to years of discretion and wishes to assume the charge of protector and defender.'

Unlike his first appointment to this role, York was in the ascendancy when invited to take it. This does not mean that he had a consensus government, though: his power bloc was the Neville family and their followers.

He faced problems almost immediately. Lawlessness between nobles in the South-West had flared up and had to be dealt with. Richard sent the offending parties to the Tower. There was also the matter of the nation's finances. Much land had been granted in such a way that it would generate income for the crown. This had been to the dismay of some of the nobility.

The Duke attempted to resolve the matter through a Bill of Resumption. By the time King Henry recovered, this Bill had not been fully implemented due to many requests for exemptions and was quickly dropped upon Henry's return to the throne.

20th November 1459

Parliament of Devils

Following the Battle of Blore Heath, the political situation was complicated. Forces loyal to the crown had attacked the Earl of Salisbury and lost. The Yorkists had not retaliated with the use of force. They had continued to make the point that they were loyal subjects wanting reform.

This presented the King, his advisors, and the highly influential Queen Margaret with a dilemma. As the Yorkists had not attacked, it was not them at fault. So, a political and military solution to the situation had to be planned.

The solution was twofold. Militarily a royal army, was sent to face the Yorkists. Politically, a Parliament was called to be held in the Lancastrian stronghold of Coventry. The summons to the Parliament was quite telling. The Duke of York and Earls of Salisbury and Warwick were not invited. This sent a clear message to the Yorkist lords. They would be impeached at best, more likely they would be attained, and if charged with treason, they could be executed.

As a result, the Yorkist lords were pushed into a corner. At Ludford, they set out to face the royal army in battle but had to flee when men defected.

This left the royal party free to proceed at Parliament. In Coventry, many Yorkists were attained. Some were charged with wishing the kings death, a treasonable offence. Lands and titles were stripped, and the Yorkists were forced into exile. For Queen Margaret, this was a huge political victory. Her opponents were overseas, their estates confiscated, and their strength significantly diminished. In theory, she had wrestled control of the country from York and his allies.

21st November 1485

Reversal of the attainder on King Henry VI

One aspect of the Tudor regime's establishment was the restoration of King Henry VI. Henry VI, and his family had been attained by the Yorkists.

This needed to be reversed by Henry VII as part of the legitimisation process. Henry VI was his uncle. His father and other uncles, the late King Henry Vis half-brothers, were also affected by this attainder and so, through birth, was the new King himself.

His own attainder had been accepted as being overturned by virtue of his victory at Bosworth. He now set about the process of legally restoring his family's rights and privileges.

This extract from the Parliamentary roll outlines the key points:

"…and all actes of atteynder, forfeture and disablement made or hadde in the said parliament or in any parliament of the said late Kynge Edwarde, ayenst the said moste blessed prince Kyng Herry, or ayenst the right famous princesse Margarete, late quene of Englande, his wife, or the right victorious prince Edwarde, late prince of Wales, sonne of the same blessed Kynge Herry and Margarete, Jasper duke of Bedford, late erle of Penbroke, or Herry late duke of Somerset, the whiche Jasper and Herry late duke of Somerset, for their true allegeaunces and servicez doon to the same blessed Kynge Herry, were atteynted of high treason, or eny of theym, by what name or names they or any of theym be named in any of the said actes, be ayenst the said blessed Kynge Herry, Quene Margarete, Edwarde late prince, and the same dukes, and the heires of every of theym, voyde, adnulled, repelled and of no force ne effecte".

22nd November 1455

Requests made to the City of Exeter

On 22nd November 1455, the Earl of Devon asked the Mayor of Exeter, Hugh Germyn, to keep the Bonville family's forces away from the city in the absence of his own men. Germyn replied that the people of Exeter 'were and beth the kynges tenaunts and this is the kynges Cite'. The city was at the heart of lands in which the violent dispute between the Courtenay's and Bonville's was being fought out.

The rivalry between the Courtenay's, the Earl of Devon, and the Bonville's, a prominent local baronial family, had developed over several years. Traditionally the Earl of Devon would be the most prominent noble in the region. However, the Bonville family had grown in importance and power. This led to disputes over land and appointments to regional offices of government.

In the 1440s, there were attempts at arbitration between the two families. The peace ended abruptly in 1449 when the Earl of Devon lay siege to a Bonville held Castle. There followed a period in which the Courtenay's raided manors held by the Bonville's and their retainers. A lawyer, Nicholas Radford, was murdered by the Earls men, leading to widespread condemnation of their actions.

The Earl of Devon's request to the City of Exeter was designed to further those raids. Exeter, knowing of the actions of liveried men inside London's walls, chose to refuse the request. It was in their interests to remain neutral.

The feud led to intervention by Richard duke of York during his protectorate. It was prompted by a small battle at Clyst. Richard's involvement complicated things as the Bonville family were allied to Yorkist lords. Consequently, the regional dispute fed into the growing problems nationally.

23rd November 1450

Richard Duke of York enters London brandishing his sword

The Parliament of 1450 began at a time of great unrest. Earlier in the year, there had been two rebellions. The revolt led by Jack Cade being the most serious. The complaints of those rebels were shared by some of the nobility. The Dukes of York and Norfolk and the earls of Salisbury and Warwick were chief among those complainants. This parliamentary session was set to be a contentious one. The 'loyal opposition' argued that the government was being mismanaged by men such as the Duke of Somerset.

To reinforce their position and influence parliament, the Yorkist lords made a show of strength. Each of them riding into London in armour and at the head of a body of men. Bale's Chronicle summarises the events of 23rd November and the following days:

'the Duke of York, with him 3000 men and more, came riding through the city, his sword borne before him, and rode to Parliament and the King. And on the following morning, came riding through the city the Duke of Norfolk with a great crowd of men in body armour, and six trumpets blowing before him. The, on the following morning, the Earl of Warwick came through the city with a great company arrayed for war, and there was [on the 30th] a dreadful storming and noise of the commons, crying and saying to the lords: 'do justice upon the false traitors or let us be avenged.'

This show of strength is partly to press for reform and target the Duke of Somerset, who was a political foe of the Yorkists. The action can be seen as the start of the road to Dartford' where the two factions faced each other without blows in 1452.

24th November 1492

Death of Louis of Gruuthuse Earl of Winchester.

Louis of Gruuthuse is an unusual English noble. He was not English. Nor was he resident in England. Indeed, Gruuthuse never really did anything of note concerning affairs on English soil or in terms of his title. So, who was he, and how did he become the Earl of Winchester?

In times of conflict, it was typical of the victors to reward their supporters. Most common were those who had fought, provided retainers and men at arms, finance or managed the administrative side of the conflict.

Yet Louis of Gruuthuse was none of those.

He was Flemish. Louis fought in the army of Burgundy in continental wars against Ghent. A regular at the Burgundian court, he was created a Knight of the Golden Fleece. He was later appointed as the lieutenant-general of The Hague, with administrative control over Zeeland, Frisia and Holland.

A patron of the arts, Gruuthuse was one of the foremost collectors of the era's illuminated manuscripts and commissioned several books.

Hardly the type of background to earn somebody an English Earldom.

There are two reasons why he was created the Earl of Winchester. First, was the fact that he had negotiated the marriage of Margaret of York to Charles the Bold of Burgundy. More pertinent is the second reason. When Edward IV and other leading Yorkists were forced into exile, Louis arranged their accommodation and ensured their safety. Once Burgundy chose to support an invasion, he oversaw the administrative side of the plans. Put simply, without Louis of Gruuthuse's assistance, Edward may not have regained his throne.

25th November 1487

Coronation of Elizabeth of York

In September 1487, writs were dispatched summoning the nobility to the Coronation of Elizabeth. The ceremony was to be held at Westminster Abbey on 25th November. Evidence suggests that the original plan had been for a joint coronation, as a book of ceremonial for both Elizabeth and Henry had been drawn up before Henry's enthronement.

Elizabeth's own coronation plans were hampered by her pregnancy with Prince Arthur and the rebellion by Yorkists led by the Earl of Lincoln. Once Elizabeth was recovered from her pregnancy, and the rebellion quashed, plans were made in earnest.

Elizabeth arrived in London by barge. She was escorted by many others, including one that carried a fire breathing Welsh Dragon. New Knights of the Bath were created to mark the occasion. The following day a grand procession through the City of London took place. She was dressed in white cloth of gold, and there was wine flowing from the conduits.

On the day of the coronation, Elizabeth wore a purple cloak and ermine. She was escorted by the officers of state whilst her train was carried by her sister. With unity perhaps in mind, her Ladies in Waiting came from all sides of earlier conflicts. The curious missing guest was her mother, Elizabeth Woodville, who was not present for reasons we can only speculate upon.

The ceremony itself took place in Westminster Abbey. Elizabeth walked barefoot from Westminster Hall and then was anointed as Queen of England. Following the coronation, she returned to Westminster Hall, where a banquet was held in her honour.

26th November 1470

Parliament attains Edward IV and Richard, Duke of Gloucester.

November 1470 saw Parliament under the control of the Earl of Warwick. This followed Warwick's pact with Margaret of Anjou, carefully orchestrated uprisings in the north and Warwick's return in the south.

Edward, facing overwhelming odds, had little choice but to evade being captured. He chose to go to the safety of his sister's court in Burgundy. Following the flight into exile of the King and Duke of Gloucester, Warwick sought to consolidate his position.

With King Henry VI's readaptation in mind, crown properties needed to be taken from the outgoing regime and passed to the returning Lancastrian Monarch. Furthermore, the rights of Edward and his children to the crown needed to be extinguished. The legal mechanism through which this could be achieved was an Act of Attainder. The parliamentary roll containing the wording of the attainder has been lost. We do know that Edward IV and Richard Duke of Gloucester were both attained, though.

An Act of Attainder typically strips somebody of their lands, income, titles, rank, rights to inherit and rights to legal recourse. Some attainders extended to the attained person's line, thus removing any possibility of an heir making a claim in years to come. In Edward and Richard's case, it is almost certain that the full range of measures would have been applied. It was a punitive measure designed to remove all influence that the pair had on English soil.

An Act of Attainder against an anointed king would be one of the first items of business, and so 26th November is assumed to be the date upon which the Act was passed.

27th November 1469

General pardon issued by King Edward IV

In 1469 the Earl of Warwick had seized control of King Edward IV and placed him under close guard. The earl then attempted to rule in the Kings name. Parliament and the Lords, however, were not warm to the idea of Warwick taking control. Powerful he may be, popular he was not. The King was released, presumably with Warwick believing he could still be controlled through the sheer weight of economic and military might.

The return of the King to his throne and seat of government presented a political challenge for Warwick. Arms had been raised against royal forces. The King himself had been taken into custody. Many men, including Warwick and the King's brother, the Duke of Clarence, were guilty of treasonable acts. Edward may not be easy to control. Especially as he knew that many of the Lords had opposed rule by Warwick. The Milanese State Papers provide an insight as to the mood at the time:

"...as it seems that king is much beloved by the men of that city, while the earl is hated, and the king is making efforts to raise as large a force as he can to go against the Earl of Warwick" Milanese State Papers, 20th November

So, he had to decide how to deal with the rebels. If he attained them, he risked a return of warfare. If he did nothing, he appears weak. He needed a middle ground that enabled the Duke of Clarence and Earl of Warwick an opportunity to be involved in elements of government whilst also making a statement.

The statement came in the form of a general pardon. At first glance, it may appear that this is doing nothing. It is not, it is giving a clear sign to those who have been pardoned that they have had their chance.

28th November 1499

Execution of Edward Plantagenet, Earl of Warwick

Edward Plantagenet Earl of Warwick was born in 1475. His parents were George Duke of Clarence and Isabel Neville, through whom he inherited the earldom of Warwick. With such illustrious parents, Edward was a significant person from birth. On one side of his family, he had royal blood. On the other, he had the Neville connections and the power that this line could bring to bear.

Following his father's trial, execution and posthumous attainder, Edward had been removed from the line of succession to the throne.

His status was such that his uncle, Richard III, saw little threat from the young boy either at the time or in the longer term. In 1485 when Henry Tudor was victorious at the Battle of Bosworth, Edward was taken into safekeeping in the Palace of the Tower of London. Here he was detained but in comfortable quarters.

Edward's significance increased following the failure of the 1487 invasion led by the Earl of Lincoln and the later capture of Perkin Warbeck. With the pretenders to the throne captured, the Princes in the Tower presumably dead and Lincoln himself dead, Edward was the remaining male from the House of York. If there was to be another Yorkist revolt, it would need to be in his name.

Edward and Perkin Warbeck were imprisoned in adjacent cells. It was alleged by their gaoler that the pair had been overheard plotting to escape from the Tower. We can only guess how true this is, and it is possible that the allegation was concocted. Nonetheless, it provided Henry VII with the grounds to have the pair tried. They were found guilty, and on 28th November 1499, Edward Plantagenet was beheaded on Tower Hill.

29th November 1422

Thomas Percy Lord Egremont, born in 1422

Thomas Percy was the second son of Henry Percy, 2nd Earl of Northumberland. As a young man, he demonstrated a violent aptitude. He and a band of his men became renowned for troublemaking in the north. In 1447, this led to Thomas and a group of his men being imprisoned in York gaol because of their repeated misconduct.

Upon release from gaol, Thomas soon found himself fighting again. This time, however, it was defending Cumberland against a Scottish raid. He performed this task well and, as a result, was created Lord Egremont on 10th November 1449. The grant of a title provided him with an annuity that he used to form a group of retainers.

With these men, Lord Egremont then began a series of raids against the family's fierce rivals, the Neville family. These raids raised tensions in Yorkshire and the North East, driving a wedge between the two most powerful landholders in the region and contributing to the factionalism regionally and nationally.

The most significant of Egremont's attacks were the Battles of Heworth Moor (1453) and Stamford Bridge (1454). His troublesome nature led to demands that he appear in court and prepare to fight in Gascony, neither of which he did.

As the Wars of the Roses began, Egremont and the rest of the Percy family fought on the Lancastrian side. He was present at the First Battle of St. Albans and was summoned to the Great Council and Loveday. As war erupted again, he fought at the Battle of Northampton, where he was killed in the fighting.

30th November 1472

With England at peace and little threat to his throne, Edward IV decided to resurrect the English claim to the French crown. He mooted the idea before the uprisings of 1469 but had squandered the monies granted by Parliament.

Edward approached Parliament to ask for funding for a new expedition. Parliament was wary, given the previous grant had not been used for the intended purpose. It agreed but on condition that it was to be released following muster and with deadlines in place for the last date of the expedition setting sail.

That Parliament even entertained such a grant is due to the planning that had made such an invasion viable. France and Normandy had been lost in part due to the collapse of support from continental powers.

Edward had sent envoys to negotiate with the key states who could make an invasion successful. An agreement was made with the powerful Duchy of Burgundy, which would see their army attack France at the same time as the English further to the west. This would split the French army and make victory and the road to Paris much more achievable. Agreements were also made with the Bretons. An assault by their forces, supported by some English archers, would have France attacked from the northeast on two fronts and from the west.

Edward agreed on a truce with Scotland and negotiated with Castile and Aragon relating to trade with the French. He presented to Parliament a thoroughly planned campaign that resulted in the award of funds being made on 30th November 1472.

December

1ˢᵗ December 1450

The Duke of Somerset's lodgings in Blackfriars were set upon by supporters of York and Norfolk.

1450 had proven to be a politically difficult year. It had begun with a series of rebellions in the South East, ruthlessly put down by the King and his men. From there, Richard Duke of York had emerged as the leader of the 'loyal opposition'. He argued that the nation's financial state and military defeats were due to poor decision-making, that lawlessness was rife and that some of the Kings key advisors were corrupt.

These were serious charges, primarily as each of these areas was managed by other senior nobles. Chief among these nobles was the Duke of Somerset. He was a Queen's favourite, had the Kings ear, had been Lieutenant of France and was involved in financial decision making on a much larger scale following the murders of the Duke of Suffolk and Moleyns earlier in the year.

The animosity between the Dukes was well known, and their followers were fiercely loyal. It led to an assault on the Duke of Somerset on 1st December 1450:

"When Parliament met in November [1450], the Duke of York cam with considerable numbers of knights and other armed men, as did the Duke of Norfolk. When these lords had been in London about a fortnight, their servants attacked the Duke of Somerset as he, with a few men but no fear of violence, dined at Blackfriars. Then, embarrassed by these occurrences, the lords left, nothing having been achieved in Parliament..."

Note: Most sources say the 1ˢᵗ, but some suggest 2nd December.

2nd December 1460

Richard Duke of York and the earls of Rutland and Salisbury march north to confront the Lancastrians.

Following the Act of Accord the divisions between the court of Queen Margaret, in the name of Prince Edward and the Yorkist faction increased rapidly. The compromise solution to appease the Duke of York provoked anger from those loyal to the House of Lancaster.

Margaret had retreated to Wales, then Scotland, following setbacks in Council and the South. From Scotland, she orchestrated a response to events in the south.

Her northern allies included the powerful Earl of Northumberland and the Earl of Westmoreland. They quickly gathered their armies and marched them to strategic locations near York and Pontefract.

News of this rapid array and deployment alarmed the Yorkists. Their response was to gather an army and make haste to the north to tackle the problem head-on.

The Duke of York and his son the Earl of Rutland, along with the Earl of Salisbury would march north. The Earl of Warwick would safeguard the south and the midlands.

Logistically such a march is quite hard to arrange for an army of any size. Messengers were sent ahead to try and secure victuals and the castle at Sandal, the final destination, would be warned of the impending arrival of a large host of men.

The route to be travelled was the Great North Road. This route was not entirely welcoming to a Yorkist force, so not only were supplies and speed of the essence but so too was readiness for an attack at any time.

3rd December 1450

A grand Royal Procession took place in London including many of the leading nobles.

Men from the Dukes of Norfolk and York households attacked the Duke of Somerset on 1st December 1450. The Duke of Norfolk removed Somerset from the affray, and, 'for his safety', placed in the Tower of London. The attack triggered looting in the Blackfriar's region.

The events surrounding the attack on the Duke of Somerset appear to have been well coordinated. The Duke was arrested and sent to the Tower. The Duke of York and his followers looked like the enforcers of the King's peace.

There followed a large military procession; no doubt intended to warn off any who contemplated further riots. Benet's Chronicle describes the events:

"The following afternoon, almost 1000 well-armed men attacked the Duke of Somerset without warning, and would have slain him, had not the Earl of Devon, at the Duke of York's request, pacified them and discreetly arrested Somerset, brought him from Blackfriars to the Thames, and thence to the Tower of London, leaving the rioters in Blackfriars to pillage… On Thursday 3rd December the King, accompanied by his dukes, earls, barons, knights and squires and others, all in full armour and about 10000 in number, marched in solemn procession through London. The Duke of Norfolk and the Earl of Devon, with 3000 men, provided the vanguard; the King, the Duke of York, the Earl of Salisbury, the Earl of Arundel, the Earl of Oxford, the Earl of Wiltshire, the Earl of Worcester and others, with 4000 men, followed; and the Duke of Buckingham, the Earl of Warwick and others, with 3000 men, brought up the rear…"

4th December 1457

Bishop Reginald Peacock was removed from the Privy Council.

Born in 1395 he was very well educated, becoming a fellow of Oriel College, Oxford in 1417. In 1420 he was ordained a subdeacon, and in the following year, he rose to deacon, then priest. In 1425, Peacock graduated with a Bachelor's degree in Divinity, and at about this time he attracted the attention of Humphrey, Duke of Gloucester.

Duke Humphrey introduced Peacock to court, and he soon gained positions of note. In 1431 he became master of Whittington College, London where he excelled. He then became the rector of St. Michaels in Riola before, in 1444, being created Bishop of Asaph. He was later translated to the bishop's seat at Chichester in 1450.

In 1454 Peacock's genius earned him a place on the Privy Council. However, there was a problem. Peacock had addressed the issue of Lollardy head-on. He wrote the Repressor of overmuch Blaming of the Clergy and other theological books. The books were highly controversial. He had written in English and suggested that non-clerics could question teachings.

The opinion that an ordinary layperson could question spiritual matters was his undoing. In 1457 he was removed from the Privy Council. Archbishop Bourchier investigated his works. Peacock's works were found to be inviting heresy which was an ecclesiastical crime.

He was stripped of his ecclesiastical roles and given a simple choice: retract and repent or be burnt at the stake.

Peacock chose to repent and retract. He delivered his books to the authorities and gave penance for his sins.

5th December 1469

Estate management by the officers of the Plumpton family

The Plumpton letters cover a wide range of issues, from national politics and economic issues to their manors' day-to-day administration. The estate management aspect of the letters is quite revealing, as they show the family undertook the way lordship. In the example below, this administration continues in the middle of a national political crisis, illustrating that for most people, life went on as usual regardless of high politics. It combines protecting the families interests with ensuring tenants are correctly treated. This letter was written by one of the Plumpton officials, George Greene, to Sir William Plumpton on 5th December 1469:

"...Sir, I have sent to you by the bringer of this letter a venire facias against the minister of St. Roberts, for he hath pleaded not guiltie for fishing your ponds att Plompton. If so your writ be well served and the issue tried for you, be punishments will be grecuieous to them, for it is gyffyn by a statute. Also I haue sent you a venis facias against Dromonby, parson of Kynalton; he hath pleaded he withholds you nothing in accion of detynue of the goods deliuered him by Heynes. Also the copie of the pleadings betwixt you and the minister for your milne at Plompton; it were wele don the ye had a speech with Mr Middleton of the forme of pleadings, and of the matter of both sides the water, soe that your council may haue instuccion thereof... next tearme at the pleasure of be partis. Mr Midleton had great labour thereof; I profferd him no rewards because ye may reward him yourselfe as it please you. Maister Fairfax has xs for that matter allon. Mr Suttil laboured effectually; I tould him he should be rewarded of the money in his hands, and said lightly he would haue none, so I wot whether he will take, or no; he hath not all paid yet..."

6th December 1485

Henry Percy was released from imprisonment.

Henry Tudor had gaoled Percy following the Battle of Bosworth, at which Percy had fought on the side of Richard III. However, his loyalty to Richard was questioned by some chroniclers at the time. The Croyland Chronicle called him a 'traitor to the north'.

Henry Percy, Earl of Northumberland, was a complex character. He had fought for both the Lancastrians and Yorkists in the Wars of the Roses, leading to his imprisonment by Edward IV. Following his release by Edward, he chose to avoid becoming embroiled in the clashes of 1471.

Percy seemed to prosper under the influence of Richard Duke of Gloucester in the north. The bitter rivalries that had scarred the north-east before the Earl of Warwick's death seemed to be a thing of the past as Percy worked in conjunction with Richard to improve local governance and the border's security.

His loyalty, though, was questioned. Though he and his retinue were present, on Richard's side, at the Battle of Bosworth, some accounts suggest he deliberately held back from engaging at a critical moment in the battle.

Nonetheless, after the battle, he was taken to the Tower of London and incarcerated there from August until 6th December. This is an unusually short amount of time for a man who had fought as a commander against the newly crowned King Henry VII. It could well be that Henry Tudor was simply trying to ensure continuity and good order in a troublesome part of the country. Instead, it was interpreted by some as evidence that Percy had been in contact with the Tudor invader and had prior agreements with him. That belief contributed to his murder in his manor of Topcliffe in 1489.

7th December 1484

A Royal Proclamation was made regarding the expected invasion by Henry Tudor. Reissued in June 1485 it outlined the concerns that the crown had about Henry and warned citizens to resist his invasion and to array when commanded.

By December of 1484, the expectation was that Henry Tudor would mount an invasion of England and Wales. The evidence was unequivocal. Tudor had attempted to land once already, before realising that the rebellions in the South had failed. The build-up of a large group of disaffected nobles in exile was another sign that plans were being made. Intelligence reports too would have reached the ear of Richard III and his council, making the prospect of invasion seem to be inevitable.

And so, the King began planning for the event of an invasion. He appointed Captains to take charge of different coastal areas and have systems in place for a quick array against enemy forces. Viscount Lovell took a key command role along England's South Coast. Richard charged the Earl of Pembroke and Rhys ap Thomas with securing their territories in the South of Wales.

The issuing of Royal Proclamations relating to the likelihood of invasion is effectively giving the population advanced warning of what is about to happen. The men who would be expected to answer the call to array could begin to plan for the management of their lands or trades in the event of their absence, or death, on the campaign. Such a proclamation gave time to prepare enfeoffments, pay debts, collect debts, make provisions for their families, whilst providing the gentry and nobility time to prepare for war.

8th December 1473

Commissioners began to purchase provisions and arms for the planned invasion of France.

Edward IVs intended invasion of France was to be a large undertaking. Construction of a large fleet began in ports along the South Coast. Lords and nobles were instructed to ready themselves. Arrangements were made to collect the taxes granted to finance the venture. Edward now needed to ensure that the invading army was well equipped and that sufficient victuals were secured for the campaign.

Planning an invasion is logistically challenging. More so when it is into entirely hostile territory. When Edward had landed at Ravenspur two years earlier, he had the advantage of knowing which parts of the country were likely to be sympathetic to his cause. That meant he could be confident of being supplied. Furthermore, he had been provisioned with victuals and arms by the Duchy of Burgundy.

In 1473 the situation was somewhat different. The King's stated intention was to invade France and reclaim the crown that Henry VI had worn. Here, there would be no warm welcome. Supplies would be collected by the French and taken into their reserve or destroyed. The French would be well-armed. The English army would need to be prepared for modern, continental tactics. This meant investment.

On 8th December 1473, the King's Commissioners began the process of ordering the supplies and arms. Armouries had time to fashion armour and artillery; the bowyers to fashion longbows; the swordsmiths and blacksmiths to hammer new weapons and, for the nobility to devise methods of producing sufficient supplies for the campaign. Pigs to be fattened, slaughtered, and cured; biscuits to be baked, the list was long and would take time. And it needed to be done as secretly as possible.

9th December 1463

An Anglo-Scottish truce was agreed upon.

In late 1463 the political situation in Scotland changed. Mary of Gueldres died. It had been the Dowager Queen who, as head of the Regency Council, had agreed with terms with Margaret of Anjou. Those terms had promised, and delivered, military assistance to the Lancastrian cause in return for the handover to Scotland of the border town of Berwick.

This military assistance had extended beyond the Lancastrians defeat at Towton. They supplied and supported the Lancastrian enclave on the Northumbrian coast and were willing to accept senior Lancastrians into Scotland for safety.

By the time Mary died, many Scottish lords were weary of the continued support for King Henry and Queen Margaret. The cause seemed irretrievably lost and the expense of the ongoing support was hard to justify as there would be little, bar Berwick which had already been ceded, in return.

With the political climate changing, Edward IV sought to bring an end to the Scots' support to the Lancastrians. A formal treaty would be discussed and agreed upon in 1464. In the interim, both nations agreed to a truce to last until those treaty negotiations were concluded.

10th December 1485

The speaker of the commons urges King Henry VII to marry Elizabeth of York.

A key negotiation in the build-up to the invasion of England and Wales by Henry Tudor was between his mother and Elizabeth Woodville. A contract of marriage between Henry and Elizabeth of York, daughter of Edward IV, would provide the new regime with focal points for supporters of all factions at the head of government and reduce any further bloodshed risk.

The agreement was made, and the expectation was that the wedding ceremony would occur shortly after the victory at Bosworth. By December, it still had not taken place. The speaker of the commons, Thomas Lovell, raised the matter and implored the King to proceed with the marriage for the country's good promptly. The following is a translation of the Parliamentary roll as provided by British History Online:

"Be it remembered that on 10th December in the present year, the commons of the realm of England, appearing before the lord king in full parliament through Thomas Lovell their speaker, humbly petitioned his royal highness, earnestly requesting his highness that, considering that by authority of the said parliament it was decreed and enacted that the inheritance of the realms of England and France, with the royal pre-eminence and power, should be, rest, remain and stay in the person of the same lord king, and the heirs lawfully begotten of his body, the same royal highness should take to himself that illustrious lady Elizabeth, daughter of King Edward IV, as his wife and consort; whereby, by God's grace, many hope to see the propagation of offspring from the stock of kings, to comfort the whole realm."

11th December 1459

The Lords swear oaths of allegiance to King Henry VI.

The Coventry Parliament, known as the Parliament of Devils, ended its session on 11th December 1459. It had been a hugely significant session with the leading Yorkist nobles and many of their retainers having been attained.

The purpose of the Coventry Parliament had been to strip the opposition of its power base. The attainders removed land, titles, wealth and therefore, authority. The Yorkists, having not been invited to the session, were well aware of the likely outcome and had removed themselves from England: The Duke of York to Ireland, the Earls of March, Salisbury and Warwick to Calais.

One of the last items on the agenda was an Oath of Allegiance to the King. The lords spiritual and temporal who were present swearing to be ready to serve the King and to aid in any resistance to acts against him.

One curiosity here is that Lord Fitzhugh was among the lords who made this oath. Fitzhugh was the Earl of Salisbury's son-in-law. He had stood firmly behind the Neville family throughout the northern clashes of 1453-4. Now, he was swearing an oath to defend the King against them. Fitzhugh was rewarded for his action against the rebellious Yorkists: much of his fathers-in-law's land was granted to him.

12th December 1455

Grooms of the chamber present a signed petition.

Grooms of the chamber were the equivalent of a valet today. They ensured the smooth running of the various elements of the Royal Household.

On the lowest level, they were responsible for public-facing rooms within the court and would ensure that they were well maintained and appropriately dressed for any given occasion.

Above this level were Grooms of the chamber who had responsibilities for the Privy Council's chambers and other official meeting rooms. Again, they dealt with things such as the layout of rooms, décor and ensuring that officials were well looked after.

There were also Grooms of the Bedchamber. These had close contact with the Royal family and were the most trusted of the Grooms. They maintained the monarch's living quarters and answered to the Lord High Steward and the King himself.

On 12th December 1455, the Grooms of the Chamber presented a petition signed by the King to his council. At first glance, there appears to be nothing unusual about this. They had access to the royal apartments and could make petitions, or collect ones sent directly to the monarch instead of Parliament.

What makes the petition remarkable is its date. It is during Henry Vis incapacity. There was a Protector, the Duke of York, along with a Council running the country. Reforms were being made at all levels, including reducing the spending of the royal household.

Yet during Henry's period of being able to rule, they acquired his signature on a petition.

13th December 1470

Marriage of Prince Edward of Westminster to Anne Neville

The union of Prince Edward of Westminster, Prince of Wales and Anne Neville is one of the more unlikely marriage contracts entered into during the Wars of the Roses era. The Prince was the son of King Henry VI and Margaret of Anjou. His bride, the daughter of Richard Neville, Earl of Warwick. The marital couple's parents had spent much of the previous two decades bickering and waging war against each other, so for a contract to be entered into may seem unusual.

The marriage contract was drawn up alongside the Angers Agreement. That agreement suited both Queen Margaret and the Earl of Warwick. Both parties wanted their rights, titles, power, and their offspring's inheritances to be secured. Both parties would wage war against Edward IV and, once successful, would both have what they wanted.

As a sign of trust between the erstwhile enemies, the Prince's marriage to the Earls daughter was arranged. The Earl of Warwick then left Angers, returned to England, and ousted Edward IV from the throne. This left the route open for the wedding to take place.

The ceremony was held at the Chateau of Amboise in France in the presence of Queen Margaret and King Louis XI of France. It created Anne Neville, the Princess of Wales. There is lots of speculation about the nature of the couple's marriage. No hard evidence exists though of consummation. Nor, or whether it was happy, or as rumour has it, a violent, marriage.

The marriage was short-lived. Prince Edward died at the Battle of Tewkesbury in 1471.

14th December 1450

The Duke of York and Bishop Bourchier appointed to lead a commission of oyer and terminer

Kent and Sussex had risen in revolt on two occasions in 1450. The first, led by Thomas Cheyne, the second, led by Jack Cade. It was clear that the area had grave concerns, but is equally clear that there were agitators at large within the Kentish and Sussex communities.

Worries about Lollardy and memories of Cade complaints remained fresh in the minds of many in the South-East. Council established a commission to identify the agitators and mete out punishment where due.

The King's choice of Lords and Bishops to manage the investigations was Richard Duke of York and his brother-in-law, Bishop Bourchier. These appointments show that King Henry, or his closest advisors, were savvy in understanding the political situation.

Following Richard's return from Ireland, he had been championed as the leader of the loyal opposition. Even in his absence in early 1450, the South East's commoners had called for him to have a much more prominent government position. They, nor Richard, had not anticipated that the role would include exacting punishments in the areas that were crying out for his inclusion in state affairs.

The appointment placed Richard in an awkward political situation. If he failed to undertake the commission in full and to the best of his ability, including trials, fines, imprisonments, and executions, he would be undermined at court. If he did fulfil these duties and administer punishment in the manner that Henry's courts had done at Canterbury and Rochester earlier in the year, he would stand to lose a lot of support from an already an area of significant Yorkist support.

15th December 1455

Battle of Clyst Heath between the retinues of the Courtenay's and Bonville's

Clyst Heath lay to the east of Exeter in an area that had Exeter Castle to its west, Tiverton Castle to the North, Colcombe Castle to the east and Powderham Castle south-west. It was adjacent to the Clyst River and a strategically important position in the local area.

In 1455 this area was experiencing great unrest. The Earl of Devon, Thomas Courtenay, and Baron Bonville were engaged in a bitter conflict over local rights, positions and land.

Both parties had engaged in raids on the other family's manors, including murders, one of a Justice of the Peace, which added to tensions and animosity between the two families.

On 15th December 1455 retinues of the two noble families formed up against each other at Clyst Heath. The intention for both was to enforce their superiority over the region and gain control of regional positions that would serve their interests well.

The Battle was a decisive victory for the Earl of Devon. The Bonville retinue was unable to counter their attack and was forced into flight. The Earl and his men then went on the rampage in Bonville lands, sacking the Manor of Shute.

News of events such as this led to intervention from the Protector, Richard Duke of York. Both nobles were briefly imprisoned before being bound over to keep the peace. Their private feud though contributed to national tensions. Both nobles had allies within the factions at court which meant that they became more entrenched in their opposition to one another, safe knowing that they had the Dukes of Somerset or York as allies.

16th December 1431

King Henry VI is crowned King of France in Paris

One of the outcomes of King Henry Vs successful campaigns in France was a Treaty that agreed that upon the King of France's death, the crown would pass by right to England's Kings. This claim stretched back several generations and was the justification for English expansion and campaigning into French controlled lands.

When King Henry V died, this right was passed to King Henry VI. In 1431 the English retained control of large parts of France, though were being challenged and pressed hard by a French army that the recently executed Joan of Arc had inspired.

With King Charles VI of France's passing, the terms of the Treaty were activated by the English. Henry VI was now the King of England and France. Henry was still young though and had not been crowned King of England due to his tender age.

Following Henry's coronation as King of England, attention was turned to his French domain. The issue was symbolically important and would lift the English forces' spirits in France at a time of military struggle.

Traditionally the Kings of France were crowned at Notre Dame Cathedral in Reims. The Dauphin, disinherited under the terms of the peace agreements, had seized Reims as part of the campaigns of the 1420s. So, the English prepared for Henry to be crowned in Paris.

Henry was crowned King of France on 16th December 1431. He remains the only monarch to have been crowned King of both countries. He retained his title and claim to the crown, theoretically, until after the French were victorious in the Hundred Years War.

17th December 1455

Breach of Wool exportation laws

William Bert, an alien (foreigner) and a London woolpacker named William Denys are in the memoranda rolls for having secreted 8000 woolfells from the wool quays. From elsewhere on the Thames, they then illegally exported the wool. Practices such as this took place to avoid the tonnage duties placed on textiles, England's staple export. Denys is cited for doing the same on a smaller scale elsewhere in the records.

In the 15th century wool was the main export from England. It took several forms, from course wool through to extremely fine. The wool was packed into bundles, and a customs duty was payable based on its value.

The duties were a source of much consternation among the wool merchants both in England and the continent. Any change impacted on the profitability of their businesses. Tariffs, coupled with the very real risk of losing the cargo due to sinking, made the trade rather precarious at times.

The volatile nature of business and uncertainties over profit sometimes contributed to illegal activities such as those described above. In London, Wool had to be loaded onto ships at specified quays so that officials could check the quality and weight of goods and charge the appropriate tolls.

Fees for 'aliens' were often higher than those for English merchants because of the Staplers' petitions. The vessels also had to sail to Calais, unless they were from some northern ports who had an exemption. This was to ensure that the treasury had bullion which there was a shortage of at the time.

18th December 1478

Envoys from Burgundy and England renew parts of the 1474 Treaty

Diplomatic relations with France, Burgundy and Brittany had been of great importance throughout the Wars of the Roses. In the 1470s alone, Treaties had been agreed upon with each of these continental powers. With Burgundy and Brittany, they were alliances. With France, the Treaty of Picquigny.

By 1478 the agreement with France was being tested. The French King, Louis XI, was attempting to broker marriage contracts. So too were the Burgundians and King Edward IV of England. It led to tension between the three states, which could have repercussions for England's economy and potentially require military intervention.

Maximillian and Mary ruled Burgundy by now. They sought the marriage of their son to Princess Elizabeth, eldest daughter of King Edward IV. They offered a sum of 10,000 crowns to Edward to secure a marriage contract.

Edward received an annual pension from the French because of the 1475 campaign, and he would stand to lose out under this deal. At the same time, the French were making overtures regarding Princess Anne. Edward would anger one, or both, of the continental powers no matter what his decision was.

He chose to remain allies with Burgundy. He did not agree to a marriage contract but instead negotiated a renewal of the agreements made in 1474. This agreement was for joint campaigning against France. The message to King Louis XI was clear, stop interfering in the affairs of England and Burgundy.

19th December 1483

Richard III issues orders relating to the Duchess of Buckingham

In 1483 the Duke of Buckingham had risen in revolt against the rule of King Richard III. The rebellion had failed, and upon his capture, the Duke had been tried for treason, found guilty and executed.

The family of the Duke had gone into hiding because of the rebellion, for fear of reprisals. What happened after the uprising's failure is a good example of how medieval Society treated noblewomen.

The Duchess and some of Buckingham's children were found hiding in Weobley by Christopher Wellesbourne. Wellesbourne requested instruction from the King who on 19th December 1483 ordered that the Duchess and children be conveyed 'to these parts', meaning London.

The Duchess is thereafter not attained, nor stripped of her title. There were no reprisals against her whatsoever for her husband's treasonable acts.

Also implicated in plotting the revolt was Margaret Beaufort. Any nobleman would be executed for such a deed. Margaret, however, was not. Her acts had to be acknowledged, but the punishment amounted to stripping her of lands. However, her husband, Lord Stanley, could collect the revenues of those lands himself. So, the penalty was a token gesture as Margaret could be maintained by the same lands, albeit now through her husband's income rather than her own.

Both are a stark contrast with the punitive measures exacted upon any men who dared to cross a medieval monarch.

20th December 1463

The Duke of Somerset leaves North Wales without Royal Consent

The Duke of Somerset had been pardoned by King Edward IV and taken back into the court. The King sent him to North Wales for his safety as many Yorkists did not trust him.

That the King himself still trusted Somerset is in no doubt. In 1463 men from the Duke of Somerset's retinue were sent north to act as the guard at the port of Newcastle. It was a trust that was ill-judged.

On or before 20th December 1463 the Duke of Somerset left North Wales. He had sought no permission to do so. The Duke headed north, towards his men in Newcastle. It is assumed that he intended to betray the port and adjoining town to the Lancastrians.

When King Edward heard of Somerset absconding, he quickly realised that the Duke was returning to the Lancastrian cause. A force of men loyal to himself personally was dispatched to the north to take Newcastle and hold it for the Yorkist regime.

Somerset managed to travel as far as Durham before anybody recognised and questioned him. He narrowly evaded capture by running from his lodgings in just his nightshirt.

The Yorkist force approaching Newcastle was far stronger than the guard from Somerset's retinue. As it neared, they fled.

Somerset and his men then made their way to the castles that remained in Lancastrian hands in the north-east. The Duke himself going to Bamburgh from where he harassed Yorkists until his eventual capture and battlefield execution in 1464.

21st December 1495

Death of Jasper Tudor

Jasper Tudor was the uncle of Henry Tudor, King Henry VII. He played a pivotal role in securing the crown for Henry and had been an active captain in the Lancastrian army throughout the Wars of the Roses.

Jasper Tudor was the Earl of Pembroke. When his brother died, he took in Margaret Beaufort and his infant nephew, Henry, and cared for them.

With the onset of hostilities, Jasper fought for the Lancastrians, supporting his half-brother, King Henry VI. Following the defeat at the Battle of Towton, Jasper oversaw resistance to the Yorkists in Wales. He and his retainers withdrew to the north of Wales, mounting attacks from Snowdonia. At the Battle of Twt Hill Jasper's force was defeated, leading to his exile in Ireland.

Exile did not prevent him from continuing to have an active role in the Wars. Harlech held firm for the Lancastrian cause, and Jasper arranged for its regular resupply by sea, enabling harassment of the Yorkists.

When Henry VI was reinstated to his throne, Jasper returned and briefly held his Earldom again. The royal army including Prince Edward and accompanied by Queen Margaret was on route to merge forces with his Welsh contingent when they were defeated at Tewkesbury.

The Lancastrian line eliminated; Jasper headed once more into exile. He became involved in the planning and execution of his nephew, Henry Tudor's invasion. On the Bosworth campaign, he commanded one of the battles, helping Henry Tudor defeat Richard III.

Jasper's loyalty to his nephew was rewarded, and in the formative years of the Tudor era, he was one of Henry's most trusted counsellors.

22nd December 1476

Death of Isabel Neville, Duchess of Clarence

Isabel Neville, the wife of George Duke of Clarence, died at Warwick Castle on 22nd December 1476. Isabel was a daughter of the Earl of Warwick and co-heiress, with her sister Anne, to his estates following his death at the Battle of Barnet.

Isabel was raised in the Neville stronghold of Middleham Castle. From an early age, she was acquainted with the sons of the Duke of York. Her family's standing made her a suitable bride for the Duke of Clarence and so, against the Kings wishes, the couple had married in Calais.

Isabel then inherited half of the vast estates that her father had held. These, along with those passing to her sister, were then granted to their husbands by Act of Parliament.

Isabel gave birth to Edward Plantagenet in February 1475. That son was to become the last male of the Yorkist line with any real claim to the throne. The birth of the couples next son, Richard, was to prove fatal. The birth was complicated, and Isabel died on 22nd December, not long after labour.

The grief that the Duke of Clarence had over her loss led to him summarily executing the midwife, whom he accused of poisoning his beloved wife.

23rd December 1482

Franco-Burgundian Treaty of Arras

Charles the Bold of Burgundy and Frederick, Holy Roman Emperor, had agreed on a marriage contract between their children, Mary of Burgundy and Maximillian. When Charles died in battle in January 1477, a decision was made, involving input from Charles' wife, Margaret of York, to retain the marriage contract. The marriage then took place in August 1477.

The French though took advantage of Charles the Bold's passing and quickly claimed the lands he had ruled: Burgundy was a Duchy of France. Maximillian decided to fight for his wife's inheritance. In 1479 he crushed the army of the French King Louis XI at the Battle of Guinegate.

Control of Burgundy was now settled. Until, in March 1482, Mary died. This left the inheritance of the Duchy in the hands of Mary and Maximillian's son, Philip. Philip was only an infant, and so a Regent was required. It soon became apparent to Maximillian that he would not be accepted as Regent by the people of Burgundy. This presented a problem as it opened the prospect of renewed attacks from France.

The solution was the Treaty of Arras. The daughter of Mary and Maximillian was contracted to marry the Dauphin of France. Her dowry was the Duchy of Burgundy.

This Treaty was a hammer blow to the English. It removed the prospect of an alliance against the French and had severe economic implications. As the Dowager Duchess of Burgundy was also a senior member of the House of York is also presented a diplomatic concern.

Fortunately for the English, Maximillian changed his mind and forced the French to sign a different Treaty the following year.

24th December 1446

Appointment of the Earl of Dorset as Lieutenant of France

1446 was an important year for the English in France. The Treaty of Tours was drawing to the end of its extension and Henry's bride, Margaret of Anjou, was recently arrived from French lands. Much was to be done in terms of Anglo-French relations: The Treaty needed extending. The terms of the marriage contract required implementation, and the English needed further respite from attacks on Normandy.

The appointment of the Earl of Dorset was likely to have disappointed the Duke of York. Dorset gave York and his counsel little confidence, furthered by the King's failure to travel to English held lands there as previously agreed.

In France, the situation was one that needed careful consideration. Under the Duke of York's Lieutenancy, the French had been kept at arm's length, and losses had been minimised before the Treaty of Tours. Now there was the prospect of a renewal of attacks on Normandy.

Coupled with this was the handing over of Maine to the French. This was a controversial and initially hidden clause of the marriage contract drawn up for the King and Margaret. Its loss angered many at court, the Earl of Dorset would now need to handle the transition, compensation, and the subsequent changes it made to English military plans in the region.

The transfer of duties from one Lieutenant to another was not an overnight task. Though the Duke of York was in London, then his Welsh estates, his appointees and men effectively ran Normandy until April of the following year.

25th December 1454

Henry VI regains his senses

King Henry VI had been in an incapacitated state since August of 1453. The cause of the illness is subject to debate with suggestions of schizophrenia, catalepsy, mutism, and nervous breakdown suggested by various historians. However, there is no substantive evidence to support any of the claims. All that is known for a fact is that the King was in some form of dissociative state from August 1453 onwards.

Speculation suggests that the cause of Henry's condition was news of the final fall of Gascony with the fall of Talbot's men at Castillon and then of Bordeaux following a siege. Such events can overwhelm a person, so some psychiatric analysis suggests that this triggered the King's illness.

The Duke of York acted as Protector of the realm during the King's incapacity. This period had seen some Lancastrian loyalists removed from posts and imprisoned. Overall though, the Duke had attempted to rule fairly and to improve the administration of government.

Suddenly and unexpectedly, the King regained full awareness on Christmas Day of 1454. He was introduced to his son, Prince Edward, who had been born whilst the King was ill. Henry quickly set about restoring himself to his seat of power. Richard Duke of York stepped down as Protector and old favourites soon returned to court.

Henry was to suffer a second period of incapacity in 1455, shortly after the Battle of St. Albans. This has led some to argue that he was mentally weak, though there is as much evidence to suggest that the Duke of York's Protectorate on that occasion was forced, with the illness being a given excuse for Yorkist control of the Government.

26th December 1462

Bamburgh Surrenders

On 26th December 1462, Bamburgh Castle surrendered to the Yorkists. At the time it was a significant gain. In October of that year, the Queen and Prince Edward had landed at Bamburgh and used it as the headquarters of Lancastrian resistance in the North East.

The Earl of Warwick besieged the castle. His plan was quite simple and typical of many medieval sieges; he would starve the defenders into submission.

Warwick had a large army at his disposal to tackle the castles that were resisting Yorkist rule. At Bamburgh, this force to block any relief for the castle from the land. Warwick also utilised the fleet based at Newcastle to instigate a naval blockade of the castle.

Despite the blockade, Queen Margaret was able to escape, by sea, to Berwick. A Scottish relief force for the castle was raised but failed to materialise on time to aid the beleaguered defenders.

With supplies low and little hope of assistance reaching them, the garrison commanders sued for terms. This is quite normal for a medieval siege, castles or towns that surrender were typically granted favourable terms.

This siege was different though. The garrison commanders were the Duke of Somerset and Earl of Northumberland, two of the men most despised by the Yorkists.

Remarkably, the men were both granted pardons in exchange for the handing over of Bamburgh and taken back into court circles. Somerset even advising the King on matters about the North East. He soon returned to the Lancastrian fold though, and Bamburgh too was returned to Lancastrian hands within months of this surrender.

27th December 1462

Dunstanburgh surrenders

Remarkably the North Eastern Castle of Dunstanburgh surrendered to the Yorkists the day after Bamburgh surrendered. It marked a significant change in the fortunes of both sides in the north east as it, for a period at least, meant that the whole area was in Yorkist hands.

The Castle of Dunstanburgh, on the Northumberland coastline, was commanded by three men who had been attained by Edward IVs first parliament. Henry Beaufort, Sir Henry Lewis, and Sir Nicholas Latimer had all fought against Edward IV.

For them to surrender was courageous, they would undoubtedly have heard of the no prisoner's policy enacted at Towton and must have been wary of the consequences of their capture.

By late 1462 the politics of the region demanded a degree of leniency though. For Edward IV or the Earl of Warwick, to have actual control over the region, they needed the local population's compliance. Executing these men, or indeed the Earl of Northumberland who had surrendered the day before, would simply antagonise the locals and make land management incredibly difficult.

So not only were the three men treated with leniency, but the custody of the castle was also actually given to the Earl of Northumberland, rather than a Yorkist Lord.

It may seem odd given that had he, or Somerset, been captured at Towton they would probably have faced execution. It reflects a need to manage a problematic part of the country with continuity in mind whilst retaining systems against Scottish incursions.

Dunstanburgh, like Bamburgh, soon reverted to the Lancastrian cause and had to be besieged again.

28th December 1471

Pilgrims at Canterbury allowed into the Cathedral overnight

Even during the uncertain times of a civil war, pilgrims still flocked to the shrine of St. Thomas at Canterbury. The practice, described in the Canterbury Tales, was subject to a range of customs, traditions, and rules.

One of the rules that the monks adhered to was to provide warmth, shelter and food for those pilgrims who were in need. Records show that this is precisely what the monks did on the evening of 28th December 1471.

On a cold night, a group of pilgrims were waiting outside the Cathedral. They wanted to see the relics associated with Thomas Becket, and would, under the careful watch of monks, even be allowed to kiss the relics.

Queues for entry to the shrine of St. Thomas could be quite long especially as the following day was the feast of St. Thomas the Martyr. Despite it being one of the 12 days of Christmas, pilgrims had begun to gather outside in the evening.

The monks opened the Cathedral doors and allowed the group to sleep in the nave's relative warmth. They were then permitted to enter the saint's shrine following Matins, which was highly unusual.

Further to giving the pilgrims the warmth of the cathedral to sleep in, and unprecedented access to the shrine, they were also fed. It was a basic meal of bread, cheese, and ale, much like the food that the monks themselves would have eaten that evening.

Such acts helped the Cathedral spread the news of St. Thomas and, cynically, were advertising that would help ensure continued revenue for the Cathedral.

29th December 1484

Commission established to seize the assets of William Colyngbourne.

On 18th July 1483, a rhyme had been pinned to the door of St. Paul's Cathedral. It read:

The Cat, The Rat and Lovel our dog,

Ruleth all England under a Hog.

The rhyme was considered seditious and inflammatory. It was aimed directly at King Richard III and his closest advisors.

Such acts were treasonable, and soon it became clear who had written the rhyme. A man named William Colyngbourne, who made little attempt to hide his dislike of the new King, was determined to be guilty of having written the rhyme.

Colyngbourne favoured closer relations with France and was particularly disgruntled with the King's stance throughout his time as Duke of Gloucester on Anglo-French relations. Richard's elevation to the throne seems to have been the final straw for him, leading him to plot and to post the rhyme.

His plotting to put Henry Tudor on the throne, and authorship of the rhyme appears to have taken the authorities some time to determine. It was over a year before he was arrested and put on trial.

At the trial, Colyngbourne was found guilty. He was sentenced to death by being hanged, drawn, and quartered, carried out in early December at Tower Hill.

The Commission of 29th December 1484 was to strip all his assets for the crown. In effect removing anything of value from his family as punishment for William's crime.

30th December 1460

Battle of Wakefield

Following the Act of Accord Margaret of Anjou had gathered a large army quickly in the North of England. The Earls of Northumberland and Westmoreland issued arrays to answer her call to arms. So too did members of her inner circle such as the Duke of Somerset.

In response, the Duke of York, Earl of Rutland and Earl of Salisbury gathered an army and marched to the Yorkist castle at Sandal, Wakefield.

On 30th December 1460, the Yorkists left the castle in large numbers. The reasons why they did this are unclear. Speculation suggests that they were foraging, tricked into thinking a small number of the enemy were in the vicinity or even that they believed a supporting force sent by the Earl of Warwick was close and in need of support.

They soon found themselves facing a large Lancastrian force. Instead of retreating to the castle, the Yorkist lords entered into battle. It was a hopeless fight. The Lancastrian force had more archers, more men, and a better position from which to fight.

Soon, the Duke of York lay dead on the battlefield. The Yorkist army turned and fled, trying to escape the rout that followed a medieval battlefield defeat. The Earl of Rutland, only a young man, was found by men of Baron Clifford's company. Clifford killed the Earl.

The Earl of Salisbury was captured. He was taken to Pontefract Castle where he was imprisoned under the Duke of Somerset's careful eye.

In one day, the Yorkists had gone from being in the ascendancy to losing a Duke and two Earls. Their leadership was shattered. The future now looked very uncertain.

31st December 1460

The Execution of the Earl of Salisbury and posthumous beheading of Richard, Duke of York.

Following the Battle of Wakefield, the Lancastrian forces cleared the battlefield. They were looking for well-known faces and gathering arms and equipment for their cause. During the clearance, they found the body of Richard, Duke of York. It was taken to the nearby castle at Pontefract.

At Pontefract, the Duke of Somerset found himself facing demands from the local population for the Earl of Salisbury's head. The Earl would fetch a handsome ransom, but the baying mob wanted blood.

So too was the body of the Earl of Rutland taken to the castle.

Somerset decided. The Earl of Salisbury was led to the centre of the Bailey and beheaded. The Duke of York's corpses and that of his son, the Earl of Rutland, were then decapitated.

The heads were gathered up and sent to the City of York.

The Battle of Wakefield triggered the busiest period of fighting in the whole of the Wars of the Roses. Upon the arrival of Queen Margaret, the Lancastrians marched on London. Elsewhere, Edward, Earl of March, and the Earl of Warwick then took the fight to the Lancastrians.

There was now an incredibly determined Queen facing an angry Earl of March. The Wars of the Roses had just become very serious.

Wars of the Roses – Chronology

31st August 1422 Death of King Henry V.

14th January 1423 The opening of Henry Vis first Parliament.

23rd April 1445 Marriage of King Henry VI and Margaret of Anjou.

23rd February 1447 Duke Humphrey arrested on charges of treason.

30th July 1447 Richard Duke of York appointed Lieutenant of Ireland.

9th January 1450 Adam Moleyns murdered by sailors at Portsmouth.

2nd May 1450 Murder of William de la Pole Duke of Suffolk.

3 July 1450 Jack Cade crosses London Bridge and declares himself Mayor.

7th September 1450 Richard Duke of York returns from Ireland.

3rd March 1452 Standoff at Dartford.

17 July 1453 Battle of Castillon (Last battle of the Hundred Years War).

10th August 1453 Henry VI suffered mental breakdown.

25th December 1454 Henry VI regained his senses.

22nd May 1455 First Battle of St. Albans.

13th January 1456 Resignation of Richard Duke of York as Protector.

20th April 1456 The Earl of Warwick appointed Captain of Calais.

28th January 1457 Henry Tudor born.

24th March 1458 Loveday Parade at St. Pauls Cathedral.

23rd September 1459 The Battle of Blore Heath.

12th **October 1459** The Battle of Ludford.

20th **November 1459** Parliament of Devils opens.

15th **January 1460** Raid on Sandwich.

2 July 1460 Siege of the Tower of London.

10 July 1460 Battle of Northampton.

9th September 1460 Richard Duke of York landed in England.

25th **October 1460** Act of Accord.

31st **October 1460** Battle of Stamford Bridge.

30th December 1460 Battle of Wakefield.

5th **January 1461** Agreement between Lancastrians and Scots.

2nd **February 1461** Battle of Mortimer's Cross.

17th **February 1461** Lancastrian victory at the Second Battle of St. Albans.

29th March 1461 Battle of Towton.

28th **June 1461** Coronation of Edward IV.

16th **October 1461** Battle of Towt Hill.

6th **January 1463** Alnwick falls.

4th March 1464 Lancastrian rebels are defeated at Dryslwyn.

25th **April 1464** Battle of Hedgeley Moor.

1st **May 1464** Secret marriage of Edward IV and Elizabeth Woodville.

15th **May 1464** Battle of Hexham.

24 July 1465 Henry VI captured by Yorkists.

26 July 1469 Battle of Edgcote.

12th March 1470 Battle of Losecote Field.

22 July 1470 Angers Agreement.

26th November 1470 Parliament attains Edward IV.

2nd January 1471 Edward IV and Charles of Burgundy discuss invasion.

30th September 1473 The beginning of the siege of St. Michael's Mount.

14th April 1471 Battle of Barnet.

4th May 1471 The Battle of Tewkesbury.

21st May 1471 Death of King Henry VI.

29th August 1475 Treaty of Picquigny.

18th February 1478 The trial of the Duke of Clarence.

9th April 1483 Death of King Edward IV.

19th May 1483 Edward V enters the Tower of London to prepare for his coronation.

26th June 1483 Richard III accedes to the throne.

6 July 1483 Coronation of King Richard III.

23rd January 1484 Titulus Regius is passed.

16th March 1485 Queen Anne Neville dies.

7th August 1485 Henry Tudor lands at Milford Haven.

22nd August 1485 Battle of Bosworth.

18th January 1486 Marriage of King Henry VII to Elizabeth of York.

16th June 1487 Battle of Stoke Field.

Bibliography

Amin, Nathen. The House of Beaufort: The Bastard line that captured the crown. Amberley (2018).

Ashdown-Hill, John. The Private Life of Edward IV. Amberley (2016).

Barber, Richard (ed) The Pastons. The letters of a family in the Wars of the Roses. Penguin (1981).

Benet, John. Chronicle for the years 1400-1462. Royal Historical Society (1972).

Boardman, Andrew W. The Medieval Soldier in The Wars of the Roses. Sutton Publishing (1998).

Boardman, Andrew W. The Battle of Towton. Sutton Publishing (2000).

Bohn, James 9ed). The Chronicles of the White Rose of York. A Series of Historical Fragments, Proclamations, Letters, and Other Contemporary Documents Relating to the Reign of King Edward the Fourth. James Bohn (1845)

Bolton, J. L. Money in the Medieval Economy: 973-1489. Manchester Medieval Studies (2012)

Bret, David. The Yorkist Kings and the Wars of the Roses: Part One: Edward IV. Lulu (2014)

Carpenter, Christine. The Wars of the Roses, Politics and the constitution in England c1437-1509. Cambridge Medieval Textbooks (2002).

Childs, Dr. Wendy R (ed) The Customs Accounts of Hull 1453-1490. Yorkshire Archaeological Society (1986)

Clark, K. L. The Nevills of Middleham: England's most powerful family in the Wars of the Roses. The History Press (2016).

Clayton, D and Moore Bennet, E. The Administration of the County Palatine of Chester, 1442-1485. Manchester University Press (1990)

Dockray, Keith. Edward IV, From contemporary chronicles, letters & records. Fonthill Media (2015)

Dockray, Keith. Henry VI, Margaret of Anjou. From contemporary chronicles, letters & records. Fonthill Media (2016)

Dyer, Christopher. Standards of Living in the later Middle Ages, Social change in England c1200-1500. Cambridge Medieval Textbooks (1989).

Gillingham, John. The Wars of the Roses: Peace and Conflict in the 15th century. Phoenix Press (2005).

Goodwin, George. Fatal Colours: Towton, 1461… England's most brutal battle. Weidenfeld & Nicolson (2012).

Haigh, Philip A. From Wakefield to Towton: The Wars of the Roses. Pen and Sword Military (2014).

Hartrich, Eliza. Politics and the Urban Sector in Fifteenth-Century England, 1413-1471. Oxford University Press (2019).

Hicks, Michael. The Wars of the Roses. Yale University Press (2010).

Horrox, Rosemary. Richard III, a failed king? Penguin Monarchs (2020).

James, Jefferey. Edward IV, Glorious son of York. Amberley (2017).

Johnson, Lauren. Shadow King, The Life and Death of Henry VI. HeadofZeus (2019).

Johnson, P.A. Duke Richard of York 1411-1460. Oxford Historical Monographs (1988).

Jones, Michael. Bosworth 1485, The Psychology of a Battle. John Murray (2002).

Lewis, Matthew. The Wars of the Roses The Key Players in the Struggle for Supremacy. Amberley (2016).

Lewis, Matthew. Richard III Loyalty Binds Me. Amberley (2020).

Miller, Fredric .P. ,Vandome, Agnes, McBrewster John (eds). Dominic Macini. VDM Publishing (2010).

Murray Kendal, Paul. Warwick the Kingmaker and the Wars of the Roses. Cardinal (1973).

Pollard, A. J. North-Eastern England during the Wars of the Roses, Lay Society, Wars and Politics 1450-1500. Clarendon Press Oxford (1990).

Pollard, A. J. The Wars of the Roses (3rd edition) British History in Perspective. Palgrave MacMillan (2013).

Ross, Charles. Richard III. University of California Press (1981)

Santiuste, David. Edward IV and the Wars of the Roses. Pen and Sword (2010).

Seward, Desmond. The Wars of the Roses and the lives of Five Men and Women in the Fifteenth Century. Constable and Company (1995).

Soberton, Sylvia Barbara. Women of the Wars of the Roses: Jaquetta Woodville, Margaret of Anjou and Cecily Neville. Self-Published (2020).

Spencer, Dan. The Castle in the Wars of the Roses. Pen and Sword (2020).

Watts, John Henry VI and the Politics of Kingship. Cambridge University Press. 1999.

Weir, Alison. Lancaster and York. Arrow Books (1996).

Wright, S. M. The Derbyshire Gentry in the Fifteenth Century. Derbyshire Record Society (1983).

Online Resources

A wide range of official documents are available online, via subscription to: https://www.british-history.ac.uk/ These sources include:

Close Rolls of King Henry VI

Close Rolls of King Edward IV

Close Rolls of King Richard III

Close Rolls of King Henry VII

Parliamentary Rolls of Medieval England (Including Acts of Parliament, Petitions and Attainders)

Inquisitions Post-mortem

Milanese State Papers

Venetian State Papers

Printed in Great Britain
by Amazon

10037814R00223